A Harmony Of The Gospels In The Words Of The Revised Version

A HARMONY

OF THE

GOSPELS

IN THE WORDS OF THE REVISED VERSION,
WITH COPIOUS REFERENCES,
TABLES, ETC.

ARRANGED BY

C. C. JAMES, M.A.,

RECTOR OF WORTHAM, SUFFOLK;
FORMERLY FELLOW OF KING'S COLLEGE, CAMBRIDGE,
AND ASSISTANT MASTER AT ETON COLLEGE.

LONDON:
C. J. CLAY AND SONS,
CAMBRIDGE UNIVERSITY PRESS WAREHOUSE,
AVE MARIA LANE.
1892

𝕮𝖆𝖒𝖇𝖗𝖎𝖉𝖌𝖊:

PRINTED BY C. J. CLAY, M.A. AND SONS,

AT THE UNIVERSITY PRESS.

INDEX.

PREFACE.

THE uses of a "Harmony of the Gospels" are twofold: first to enable each reader to draw up for himself a connected narrative of our Lord's History containing the fullest possible account that can be given: this I have endeavoured to do in my "Gospel History," which I have published for the use of others. I have been surprised by the number of correspondents, both men and women, who have told me that they had attempted this, but had not time or patience enough to complete it, and have thanked me for doing it for them. The second use is to enable the reader, by seeing all the different accounts of each event before his eyes at the same moment, to judge how very few and unimportant the actual variations are, and how utterly mistaken are those persons who would represent the holy witnesses as "contradicting each other" in any essential matters. No two persons ever give precisely the same account of the same event; if they did, their testimony would at once be open to the suspicion of having been made up and agreed upon beforehand; and the honest, independent witness of two or more would be reduced to the suspected testimony of one.

In this Harmony, which follows the order of S. Luke and the same arrangement of sections as my "Gospel History," I have endeavoured to set forth the parallel passages in a clearer and therefore more useful form than has generally been the case in similar publications; avoiding, at the cost of increased bulk, that snake-like wriggling about of the text which mars the beauty of the page and fatigues the eye. Wherever it has been necessary on account of their length to

present the parallels of any section on more than two pages,
I have tried to divide them at the same points of the narrative,
adding "T. O." at the foot of the unfinished extracts, the com-
pletion of which will be found in the same order on the next
page or pages, so that the same portions of the histories are
always before the eye simultaneously.   The necessity of ar-
ranging the parallels so that the eye could take in both or all
at the same moment, entailed in several places some vacant
spaces, and these I have for the most part filled with what I
have called Quasi-parallels, or passages from other parts of
Scripture illustrative of the text, which a student might find
it very convenient to have before his eye together; such as,
all of our Lord's words about the Sabbath, on page 29; all
the Scriptural accounts of the raising of the dead, p. 162; and
others, of which a list is given in the Table of Contents, after
the list of the Sections, on page xx.   Such passages are printed
in *Italics*, to avoid any possibility of mistake.   The Italics of
the Revised Version are printed in the same Roman type with
the rest of the text.   For my own part, I do not see any need
of retaining these Italics in our Bibles at all: if the words so
printed are not necessary to the translation they ought not to
have been introduced: if they are necessary, they form part of
the translation.   Certainly they are very misleading to many
simple people, who imagine that they ought to be read with
special emphasis.

In most sections, the fullest account is printed first.   The
reader cannot fail to notice how very often, from Section 31
onwards, this is the account of S. Mark.   One can scarcely
study these extracts without feeling that we have the words of
an eye-witness very observant of little details, who was almost
certainly S. Peter.   Nothing can be more mistaken than the
common notion that S. Mark's Gospel is merely an epitome of
S. Matthew's; Section 73 is a sufficient refutation of that
idea.   I cannot see any indications which would lead me to
think that any one of the first three Evangelists had seen the

work of another, except that perhaps S. Matthew's "Blessed are the poor in spirit," "Blessed are they that hunger and thirst after righteousness" (v. 3, 6), may contain a correction of possible misinterpretations of S. Luke's "Blessed are ye poor," "Blessed are ye that hunger now" (vi. 20, 21). If there be any force in this remark, it would place S. Matthew's last of the three in point of time. But in all probability the three appeared in their complete form about the same time (A.D. 65 or thereabouts) in different parts of the world. S. John, writing fully a generation later, was doubtless familiar with the three others, and supposes his readers to be also familiar with them, for he purposely avoids for the most part repeating what they had already said, except in one instance (ch. vi), where he had much new matter to add to the narrative, and some most important teaching to append to it. Having been himself present throughout the Passion, he could not have added his testimony in this part without repeating the main outlines of the history, but he has done this as little as possible.

Everybody can see that there is a close verbal resemblance in many passages between the narratives of the three first Evangelists (often called the Synoptics), and this is even more apparent in the Greek than in the English, at least of the Authorised Version: a resemblance far too great to admit of our supposing that the three histories are altogether the separate productions of three different minds. At the same time there is even in these very passages sufficient variety to shew that no original document was slavishly copied or incorporated into the text, as we find in parts of the Old Testament (e.g. 2 Kings xviii. 13—xx. 19 compared with Isaiah xxxvi—xxxix), and it is closer between S. Mark (S. Peter) and S. Matthew, than between either of them and S. Luke. This is exactly what we might expect to find if the two former, having been eye-witnesses, while recording what they had seen used much of the language with which they were very familiar of an unwritten record constantly recited in Church. Such a record would necessarily begin to grow up from the first day on which the Apostles and early disciples adjourned after attending the Temple Service, to "break bread at home" (Acts ii. 47), i.e. to receive the Holy Communion in a house belonging to one of themselves. Having been accustomed to the reading of the Law and the Prophets at the Temple and Synagogue Services, they would necessarily wish to have something about their beloved Master read or recited at their own, and anything so read or recited would have a tendency to grow into a definite form, much of which would naturally be reproduced by those eye-witnesses who were committing to writing their own testimony. S. Luke, being as he tells us one degree further off from original testimony, would reproduce this language a little less closely, as we find to be the case.

The central idea of the Gospel of S. Mark may be briefly expressed as, Jesus Christ the Son of God;

of S. Matthew, Jesus Christ the Son of Abraham and of David, the King of Israel;

of S. Luke, Jesus Christ the Son of Man, the seed of the woman, that should bruise the serpent's head;

of S. John, Jesus Christ the Light and Life of the world.

The more carefully these holy witnesses are compared together, the more clearly will it be seen that all are alive with the breath of that one Holy Spirit who alone can bless their use to quicken or revive the hearts of the children of God.

C. C. JAMES.

WORTHAM RECTORY, DISS,
Jan. 1, 1892.

NOTE ON THE VERSIONS OF 1611 (A) AND 1881 (R).

The Version of 1611 commonly called the "Authorised Version," and stating on its title-page that it is "appointed to be read in Churches," though there is I believe no record of such Authorisation or appointment, delights throughout to indulge in what used to be considered a great beauty in composition, and a mark of good taste, namely, to introduce as much variety as possible into the language used; not only rendering the same Greek word differently where the meaning appeared to be in any way different, but changing about the English words employed merely for the sake of avoiding the repetition of the same sound[1], and in very many cases translating differently the same Greek word or phrase in the parallel passage from two Gospels[2], thereby giving an appearance of Variation between the Witnesses which does not really exist. This artificial variety is frequent throughout the whole Version. R has endeavoured to translate the same Greek word by the same English word wherever it can be done.

The following defects may also be observed in A, which are altogether removed in R.

Notes of time scattered arbitrarily about the narrative, by giving "when," "then" as translations of the conjunction δὲ.

A certain Predestinarian bias arbitrarily introduced into a few passages: as ἀλλ' οἷς ἡτοίμασται "but it shall be given to them for whom it is prepared" Mt. xx. 23 and parallels; εἰ δυνατὸν "if it were possible" Mt. xxiv. 24 and parallels.

The neglect of distinguishing between aorists and perfects, the inaccurate rendering of prepositions, and the indifference of A to the force of the Greek article in many cases, are well known.

"You" and "ye" are often used the one for the other, so are "would" and "should," and sometimes even "shall" and "will:" "might" is often used where we should now say "may."

---

[1] e.g. ἀρχιτρίκλινος Jn. ii. 8, 9; ἐγερῶ Jn. ii. 19; χώρα Lk. xv. 13, 14, 15.
[2] e.g. ἀξίους Mt. iii. 8 and Lk. iii. 8; ἀφέντες Mk. i. 18 and Mt. iv. 20.

Many words have quite lost their old-fashioned use, so that they no longer adequately represent the original: as "coasts," "meat," "doctrine," "fowls," "prevent," &c.

Οὐδείς is generally rendered "no man" in A, which logically involves a most astounding consequence in Mk. x. 18, "There is no man good but one, that is God" (therefore God is man!).

It should be borne in mind that so far as we deviate in our translation from the exact sense of the original writings, so far are we substituting words of mere human authority for the words of Scripture, and are knowingly, so far, teaching error.

NOTE ON THE DIVISIONS OF THE GOSPEL HISTORY.

The Gospel History seems naturally to divide itself into five parts, which are separated by a line both in the text and the Index :—

   I.   Early History, §§ 1—14.

   II.   From John's preaching to the Great Confession, §§ 15—71.

   III. From the Transfiguration to the Supper at Bethany, §§ 72—125.

   IV. From the Triumphal Entry to our Lord's burial, §§ 126—173.

   V.   The great forty days, §§ 174—186.

It may be observed of the second and third divisions, which comprise the whole of our Lord's ministry until the events immediately preceding His Passion, that each begins with circumstances of great glory and a declaration from heaven, and each closes with a special act of faith which is very highly commended by our Saviour.

NOTE ON THE SERMON ON THE MOUNT.

Whether the discourse in S. Luke vi. 20—49 is another report of the same as that in S. Matthew v. vi. vii. or not is one of those questions which must continue to be matters of opinion. I printed them independently in my Gospel History, as it is perfectly impossible to blend them into one, from their being reported from different points of view. S. Luke cannot have been acquainted with S. Matthew's report before his own was written, as the latter is so perfect a composition that had he known it he could not have varied so greatly from it ; on the other hand, S. Matthew perhaps did know S. Luke's report, and explain some phrases in it.

Many of the passages which at first sight appear peculiar to S. Matthew are found in other parts of S. Luke, mostly in chapters xi. and xii. In the Harmony these are printed in *Italics*.

An able writer has recently called the Sermon on the Mount " a collec-tion of loosely connected and aphoristic utterances." I do not know of any more perfect composition in the world, or any hortatory moral treatise in which the train of thought is more connected and logically evolved. It begins by declaring who are good citizens of the new kingdom (v. 3—12); sets forth the duties of such citizens, both in the way of example and pre-cept ; (13—17) enlarges on the principles on which the laws of that king-dom, the ancient commandments of God, are to be interpreted and kept; (17—48) treats of the great religious duties of the citizens, Almsgiving, Prayer and Fasting (vi. 1—18), and warns us against the chief hinderances to our spiritual life: worldliness (19—34); self-righteousness (vii. 1—5); irreverence (6); want of confidence (7—12), or earnestness (13—14) ; and hypocrisy, whether in teachers (15—23), or hearers (24—27). The more it is studied as a whole the more does its wonderful beauty shine forth, and the attainment of its glorious standard of perfection commend itself as the worthiest object of human ambition. He might as well have called the human skeleton a string of disconnected ossifications.

NOTE ON THE MARGINAL REFERENCES.

I have endeavoured in these to suggest every passage to which I should wish to be able to refer a class that I was teaching. I have therefore given not only the places quoted from the Old Testament, but many others also that occurred to me or were suggested by others as illustrating the text, whether by throwing light upon obscure or unusual phrases or words, or the general thought; and in many cases also passages in the Acts and Epistles, as shewing the evolution as it were of our Lord's teaching in the minds of those who first heard Him, and the application of His principles to their own circumstances and times. I know of few things more interesting than thus to trace the history of a thought, dug up from the rich mine of the Old Testament, stamped as current coin by our Saviour, and applied by His Apostles to the various uses of Christian life. The two millennia which have nearly passed since the words were spoken have added infinite variety to such application, but have in no way altered the principles themselves.

Where H. or Gr. is printed, attention is called to the Hebrew or the Greek. When more than one or two verses should be read for the reference, two or three dots are in most cases added; but the exigences of the margin have prevented this being always done, as for the sake of clearness each reference is contained for the most part in one line. For the same reason the names of the books have been abbreviated as much as possible, but not, I hope, so as to be in any case unintelligible. Other abbreviations will explain themselves : such as cp, compare ; etc.

Cross references to other sections are added where the illustration applies to the general thought of a passage, and not merely to a particular word or phrase. These are not repeated on the same page.

TABLE OF CONTENTS.

QUASI PARALLELS:

OR PASSAGES PRINTED IN ITALICS, IN ILLUSTRATION
OF THE TEXT: TO SECTIONS

27. Bethesda. The Sabbath. All of our Lord's utterances about the Sabbath-day.

43. Sermon on the Mount. Several passages from S. Luke xi. xii. xiii. xiv. xvi. also S. Mark ix. 43—48.

45. Widow's Son raised at Nain. S. Mark v. 40—43; raising of Jairus' daughter. S. John xi. 41—44; raising of Lazarus.

47. Anointing of Jesus' feet by a sinful woman. S. John xii. 1—8, S. Mark xiv. 3—9; anointing by Mary at Bethany.

59. Instructions to the twelve Apostles. S. Luke x. 3—12; instructions to the Seventy.

71. The great confession. On self-denial. S. Matthew xxv. 31—46; of the last judgement.

74. The temple-tax supplied. Exodus xxx. 11—16; the institution of the tax.

90. The Lord's Prayer, &c. S. Matthew vi. 5—15, and vii. 7—11; of prayer.

112. The raising of Lazarus. All the other Scriptural accounts of the raising of the dead, by Christ, Elijah, Elisha, Peter and Paul.

130. The king's marriage feast. S. Luke xiv. 15—24; the great supper.

139. Parable of the talents. S. Luke xix. 12—27; the ten pounds.

161. Suicide of Judas. 1 Sam. xxxi. 1—6; Saul. 2 Sam. xvii. 14, 23; Ahithophel.

164. Barabbas preferred to Jesus. S. Peter in Acts ii. 22, 23, and iii. 13—15. The high priest in Acts v. 27, 28, admitting guilt if Jesus was innocent.

TABLE FOR FINDING ANY PASSAGE.

S. MATTHEW.

S. MARK.

S. LUKE.

MIRACLES OF OUR LORD, OR ACTS SHOWING HIS SUPREMACY OVER

α. Inanimate Nature, and the lower animals.
β. Human diseases and infirmities.
γ. Evil Spirits.
δ. Death and Hades.

Besides these, several instances are recorded of the general healing of all who came or were brought to Him. Sections 33, 34, 36, 41, 46, 63, 67, 117, 127.

PARABLES OF OUR LORD.

PRINCIPAL DISCOURSES OF OUR LORD.

ADVERTISEMENT.

THE numbers of a few Sections in this Harmony correspond to different numbers in my "Gospel History" as at present published. These will be altered in the next Edition of the latter volume, so that the two books will correspond throughout.

Gospel History Sections	Harmony Sections
37, 38	27, 28
27—36	29—38
84—90	82—88
82	89
91—112	90—111
83	112

C. C. JAMES.

Feb. 1892.

A HARMONY

OF THE

GOSPELS.

_____

JESUS THE WORD OF GOD.

1. *The divinity, humanity, and office of Jesus Christ,
the Word of God, and himself God.*

S. John 1. 1—14.

1   IN the beginning was the Word, and the Word was Rev.19.13.
2 with God, and the Word was God.   The same was in Pro. 8. 22..
3 the beginning with God.   All things were made by
 him; and without him was not anything made that Col. 1. 16.
4 hath been made.   In him was life; and the life was Heb. 1. 2.
5 the light of men.   And the light shineth in the dark-
6 ness; and the darkness apprehended it not.   There Jn. 3. 19.
 came a man, sent from God, whose name was John.
7 The same came for witness, that he might bear witness
8 of the light, that all might believe through him.   He
 was not the light, but came that he might bear witness
9 of the light.   There was the true light, even the light Lk.11.35..
10 which lighteth every man, coming into the world.   He
 was in the world, and the world was made by him, Heb.11.3.
11 and the world knew him not.   He came unto his own,
12 and they that were his own received him not.   But as
 many as received him, to them gave he the right to
 become children of God, even to them that believe on Rom.8.15.
13 his name: which were born, not of blood, nor of the 1 Pet.1. 23.
 will of the flesh, nor of the will of man, but of God. Jn. 3. 5.
14 And the Word became flesh, and dwelt among us (and
 we beheld his glory, glory as of the only begotten from Col. 2. 9.
 the Father), full of grace and truth.

    J. H. G.   I

2. *The genealogy of Jesus Christ from Abraham to Joseph.*
S. Matthew 1. 1—17.

1Ch.17.12..
Ps.89.27...
Gen.22.18.

THE book of the generation of Jesus Christ, the son 1 of David, the son of Abraham.

2 Abraham begat Isaac;
and Isaac begat Jacob;
and Jacob begat Judah and his brethren;

Gen. 38.
3 and Judah begat Perez and Zerah of Tamar;
and Perez begat Hezron;
and Hezron begat Ram;
4 and Ram begat Amminadab;
and Amminadab begat Nahshon;
and Nahshon begat Salmon;

Heb.11.31.
5 and Salmon begat Boaz of Rahab;
and Boaz begat Obed of

Ruth 4. 17.
Ruth;
and Obed begat Jesse;
6 and Jesse begat David the king.

And David begat Solo-
2Sa.13.24.
mon of her that had been the wife of Uriah;
7 and Solomon begat Rehoboam;
and Rehoboam begat Abijah;
and Abijah begat Asa;
8 and Asa begat Jehoshaphat;
and Jehoshaphat begat Joram;

1 Ch. 22.1;
— 22. 11;
— 24. 27;
— 26. 1.
and Joram begat Uzziah;

and Uzziah begat Jo- 9 tham;
and Jotham begat Ahaz;
and Ahaz begat Hezekiah;
and Hezekiah begat Ma- 10 nasseh;
and Manasseh begat Amon;
and Amon begat Josiah;
and Josiah begat Jecho- 11 niah and his brethren, at
the time of the carrying away to Babylon.

1Ch.3.15...

And after the carrying 12 away to Babylon,
Jechoniah begat Shealtiel;
and Shealtiel begat Ze- 1 Ch.3.17..
rubbabel;
and Zerubbabel begat 13 Abiud;
and Abiud begat Eliakim;
and Eliakim begat Azor;
and Azor begat Sadoc; 14
and Sadoc begat Achim;
and Achim begat Eliud;
and Eliud begat Eleazar; 15
and Eleazar begat Matthan;
and Matthan begat Jacob;
and Jacob begat Joseph 16 the husband of Mary, of whom was born Jesus, who is called Christ.

So all the generations from Abraham unto David are 17 fourteen generations; and from David unto the carrying away to Babylon fourteen generations; and from the carrying away to Babylon unto the Christ fourteen generations.

3. *The age and genealogy of Christ from Joseph upwards.*

S. Luke iii. 23—38.

23   AND Jesus himself, when he began to teach, was about
thirty years of age, being the son (as was supposed) of Num. 4. 3.
Joseph,

the son of Heli,
24   the son of Matthat,
the son of Levi,
the son of Melchi,
the son of Jannai,
the son of Joseph,
25   the son of Mattathias,
the son of Amos,
the son of Nahum,
the son of Esli,
the son of Naggai,
26   the son of Maath,
the son of Mattathias,
the son of Semein,
the son of Josech,
the son of Joda,
27   the son of Joanan,
the son of Rhesa,
the son of Zerubbabel,
the son of Shealtiel,
the son of Neri,
28   the son of Melchi,
the son of Addi,
the son of Cosam,
the son of Elmadam,
the son of Er,
29   the son of Jesus,
the son of Eliezer,
the son of Jorim,
the son of Matthat,
the son of Levi,
30   the son of Symeon,
the son of Judas,
the son of Joseph,
the son of Jonam,
the son of Eliakim,
31   the son of Melea,
the son of Menna,

the son of Mattatha,
the son of Nathan,
the son of David,   1Ch.17.12..
32 the son of Jesse,   Ps.89.27...
the son of Obed,
the son of Boaz,
the son of Salmon,
the son of Nahshon,
33 the son of Amminadab,
the son of Arni,
the son of Hezron,
the son of Perez,
the son of Judah,
34 the son of Jacob,
the son of Isaac,
the son of Abraham,   Gen.22.18.
the son of Terah,
the son of Nahor,
35 the son of Serug,
the son of Reu,
the son of Peleg,
the son of Eber,
the son of Shelah,
36 the son of Cainan,
the son of Arphaxad,
the son of Shem,   Gen. 9. 26.
the son of Noah,
the son of Lamech,
37 the son of Methuselah,
the son of Enoch,
the son of Jared,
the son of Mahalaleel,
the son of Cainan,
38 the son of Enos,
the son of Seth,
the son of Adam,   Gen. 3. 15.
the son of God.

4. *The plan and purpose of S. Luke's Gospel.*
S. Luke 1. 1—4.

FORASMUCH as many have taken in hand to draw up 1
a narrative concerning those matters which have been
fulfilled among us, even as they delivered them unto us, 2
Acts 10.41. which from the beginning were eyewitnesses and ministers
of the word, it seemed good to me also, having traced 3
the course of all things accurately from the first, to write
Acts 1. 1. unto thee in order, most excellent Theophilus; that thou 4
mightest know the certainty concerning the things wherein
Gal. 6. 6   thou wast instructed.
Gr.

5. *Birth of John Baptist promised.*
S. Luke 1. 5—25.

THERE was in the days of Herod, king of Judæa, a 5
1Ch.24.10. certain priest named Zacharias, of the course of Abijah:
and he had a wife of the daughters of Aaron, and her
Gen. 7. 1. name was Elisabeth. And they were both righteous 6
before God, walking in all the commandments and
Phil. 3. 6. ordinances of the Lord blameless. And they had no 7
child, because that Elisabeth was barren, and they both
were *now* well stricken in years.
Now it came to pass, while he executed the priest's 8
2 Ch. 8. 14. office before God in the order of his course, according 9
to the custom of the priest's office, his lot was to enter
Ex. 30. 7.. into the temple of the Lord and burn incense. And 10
the whole multitude of the people were praying without at the hour of incense. And there appeared unto 11
him an angel of the Lord standing on the right side
Ex. 30. 1. of the altar of incense. And Zacharias was troubled 12
Jud.13. 22. when he saw him, and fear fell upon him. But the 13
angel said unto him, Fear not, Zacharias: because thy
supplication is heard, and thy wife Elisabeth shall bear
. thee a son, and thou shalt call his name John. And 14
thou shalt have joy and gladness; and many shall
Num. 6. 3. rejoice at his birth. For he shall be great in the sight 15
Jud. 13. 7. of the Lord, and he shall drink no wine nor strong
drink; and he shall be filled with the Holy Ghost,
even from his mother's womb. And many of the children 16
of Israel shall he turn unto the Lord their God. And he 17
Mal. 4. 5. shall go before his face in the spirit and power of Elijah,
to turn the hearts of the fathers to the children, and the
disobedient to walk in the wisdom of the just; to make

18 ready for the Lord a people prepared for him. And
Zacharias said unto the angel, Whereby shall I know
this? for I am an old man, and my wife well stricken in Gen. 17. 17.
19 years. And the angel answering said unto him, I am — 18. 12.
Gabriel, that stand in the presence of God; and I was Dan. 8. 16.
sent to speak unto thee, and to bring thee these good
20 tidings. And behold, thou shalt be silent and not able to Eze. 3. 26..
speak, until the day that these things shall come to pass, — 24. 27.
because thou believedst not my words, which shall be
21 fulfilled in their season. And the people were waiting
for Zacharias, and they marvelled while he tarried in
22 the temple. And when he came out, he could not
speak unto them: and they perceived that he had seen a
vision in the temple: and he continued making signs
23 unto them, and remained dumb. And it came to pass, 1 Ch. 9. 25.
when the days of his ministration were fulfilled, he
departed unto his house.
24   And after these days Elisabeth his wife conceived;
25 and she hid herself five months, saying, Thus hath the
Lord done unto me in the days wherein he looked upon
me, to take away my reproach among men.   Gen. 30. 23.

6. *The Annunciation. Visit to Elisabeth. Magnificat.*

S. Luke 1. 26—56.

26   Now in the sixth month the angel Gabriel was sent
27 from God unto a city of Galilee, named Nazareth, to a
virgin betrothed to a man whose name was Joseph, of
the house of David; and the virgin's name was Mary.
28 And he came in unto her, and said, Hail, thou that art
29 highly favoured, the Lord is with thee. But she was Jud. 6. 12.
greatly troubled at the saying, and cast in her mind
30 what manner of salutation this might be. And the angel
said unto her, Fear not, Mary: for thou hast found favour
31 with God. And behold, thou shalt conceive in thy womb, Is. 7. 14.
and bring forth a son, and shalt call his name JESUS.
32 He shall be great, and shall be called the Son of the
Most High: and the Lord God shall give unto him the Ps. 72. 8...
33 throne of his father David: and he shall reign over the Is. 9. 7.
house of Jacob for ever; and of his kingdom there shall Dan. 7. 14.
34 be no end. And Mary said unto the angel, How shall Mic. 4. 7.
35 this be, seeing I know not a man? And the angel
answered and said unto her, The Holy Ghost shall come

upon thee, and the power of the Most High shall over-
shadow thee: wherefore also that which is to be born
Jn. 20. 31. shall be called holy, the Son of God.   And behold, 36
Elisabeth thy kinswoman, she also hath conceived a son
in her old age: and this is the sixth month with her that
Is. 55. 11. was called barren.   For no word from God shall be 37
Rom. 4. 21. void of power.   And Mary said, Behold, the handmaid 38
of the Lord; be it unto me according to thy word.   And
the angel departed from her.

And Mary arose in these days and went into the hill 39
Jos. 21. 9.. country with haste, into a city of Judah; and entered 40
into the house of Zacharias and saluted Elisabeth.   And 41
it came to pass, when Elisabeth heard the salutation of
Mary, the babe leaped in her womb; and Elisabeth was
filled with the Holy Ghost; and she lifted up her voice 42
with a loud cry, and said, Blessed art thou among
women, and blessed is the fruit of thy womb.   And 43
whence is this to me, that the mother of my Lord should
come unto me?   For behold, when the voice of thy 44
salutation came into mine ears, the babe leaped in my
womb for joy.   And blessed is she that believed; for 45
there shall be a fulfilment of the things which have been
spoken to her from the Lord.   And Mary said,   46

1 Sa. 2. 1...   My soul doth magnify the Lord,
                And my spirit hath rejoiced in God my Saviour. 47
1 Sa. 1. 11.   For he hath looked upon the low estate of his 48
                    handmaiden:
                For behold, from henceforth all generations shall
                    call me blessed.
Ps. 126. 2..   For he that is mighty hath done to me great 49
                    things;
Ps. 111. 9.   And holy is his name.
Ps. 103. 17.   And his mercy is unto generations and generations 50
                On them that fear him.
Is. 52. 10.   He hath shewed strength with his arm;   51
Ps. 33. 10;   He hath scattered the proud in the imagination
— 89. 10.   of their heart.
Job 12. 19;   He hath put down princes from their thrones,   52
— 5. 11.   And hath exalted them of low degree.
Ps. 107. 9;   The hungry he hath filled with good things;   53
— 34. 10.   And the rich he hath sent empty away.
Is. 41. 8.   He hath holpen Israel his servant,   54
Mic. 7. 20.   That he might remember mercy

55   (As he spake unto our fathers)
     Toward Abraham and his seed for ever.   Gen.17.19.
56   And Mary abode with her about three months, and
     returned unto her house.

7.   *The conception immaculate.*
S. Matt. 1. 18—25.

18   Now the birth of Jesus Christ was on this wise:
     When his mother Mary had been betrothed to Joseph,
     before they came together she was found with child of
19   the Holy Ghost.   And Joseph her husband, being a
     righteous man, and not willing to make her a public
20   example, was minded to put her away privily.   But Deut.24.1.
     when he thought on these things, behold, an angel of the
     Lord appeared unto him in a dream, saying, Joseph,
     thou son of David, fear not to take unto thee Mary thy
     wife: for that which is conceived in her is of the Holy
21   Ghost.   And she shall bring forth a son; and thou shalt
     call his name JESUS; for it is he that shall save his Nu. 13. 16.
22   people from their sins.   Now all this is come to pass, Acts 4. 12.
     that it might be fulfilled which was spoken by the Lord
     through the prophet, saying,
23   Behold, the virgin shall be with child, and shall Is. 7. 14.
             bring forth a son,
     And they shall call his name Immanuel;
24   which is, being interpreted, God with us.   And Joseph
     arose from his sleep, and did as the angel of the Lord
25   commanded him, and took unto him his wife; and knew
     her not till she had brought forth a son: and he called
     his name JESUS.

8.   *Birth of John Baptist.   Benedictus.*
S. Luke 1. 57—80.

57   Now Elisabeth's time was fulfilled that she should be
58   delivered; and she brought forth a son.   And her neigh-
     bours and her kinsfolk heard that the Lord had magni-
     fied his mercy towards her; and they rejoiced with her.
59   And it came to pass on the eighth day, that they came Gen.17.12.
     to circumcise the child; and they would have called him Lev. 12. 3.
60   Zacharias, after the name of his father.   And his mother
     answered and said, Not so; but he shall be called John.
61   And they said unto her, There is none of thy kindred

that is called by this name. And they made signs to 62
his father, what he would have him called. And he 63
2 Cor. 3. 3. asked for a writing tablet, and wrote, saying, His name
is John. And they marvelled all. And his mouth was 64
Eze. 3. 27. opened immediately, and his tongue loosed, and he spake,
— 24. 27. blessing God. And fear came on all that dwelt round 65
about them: and all these sayings were noised abroad
throughout all the hill country of Judæa. And all that 66
heard them laid them up in their heart, saying, What
Neh. 2. 8. then shall this child be? For the hand of the Lord was
Acts 11. 21. with him.

. And his father Zacharias was filled with the Holy 67
Ghost, and prophesied, saying,

1 Ki. 1. 48.   Blessed be the Lord, the God of Israel;   68
Ex. 3. 16..   For he hath visited and wrought redemption for his
— 4. 31.   people,
Ps. 132. 17.   And hath raised up a horn of salvation for us   . 69
Jer. 23. 5;   In the house of his servant David
— 30. 9.   (As he spake by the mouth of his holy prophets 70
Acts 3. 24.   which have been since the world began),
Ps. 106. 10.   Salvation from our enemies, and from the hand of 71
                    all that hate us;
Ps. 105. 8.   To shew mercy towards our fathers,   72
— 106. 45.   And to remember his holy covenant;
Ge. 22. 16..   The oath which he sware unto Abraham our father, 73
Mic. 7. 20.   To grant unto us that we being delivered out of the 74
                    hand of our enemies
1 Jn. 4. 18.   Should serve him without fear,
Eph. 4. 24.   In holiness and righteousness before him all our 75
1 Pet. 1. 15.   days.
.   Yea and thou, child, shalt be called the prophet of 76
                    the Most High:
Is. 40. 3.   For thou shalt go before the face of the Lord to
Mal. 3. 1.   make ready his ways;
               To give knowledge of salvation unto his people   77
               In the remission of their sins,
               Because of the tender mercy of our God,   78
Nu. 24. 17.   Whereby the dayspring from on high shall visit us,
Mal. 4. 2.   To shine upon them that sit in darkness and the 79
Is. 9. 2.   shadow of death;
               To guide our feet into the way of peace.
1 Sa. 3. 19.   And the child grew, and waxed strong in spirit, and 80
was in the deserts till the day of his shewing unto Israel.

9. *Birth of Jesus.*
S. Luke ii. 1—7.

1 Now it came to pass in those days, there went out a
decree from Cæsar Augustus, that all the world should
2 be enrolled. This was the first enrolment made when Acts 5. 37.
3 Quirinius was governor of Syria. And all went to enrol
4 themselves, every one to his own city. And Joseph also
went up from Galilee, out of the city of Nazareth, into
Judæa, to the city of David, which is called Bethlehem, 1 Sa. 16. 1.
5 because he was of the house and family of David; to Jn. 7. 42.
enrol himself with Mary, who was betrothed to him,
6 being great with child. And it came to pass, while they
were there, the days were fulfilled that she should be
7 delivered. And she brought forth her firstborn son;
and she wrapped him in swaddling clothes, and laid him Ezek. 16. 4.
in a manger, because there was no room for them in the
inn.

10. *Shepherds at Bethlehem.*
S. Luke ii. 8—20.

8 AND there were shepherds in the same country abiding in the field, and keeping watch by night over their
9 flock. And an angel of the Lord stood by them, and
the glory of the Lord shone round about them: and
10 they were sore afraid. And the angel said unto them,
Be not afraid; for behold, I bring you good tidings of
11 great joy which shall be to all the people: for there is Gen. 12. 3.
born to you this day in the city of David a Saviour, Is. 9. 6.
12 which is Christ the Lord. And this is the sign unto
you; Ye shall find a babe wrapped in swaddling clothes,
13 and lying in a manger. And suddenly there was with
the angel a multitude of the heavenly host praising God, Rev. 5. 11..
and saying,
14   Glory to God in the highest,
And on earth peace among men in whom he is well Is. 26. 3.
    pleased.   — 57. 19.
15 And it came to pass, when the angels went away
from them into heaven, the shepherds said one to another, Let us now go even unto Bethlehem, and see this
thing that is come to pass, which the Lord hath made
16 known unto us. And they came with haste, and found
both Mary and Joseph, and the babe lying in the manger.
17 And when they saw it, they made known concerning the

saying which was spoken to them about this child. And 18
all that heard it wondered at the things which were
spoken unto them by the shepherds. But Mary kept 19
Gen. 37.11. all these sayings, pondering them in her heart. And 20
the shepherds returned, glorifying and praising God for
all the things that they had heard and seen, even as it
was spoken unto them.

11. *Circumcision. Presentation. Nunc Dimittis.* *Anna.*

S. Luke ii. 21—40.

Gen. 17.12.　　AND when eight days were fulfilled for circumcising 21
him, his name was called JESUS, which was so called by
the angel before he was conceived in the womb.

Lev. 12. 2.　　And when the days of their purification according to 22
the law of Moses were fulfilled, they brought him up to
Jerusalem, to present him to the Lord (as it is written in 23
Ex. 13. 2. the law of the Lord, Every male that openeth the womb
shall be called holy to the Lord), and to offer a sacrifice 24
according to that which is said in the law of the Lord,

Lev. 12. 8. A pair of turtle-doves, or two young pigeons. And be- 25
hold, there was a man in Jerusalem, whose name was
Simeon; and this man was righteous and devout, look-
Is. 40. 1. ing for the consolation of Israel: and the Holy Spirit
was upon him. And it had been revealed unto him by 26
the Holy Spirit, that he should not see death, before he
had seen the Lord's Christ. And he came in the Spirit 27
into the temple: and when the parents brought in the
child Jesus, that they might do concerning him after the
custom of the law, then he received him into his arms, 28
and blessed God, and said,

Gen. 46.30.　　Now lettest thou thy servant depart, O Lord, 　　29
　　　　According to thy word, in peace;

Is. 40. 5.　　For mine eyes have seen thy salvation, 　　30
— 52. 10.　　Which thou hast prepared before the face of all 31
　　　　　peoples;

Is. 9. 2;　　A light for revelation to the Gentiles, 　　32
— 35. 7;　　And the glory of thy people Israel.
— 49. 6.　　And his father and his mother were marvelling at the 33
things which were spoken concerning him; and Simeon 34
blessed them, and said unto Mary his mother, Behold,
Is. 8. 14. this child is set for the falling and rising up of many in
Rom. 9.32. Israel; and for a sign which is spoken against; yea 35

and a sword shall pierce through thine own soul; that Jn. 19. 25.
36 thoughts out of many hearts may be revealed.   And
there was one Anna, a prophetess, the daughter of
Phanuel, of the tribe of Asher (she was of a great age,
having lived with a husband seven years from her vir-
37 ginity, and she had been a widow even for fourscore and
four years), which departed not from the temple, worshipping with fastings and supplications night and day. 1 Tim. 5.5.
38 And coming up at that very hour she gave thanks unto
God, and spake of him to all them that were looking for
39 the redemption of Jerusalem.   And when they had accomplished all things that were according to the law of
the Lord, they returned into Galilee, to their own city
Nazareth.
40   And the child grew and waxed strong, filled with 1 Sa. 3. 19.
wisdom : and the grace of God was upon him.

12. *Epiphany.*

S. Matthew ii. 1—12.

1   Now when Jesus was born in Bethlehem of Judæa in
the days of Herod the king, behold, wise men from the 1 Ki. 4. 30.
2 east came to Jerusalem, saying, Where is he that is born
King of the Jews? for we saw his star in the east, and Nu. 24. 17.
3 are come to worship him.   And when Herod the king Is. 60. 3.
heard it, he was troubled, and all Jerusalem with him.
4 And gathering together all the chief priests and scribes 2Ch.34.13.
of the people, he inquired of them where the Christ
5 should be born.   And they said unto him, In Bethlehem
of Judæa : for thus it is written by the prophet,
6   And thou Bethlehem, land of Judah,   Mic. 5. 2.
       Art in no wise least among the princes of Judah :   Jn. 7. 42.
       For out of thee shall come forth a governor,
       Which shall be shepherd of my people Israel.   Jn. 10. 11.
7 Then Herod privily called the wise men, and learned of
8 them carefully what time the star appeared.   And he
sent them to Bethlehem, and said, Go and search out
carefully concerning the young child ; and when ye have
found him, bring me word, that I also may come and
9 worship him.   And they, having heard the king, went
their way ; and lo, the star, which they saw in the east,
went before them, till it came and stood over where the
10 young child was.   And when they saw the star, they

rejoiced with exceeding great joy. And they came into 11
the house and saw the young child with Mary his mother;
and they fell down and worshipped him; and opening
their treasures they offered unto him gifts, gold and
frankincense and myrrh. And being warned of God 12
in a dream that they should not return to Herod, they
departed into their own country another way.

Ps. 72. 10.
Is. 60. 6.
Jn. 19. 39.

13. *Flight into Egypt. Murder of the Innocents.*
S. Matthew ii. 13—23.

Now when they were departed, behold, an angel of 13
the Lord appeareth to Joseph in a dream, saying, Arise
and take the young child and his mother, and flee into
Egypt, and be thou there until I tell thee: for Herod
will seek the young child to destroy him. And he arose 14
and took the young child and his mother by night, and
departed into Egypt; and was there until the death 15
of Herod: that it might be fulfilled which was spoken
by the Lord through the prophet, saying, Out of Egypt
did I call my son. Then Herod, when he saw that he 16
was mocked of the wise men, was exceeding wroth, and
sent forth, and slew all the male children that were in
Bethlehem, and in all the borders thereof, from two
years old and under, according to the time which he
had carefully learned of the wise men. Then was ful- 17
filled that which was spoken by Jeremiah the prophet,
saying,

Hos. 11. 1.

Jer. 31. 15.

A voice was heard in Ramah,   18
   Weeping and great mourning,
   Rachel weeping for her children;
   And she would not be comforted, because they are
      not.

But when Herod was dead, behold, an angel of the 19
Lord appeareth in a dream to Joseph in Egypt, saying, 20
Arise and take the young child and his mother, and go
into the land of Israel: for they are dead that sought
the young child's life. And he arose and took the young 21
child and his mother, and came into the land of Israel.
But when he heard that Archelaus was reigning over 22
Judæa in the room of his father Herod, he was afraid
to go thither; and being warned of God in a dream, he
withdrew into the parts of Galilee, and came and dwelt 23

in a city called Nazareth : that it might be fulfilled which perhaps נצר
was spoken by the prophets, that he should be called a Branch
Nazarene.   Is. 11. 1.

14. *Jesus found in his Father's house.*

S. Luke ii. 41—52.

41 AND his parents went every year to Jerusalem at the Ex.23.14..
42 feast of the passover. And when he was twelve years Deu.16.15.
43 old, they went up after the custom of the feast; and
   when they had fulfilled the days, as they were returning,
   the boy Jesus tarried behind in Jerusalem; and his
44 parents knew it not; but supposing him to be in the
   company, they went a day's journey; and they sought
45 for him among their kinsfolk and acquaintance: and
   when they found him not, they returned to Jerusalem,
46 seeking for him. And it came to pass, after three days
   they found him in the temple, sitting in the midst of the
   doctors, both hearing them, and asking them questions :
47 and all that heard him were amazed at his understanding
48 and his answers. And when they saw him, they were
   astonished : and his mother said unto him, Son, why
   hast thou thus dealt with us? behold, thy father and I
49 sought thee sorrowing. And he said unto them, How is
   it that ye sought me? wist ye not that I must be in my Jn. 2. 16.
50 Father's house? And they understood not the saying
51 which he spake unto them. And he went down with
   them, and came to Nazareth; and he was subject unto
   them : and his mother kept all these sayings in her heart. Dan. 7. 28.
52 And Jesus advanced in wisdom and stature, and in 1 Sa. 2. 26.
   favour with God and men.

15. *Preaching of John the Baptist.*

S. Luke iii. 1—20.

Now in the fifteenth year of the reign of Tiberius 1
Cæsar, Pontius Pilate being governor of Judæa, and
Herod being tetrarch of Galilee, and his brother Philip
tetrarch of the region of Ituræa and Trachonitis, and
Lysanias tetrarch of Abilene, in the high-priesthood of 2
Jn. 18. 13. Annas and Caiaphas, the word of God came unto John
the son of Zacharias in the wilderness.   And he came 3
into all the region round about Jordan, preaching the
baptism of repentance unto remission of sins; as it is 4
written in the book of the words of Isaiah the Prophet,

Is. 40. 3...   The voice of one crying in the wilderness,
            Make ye ready the way of the Lord,
            Make his paths straight.
            Every valley shall be filled,   5
            And every mountain and hill shall be brought low;
            And the crooked shall become straight,
            And the rough ways smooth;
            And all flesh shall see the salvation of God.   6
He said therefore to the multitudes that went out 7
Is. 59. 5. to be baptized of him, Ye offspring of vipers, who warned
you to flee from the wrath to come?   Bring forth there- 8
fore fruits worthy of repentance, and begin not to say
Jn. 8. 39. within yourselves, We have Abraham to our father: for I
say unto you, that God is able of these stones to raise up
children unto Abraham.   And even now is the axe also 9
laid to the root of the trees: every tree therefore that
bringeth not forth good fruit is hewn down, and cast into
the fire.   And the multitudes asked him, saying, What 10
then must we do?   And he answered and said unto 11
Job 31. 19. them, He that hath two coats, let him impart to him
— 31. 17. that hath none; and he that hath food, let him do likewise.   And there came also publicans to be baptized, and 12
Lk. 19. 8. they said unto him, Master, what must we do?   And he 13
said unto them, Extort no more than that which is appointed you.   And soldiers also asked him, saying, And 14
·   we, what must we do?   And he said unto them, Do
violence to no man, neither exact anything wrongfully;
Acts 24. 29. and be content with your wages.   [T. O.

8. Matthew iii. 1—12.

1   And in those days cometh John the Baptist, preaching
2 in the wilderness of Judæa, saying, Repent ye ; for the
3 kingdom of heaven is at hand. For this is he that was
   spoken of by Isaiah the prophet, saying,
      The voice of one crying in the wilderness,
      Make ye ready the way of the Lord,
      Make his paths straight.
4   Now John himself had his raiment of camel's hair,
   and a leathern girdle about his loins; and his food was 2 Ki. 1. 8.
5 locusts and wild honey. Then went out to him Jerusalem, and all Judæa, and all the region round about
6 Jordan ; and they were baptized of him in the river
7 Jordan, confessing their sins. But when he saw many of Acts 19.18.
   the Pharisees and Sadducees coming to his baptism, he Jam. 5. 16.
   said unto them, Ye offspring of vipers, who warned you Is. 59. 5.
8 to flee from the wrath to come? Bring forth therefore
9 fruit worthy of repentance : and think not to say within
   yourselves, We have Abraham to our father : for I say Jn. 8. 39.
   unto you that God is able of these stones to raise up
10 children unto Abraham. And even now is the axe laid
   to the root of the trees : every tree therefore that bringeth
   not forth good fruit is hewn down, and cast into the fire.
                                [T. O.

8. Mark i. 1—8.

1   The beginning of the gospel of Jesus Christ, the
   Son of God.
2   Even as it is written in Isaiah the prophet,
      Behold, I send my messenger before thy face,   Mal. 3. 1.
      Who shall prepare thy way ;
3   The voice of one crying in the wilderness,   Is. 40. 3...
      Make ye ready the way of the Lord,
      Make his paths straight ;
4 John came, who baptized in the wilderness and preached
5 the baptism of repentance unto remission of sins. And
   there went out unto him all the country of Judæa, and
   all they of Jerusalem ; and they were baptized of him in
6 the river Jordan, confessing their sins. And John was
   clothed with camel's hair, and *had* a leathern girdle
   about his loins, and did eat locusts and wild honey.
                                [T. O.

S. Luke iii.

And as the people were in expectation, and all men 15
reasoned in their hearts concerning John, whether haply
he were the Christ; John answered, saying unto them 16
all, I indeed baptize you with water; but there cometh
after me he that is mightier than I, the latchet of whose
Acts 1. 5. shoes I am not worthy to unloose: he shall baptize you
with the Holy Ghost and with fire: whose fan is in his 17
Amos 9. 9. hand, throughly to cleanse his threshing-floor, and to
Is. 66. 24. gather the wheat into his garner; but the chaff he will
Mt. 13. 30. burn up with unquenchable fire.
51   With many other exhortations therefore preached he 18
good tidings unto the people; but Herod the tetrarch, 19
46. 60   being reproved by him for Herodias his brother's wife,
and for all the evil things which Herod had done, added 20
yet this above all, that he shut up John in prison.

S. Matthew iii.

I indeed baptize you with water unto repentance: 11
but he that cometh after me is mightier than I, whose
shoes I am not worthy to bear: he shall baptize you
with the Holy Ghost and *with* fire: whose fan is in his
hand, and he will throughly cleanse his threshing-floor; 12
and he will gather his wheat into the garner, but the
chaff he will burn up with unquenchable fire.

S. Mark i.

And he preached, saying, There cometh after me he 7
that is mightier than I, the latchet of whose shoes I am
not worthy to stoop down and unloose. I baptized you 8
with water; but he shall baptize you with the Holy
Ghost.

16. *Baptism of Jesus*

S. Matthew. iii. 13—17.

13 THEN cometh Jesus from Galilee to the Jordan unto
14 John, to be baptized of him. But John would have
hindered him, saying, I have need to be baptized of thee,
15 and comest thou to me? But Jesus answering said unto
him, Suffer it now : for thus it becometh us to fulfil all
16 righteousness. Then he suffereth him. And Jesus when
he was baptized went up straightway from the water :
and lo, the heavens were opened unto him, and he saw
the Spirit of God descending as a dove, and coming
17 upon him; and lo, a voice out of the heavens, saying, 72. 141
This is my beloved Son ; in whom I am well pleased.   Ps. 2. 7.
                                                         Is. 42. 1.

S. Mark i. 9—11.

9 And it came to pass in those days, that Jesus came
from Nazareth of Galilee, and was baptized of John in
10 the Jordan. And straightway coming up out of the
water, he saw the heavens rent asunder, and the Spirit as
11 a dove descending upon him : and a voice came out of
the heavens, Thou art my beloved Son, in thee I am
well pleased.

S. Luke iii. 21, 22.

21 Now it came to pass, when all the people were
baptized, that, Jesus also having been baptized, and
22 praying, the heaven was opened, and the Holy Ghost
descended in a bodily form, as a dove, upon him, and a
voice came out of heaven, Thou art my beloved Son ; in
thee I am well pleased.

17. *Fasting and Temptation of Jesus.*

S. Luke iv. 1—13.

AND Jesus, full of the Holy Spirit, returned from the 1
Jordan, and was led by the Spirit in the wilderness
during forty days, being tempted of the devil.   And he 2
did eat nothing in those days : and when they were
Ex. 34. 28.   completed, he hungered.   And the devil said unto him, 3
1 Ki. 19. 8.   If thou art the Son of God, command this stone that it
become bread.   And Jesus answered unto him, It is
Deu. 8. 3.   written, Man shall not live by bread alone.

And he led him up, and shewed him all the kingdoms 5
of the world in a moment of time.   And the devil said 6
unto him, To thee will I give all this authority, and the
Jn. 16. 11.   glory of them : for it hath been delivered unto me ; and
— 14, 30.   to whomsoever I will, I give it.   If thou therefore wilt 7
Rev. 13. 7.   worship before me, it shall all be thine.   And Jesus 8
Deu. 6. 13.   answered and said unto him, It is written, Thou shalt
— 10. 20.   worship the Lord thy God, and him only shalt thou
serve.

And he led him to Jerusalem, and set him on the 9
pinnacle of the temple, and said unto him, If thou art
the Son of God, cast thyself down from hence : for it is 10
written,
Ps. 91. 11.   He shall give his angels charge concerning thee, to
guard thee :
and,   11
— 12.   On their hands they shall bear thee up,
Lest haply thou dash thy foot against a stone.
Deu. 6. 16.   And Jesus answering said unto him, It is said, Thou 12
shalt not tempt the Lord thy God.

And when the devil had completed every temptation, 13
he departed from him for a season.

S. Matthew iv. 1—11.

1 Then was Jesus led up of the Spirit into the
2 wilderness to be tempted of the devil. And when he
had fasted forty days and forty nights, he afterward
3 hungered. And the tempter came and said unto him, If
thou art the Son of God, command that these stones
4 become bread. But he answered and said, It is written,
Man shall not live by bread alone, but by every word
that proceedeth out of the mouth of God.
5 Then the devil taketh him into the holy city; and
6 he set him on the pinnacle of the temple, and saith unto
him, If thou art the Son of God, cast thyself down: for
it is written,

He shall give his angels charge concerning thee:
And on their hands they shall bear thee up,
Lest haply thou dash thy foot against a stone.

7 Jesus said unto him, Again it is written, Thou shalt not
tempt the Lord thy God.
8 Again, the devil taketh him unto an exceeding high
mountain, and sheweth him all the kingdoms of the
9 world, and the glory of them; and he said unto him,
All these things will I give thee, if thou wilt fall down
10 and worship me. Then saith Jesus unto him, Get thee
hence, Satan: for it is written, Thou shalt worship the
11 Lord thy God, and him only shalt thou serve. Then the
devil leaveth him; and behold, angels came and min- Lk. 22. 43.
istered unto him.

S. Mark i. 12, 13.

12 And straightway the Spirit driveth him forth into the
13 wilderness. And he was in the wilderness forty days
tempted of Satan; and he was with the wild beasts; Gen. 2. 19.
and the angels ministered unto him.

18. *John Baptist of Jesus and of himself.*

S. John 1. 15—28.

JOHN beareth witness of him, and crieth, saying, 15
This was he of whom I said, He that cometh after me is
become before me : for he was before me.   For of his 16
Col. 1. 19. fulness we all received, and grace for grace.   For the law 17
was given by Moses ; grace and truth came by Jesus
1 Tim 6.16. Christ.   No man hath seen God at any time ; the only- 18
1 Joh.4.12. begotten Son, which is in the bosom of the Father, he
hath declared him.

And this is the witness of John, when the Jews sent 19
unto him from Jerusalem priests and Levites to ask him,
Acts 13. 25. Who art thou ?   And he confessed, and denied not ; and 20
he confessed, I am not the Christ.   And they asked him, 21
Mal. 4. 5. What then ?   Art thou Elijah ?   And he saith, I am not.
De. 18. 15.. Art thou the prophet ?   And he answered, No.   They 22
said therefore unto him, Who art thou ? that we may give
an answer to them that sent us.   What sayest thou of
Is. 40. 3. thyself ?   He said, I am the voice of one crying in the 23
wilderness, Make straight the way of the Lord, as said
Isaiah the prophet.   And they had been sent from the 24
Pharisees.   And they asked him, and said unto him, 25
Eze. 36.25. Why then baptizest thou, if thou art not the Christ,
Is. 52. 15. neither Elijah, neither the prophet ?   John answered 26
Zech.13. 1. them, saying, I baptize with water : in the midst of you
standeth one whom ye know not, even he that cometh
after me, the latchet of whose shoe I am not worthy to 27
unloose.   These things were done in Bethany beyond 28
Jordan, where John was baptizing.

19.   *The Lamb of God. Andrew, Peter, Philip, Nathanael.*

S. John 1. 29—51.

ON the morrow he seeth Jesus coming unto him, and 29
Is. 53. 7. saith, Behold, the Lamb of God, which taketh away the
Ex. 29. 38. sin of the world !   This is he of whom I said, After me 30
Ex. 12. 3. cometh a man which is become before me : for he was
before me.   And I knew him not ; but that he should be 31
made manifest to Israel, for this cause came I baptizing
with water.   And John bare witness, saying, I have 32
16   beheld the Spirit descending as a dove out of heaven ;
and it abode upon him.   And I knew him not : but he 33

that sent me to baptize with water, he said unto me,
Upon whomsoever thou shalt see the Spirit descending,
and abiding upon him, the same is he that baptizeth with Acts 1. 5.
34 the Holy Spirit. And I have seen, and have borne
witness that this is the Son of God.

35   Again on the morrow John was standing, and two of
36 his disciples; and he looked upon Jesus as he walked,
37 and saith, Behold, the Lamb of God! And the two
38 disciples heard him speak, and they followed Jesus. And
Jesus turned, and beheld them following, and saith unto
them, What seek ye? And they said unto him, Rabbi
(which is to say, being interpreted, Master), where
39 abidest thou? He saith unto them, Come, and ye shall
see. They came therefore and saw where he abode;
and they abode with him that day: it was about the tenth
40 hour. One of the two that heard John speak, and
41 followed him, was Andrew, Simon Peter's brother. He
findeth first his own brother Simon, and saith unto him,
We have found the Messiah (which is, being interpreted,
42 Christ). He brought him unto Jesus. Jesus looked upon
him, and said, Thou art Simon the son of John: thou
shalt be called Cephas (which is by interpretation, Peter). Mt. 16. 18.
43   On the morrow he was minded to go forth into   **71**
Galilee, and he findeth Philip: and Jesus saith unto him,
44 Follow me. Now Philip was from Bethsaida, of the city Jn. 12. 21.
45 of Andrew and Peter. Philip findeth Nathanael, and Jn. 21. 2.
saith unto him, We have found him, of whom Moses in Gen. 49. 10.
the law, and the prophets, did write, Jesus of Nazareth,
46 the son of Joseph. And Nathanael said unto him, Can
any good thing come out of Nazareth? Philip saith Joh. 7. 52.
47 unto him, Come and see. Jesus saw Nathanael coming
to him, and saith of him, Behold, an Israelite indeed, in
48 whom is no guile! Nathanael saith unto him, Whence Ps. 32. 2.
knowest thou me? Jesus answered and said unto him,
Before Philip called thee, when thou wast under the fig Mic. 4. 4.
49 tree, I saw thee. Nathanael answered him, Rabbi, thou Zech. 3. 10.
50 art the Son of God; thou art King of Israel. Jesus
answered and said unto him, Because I said unto thee, I
saw thee underneath the fig tree, believest thou? thou
51 shalt see greater things than these. And he saith unto
him, Verily, verily, I say unto you, Ye shall see the
heaven opened, and the angels of God ascending and Gen. 28. 12.
descending upon the Son of man.

20. *Water made wine.*

S. John ii. 1—12.

AND the third day there was a marriage in Cana of 1
Galilee; and the mother of Jesus was there: and Jesus 2
also was bidden, and his disciples, to the marriage.   And 3
when the wine failed, the mother of Jesus saith unto him,
Jn. 19. 26. They have no wine.   And Jesus saith unto her, Woman, 4
2 S. 16. 10. what have I to do with thee? mine hour is not yet come.
— 19. 22. His mother saith unto the servants, Whatsoever he saith 5
unto you, do it.   Now there were six waterpots of stone 6
Mk. 7. 3. set there after the Jews' manner of purifying, containing
two or three firkins apiece.   Jesus saith unto them, Fill 7
the waterpots with water.   And they filled them up to
the brim.   And he saith unto them, Draw out now, and 8
Ecclus. bear unto the ruler of the feast.   And they bare it.
32. 1. And when the ruler of the feast tasted the water now 9
become wine, and knew not whence it was (but the
servants which had drawn the water knew), the ruler of
the feast calleth the bridegroom, and saith unto him, 10
Every man setteth on first the good wine; and when
men have drunk freely, then that which is worse: thou
hast kept the good wine until now.   This beginning of 11
his signs did Jesus in Cana of Galilee, and manifested
Jn. 1. 14. his glory; and his disciples believed on him.   .
After this he went down to Capernaum, he, and his 12
Mt. 12. 46.. mother, and *his* brethren, and his disciples: and there
they abode not many days.

21. *Temple cleansed.   Sign.*

S. John ii. 13—25.

De. 16. 16. AND the passover of the Jews was at hand, and Jesus 13
127 went up to Jerusalem.   And he found in the temple those 14
De. 14. 24.. that sold oxen and sheep and doves, and the changers of
money sitting: and he made a scourge of cords, and cast 15
all out of the temple, both the sheep and the oxen; and
he poured out the changers' money, and overthrew their
tables; and to them that sold the doves he said, Take 16
these things hence; make not my Father's house a house
of merchandise.   His disciples remembered that it was 17
Ps. 69. 9. written, The zeal of thine house shall eat me up.   The 18
De. 18. 21.. Jews therefore answered and said unto him, What sign
shewest thou unto us, seeing that thou doest these things?

19 Jesus answered and said unto them, Destroy this temple, Mt. 26. 61.
20 and in three days I will raise it up.   The Jews therefore
   said, Forty and six years was this temple in building, and
21 wilt thou raise it up in three days?   But he spake of the
22 temple of his body.   When therefore he was raised from Col. 2. 9.
   the dead, his disciples remembered that he spake this; 1 Cor.6.19.
   and they believed the scripture, and the word which 2 Cor.6.16.
   Jesus had said.
23   Now when he was in Jerusalem at the passover,
   during the feast, many believed on his name, beholding
24 his signs which he did.   But Jesus did not trust himself
25 unto them, for that he knew all men, and because he Acts i. 24.
   needed not that any one should bear witness concerning
   man; for he himself knew what was in man.   1 Cor.2.11.

22. *Nicodemus.   The new birth.*
S. John iii. 1—21.

1   Now there was a man of the Pharisees, named Nico- Jn. 7. 50.
2 demus, a ruler of the Jews: the same came unto him by — 19. 39.
   night, and said to him, Rabbi, we know that thou art a
   teacher come from God: for no man can do these signs Jn. 9. 33.
3 that thou doest, except God be with him.   Jesus answered and said unto him, Verily, verily, I say unto
   thee, Except a man be born anew, he cannot see the Jn. 1. 13.
4 kingdom of God.   Nicodemus saith unto him, How can Gal. 6. 15.
   a man be born when he is old? can he enter a second
5 time into his mother's womb, and be born?   Jesus answered, Verily, verily, I say unto thee, Except a man
   be born of water and the Spirit, he cannot enter into the Tit. 3. 5.
6 kingdom of God.   That which is born of the flesh is 1 Pet. 1.23.
   flesh; and that which is born of the Spirit is spirit. — 3. 21.
7 Marvel not that I said unto thee, Ye must be born anew.
8 The wind bloweth where it listeth, and thou hearest the
   voice thereof, but knowest not whence it cometh, and
   whither it goeth: so is every one that is born of the
9 Spirit.   Nicodemus answered and said unto him, How
10 can these things be?   Jesus answered and said unto
   him, Art thou the teacher of Israel, and understandest
11 not these things?   Verily, verily, I say unto thee, We
   speak that we do know, and bear witness of that we
12 have seen; and ye receive not our witness.   If I told
   you earthly things, and ye believe not, how shall ye
13 believe, if I tell you heavenly things?   And no man

hath ascended into heaven, but he that descended out
of heaven, even the Son of man, which is in heaven.
Num.21.8. And as Moses lifted up the serpent in the wilderness, 14
even so must the Son of man be lifted up: that who- 15
soever believeth may in him have eternal life.
1 Joh. 4. 9.   For God so loved the world, that he gave his only 16
begotten Son, that whosoever believeth on him should
not perish, but have eternal life.   For God sent not the 17
Jn. 12. 47. Son into the world to judge the world; but that the
world should be saved through him.   He that believeth 18
on him is not judged: he that believeth not hath been
judged already, because he hath not believed on the
name of the only begotten Son of God.   And this 19
is the judgement, that the light is come into the
world, and men loved the darkness rather than the
light; for their works were evil.   For every one that 20
doeth ill hateth the light, and cometh not to the light,
lest his works should be reproved.   But he that doeth 21
Eph. 5. 13. the truth cometh to the light, that his works may be
made manifest, that they have been wrought in God.

23. *John Baptist's last testimony to Jesus.   Eternal life.*
S. John iii. 22—36.
    AFTER these things came Jesus and his disciples into 22
the land of Judæa; and there he tarried with them, and
baptized.   And John also was baptizing in Ænon near 23
to Salim, because there was much water there: and they
came, and were baptized.   For John was not yet cast 24
into prison.   There arose therefore a questioning on the 25
part of John's disciples with a Jew about purifying.
And they came unto John, and said to him, Rabbi, he 26
that was with thee beyond Jordan, to whom thou hast
borne witness, behold, the same baptizeth, and all men
come to him.   John answered and said, A man can 27
1 Cor. 4. 7. receive nothing, except it have been given him from
heaven.   Ye yourselves bear me witness, that I said, I 28
am not the Christ, but, that I am sent before him.   He 29
that hath the bride is the bridegroom: but the friend of
the bridegroom, which standeth and heareth him, re-
Mt. 9. 15. joiceth greatly because of the bridegroom's voice: this
my joy therefore is fulfilled.   He must increase, but I 30
must decrease.
    He that cometh from above is above all: he that is 31

of the earth is of the earth, and of the earth he speaketh:
32 he that cometh from heaven is above all. What he hath
seen and heard, of that he beareth witness; and no man
33 receiveth his witness. He that hath received his witness
34 hath set his seal to this, that God is true. For he whom
God hath sent speaketh the words of God: for he giveth
35 not the Spirit by measure. The Father loveth the Son,
36 and hath given all things into his hand. He that be- Mt. 28. 18.
lieveth on the Son hath eternal life; but he that obeyeth Hab. 2. 4.
not the Son shall not see life, but the wrath of God
abideth on him.

24. *The Woman of Samaria. True worship. Messiah.*
S. John iv. 1—26.

1 WHEN therefore the Lord knew how that the Pharisees had heard that Jesus was making and baptizing
2 more disciples than John (although Jesus himself bap-
3 tized not, but his disciples), he left Judæa, and departed
4 again into Galilee. And he must needs pass through
5 Samaria. So he cometh to a city of Samaria, called
Sychar, near to the parcel of ground that Jacob gave to Gen. 48. 22.
6 his son Joseph: and Jacob's well was there. Jesus Jos. 24. 32.
therefore, being wearied with his journey, sat thus by
7 the well. It was about the sixth hour. There cometh
a woman of Samaria · to draw water: Jesus saith unto
8 her, Give me to drink. For his disciples were gone
9 away into the city to buy food. The Samaritan woman
therefore saith unto him, How is it that thou, being a
Jew, askest drink of me, which am a Samaritan woman? 2 Ki. 17. 24.
10 (For Jews have no dealings with Samaritans.) Jesus
answered and said unto her, If thou knewest the gift of
God, and who it is that saith to thee, Give me to drink;
thou wouldest have asked of him, and he would have Rev. 22. 17.
11 given thee living water. The woman saith unto him,
Sir, thou hast nothing to draw with, and the well is deep:
12 from whence then hast thou that living water? Art thou
greater than our father Jacob, which gave us the well,
and drank thereof himself, and his sons, and his cattle?
13 Jesus answered and said unto her, Every one that
14 drinketh of this water shall thirst again: but whosoever drinketh of the water that I shall give him shall
never thirst; but the water that I shall give him shall Jn. 7. 37.
become in him a well of water springing up unto eternal

life. The woman saith unto him, Sir, give me this water, 15
that I thirst not, neither come all the way hither to draw.
Jesus saith unto her, Go, call thy husband, and come 16
hither. The woman answered and said unto him, I have 17
no husband. Jesus saith unto her, Thou saidst well, I
have no husband : for thou hast had five husbands ; and 18
he whom thou now hast is not thy husband : this hast
thou said truly. The woman saith unto him, Sir, I per- 19
ceive that thou art a prophet. Our fathers worshipped 20
Deu.12.13. in this mountain; and ye say, that in Jerusalem is the
place where men ought to worship. Jesus saith unto 21
her, Woman, believe me, the hour cometh, when neither
in this mountain, nor in Jerusalem, shall ye worship the
Father. Ye worship that which ye know not : we wor- 22
ship that which we know : for salvation is from the Jews.
But the hour cometh, and now is, when the true wor- 23
shippers shall worship the Father in spirit and truth :
for such doth the Father seek to be his worshippers.
2 Cor.3.17. God is a Spirit : and they that worship him must worship 24
in spirit and truth. The woman saith unto him, I know 25
that Messiah cometh (which is called Christ) : when he
is come, he will declare unto us all things. Jesus saith 26
unto her, I that speak unto thee am he.

25. *The Samaritans.*
S. John iv. 27—42.

AND upon this came his disciples; and they mar- 27
velled that he was speaking with a woman; yet no man
said, What seekest thou? or, Why speakest thou with
her? So the woman left her waterpot, and went away 28
into the city, and saith to the men, Come, see a man, 29
which told me all things that ever I did : can this be the
Christ? They went out of the city, and were coming to 30
him. In the mean while the disciples prayed him, say- 31
Rev. 2. 17. ing, Rabbi, eat. But he said unto them, I have meat to 32
eat that ye know not. The disciples therefore said one 33
to another, Hath any man brought him aught to eat?
Jesus saith unto them, My meat is to do the will of him 34
that sent me, and to accomplish his work. Say not ye, 35
There are yet four months, and then cometh the harvest?
Is. 49. 18. behold, I say unto you, Lift up your eyes, and look on
the fields, that they are white already unto harvest. He 36
that reapeth receiveth wages, and gathereth fruit unto

life eternal; that he that soweth and he that reapeth
37 may rejoice together.   For herein is the saying true,
38 One soweth, and another reapeth.   I sent you to reap
that whereon ye have not laboured: others have laboured, Jos. 24. 13.
and ye are entered into their labour.

39   And from that city many of the Samaritans believed
on him because of the word of the woman, who testified,
40 He told me all things that ever I did.   So when the
Samaritans came unto him, they besought him to abide
41 with them: and he abode there two days.   And many
42 more believed because of his word; and they said to
the woman, Now we believe, not because of thy speaking: for we have heard for ourselves, and know that this
is indeed the Saviour of the world.   1 Joh. 4. 14.

26. *Nobleman's son healed.*
S. John iv. 43—54.

43   AND after the two days he went forth from thence
44 into Galilee.   For Jesus himself testified, that a prophet
45 hath no honour in his own country.   So when he came Mt. 13. 57.
into Galilee, the Galilæans received him, having seen all
the things that he did in Jerusalem at the feast: for they
also went unto the feast.

46   He came therefore again unto Cana of Galilee, where   20
he made the water wine.   And there was a certain noble-
47 man, whose son was sick at Capernaum.   When he
heard that Jesus was come out of Judæa into Galilee,
he went unto him, and besought him that he would
come down, and heal his son; for he was at the point
48 of death.   Jesus therefore said unto him, Except ye see
49 signs and wonders, ye will in no wise believe.   The
nobleman saith unto him, Sir, come down ere my child Mk. 5. 23.
50 die.   Jesus saith unto him, Go thy way: thy son liveth.
The man believed the word that Jesus spake unto him,
51 and he went his way.   And as he was now going down,
52 his servants met him, saying, that his son lived.   So he
inquired of them the hour when he began to amend.
They said therefore unto him, Yesterday at the seventh
53 hour the fever left him.   So the father knew that it was
at that hour in which Jesus said unto him, Thy son liveth:
54 and himself believed, and his whole house.   This is again
the second sign that Jesus did, having come out of Judæa
into Galilee.

27. *Bethesda. The sabbath.*

S. John v. 1—18.

AFTER these things there was a feast of the Jews; 1
and Jesus went up to Jerusalem.

Neh. 3. 1.   Now there is in Jerusalem by the sheep gate a pool, 2
which is called in Hebrew Bethesda, having five porches.
In these lay a multitude of them that were sick, blind, 3
halt, withered. And a certain man was there, which had 5
been thirty and eight years in his infirmity. When Jesus 6
saw him lying, and knew that he had been now a long
time in that case, he saith unto him, Wouldest thou be
made whole? The sick man answered him, Sir, I have 7
no man, when the water is troubled, to put me into the
pool : but while I am coming, another steppeth down
before me. Jesus saith unto him, Arise, take up thy 8

Mt. 9. 6.

37   bed, and walk. And straightway the man was made 9
whole, and took up his bed and walked.

Jn. 9. 14.   Now it was the sabbath on that day. So the Jews 10

80   said unto him that was cured, It is the sabbath, and it is

Neh.13.19. not lawful for thee to take up thy bed. But he answered 11

Jer. 17.22. them, He that made me whole, the same said unto me,
Take up thy bed, and walk. They asked him, Who is 12
the man that said unto thee, Take up thy bed, and walk?
But he that was healed wist not who it was : for Jesus 13
had conveyed himself away, a multitude being in the

Acts 3. 8. place. Afterward Jesus findeth him in the temple, and 14

Jn. 8. 11. said unto him, Behold, thou art made whole : sin no

Mt. 12.45. more, lest a worse thing befall thee. The man went 15
away, and told the Jews that it was Jesus which had
made him whole. And for this cause did the Jews 16
persecute Jesus, because he did these things on the
sabbath. But Jesus answered them, My Father worketh 17
even until now, and I work. For this cause therefore 18

Jn. 7. 19. the Jews sought the more to kill him, because he not only
brake the sabbath, but also called God his own Father,

Jn. 10. 30. making himself equal with God.

Phil. 2. 5.

Our Lord's words about the Sabbath day.

My Father worketh even until now, and I work.   27
  S. John v. 17.

Have ye not read what David did, when he was an   39
hungred, and they that were with him; how he entered
into the house of God, and did eat the shewbread, which
it was not lawful for him to eat, neither for them that
were with him, but only for the priests?

Or have ye not read in the law, how that on the
sabbath day the priests in the temple profane the sabbath,
and are guiltless? But I say unto you that one greater
than the temple is here.

But if ye had known what this meaneth, I desire mercy,
and not sacrifice, ye would not have condemned the guiltless.
For the Son of man is lord of the Sabbath.
  S. Matthew xii. 3—8.

The sabbath was made for man, and not man for the
sabbath: so that the Son of man is lord even of the
sabbath.   S. Mark ii. 27, 28.

Is it lawful on the sabbath day to do good, or to do   40
harm? to save a life, or to kill?   S. Mark iii. 4.

What man shall there be of you, that shall have one   40
sheep, and if this fall into a pit on the sabbath day, will he
not lay hold on it, and lift it out? How much then is a
man of more value than a sheep! Wherefore it is lawful
to do good on the sabbath day.   S. Matthew xii. 11, 12.

On the sabbath ye circumcise a man. If a man receive   77
circumcision on the sabbath, that the law of Moses may not
be broken; are ye wrath with me, because I made a man
every whit whole on the sabbath? Judge not according to
appearance, but judge righteous judgement.   S. John vii. 22.

Ye hypocrites, doth not each of you on a sabbath loose   102
his ox or his ass from the stall, and lead him away to
watering? and ought not this woman, being a daughter of
Abraham, whom Satan hath bound, lo these eighteen years,
to have been loosed from this bond on the day of the
sabbath?   S. Luke xiii. 15, 16.

Which of you shall have an ass or an ox fallen into a   106
well, and will not straightway draw him up on the
sabbath day?   S. Luke xiv. 5, 6.

28. *Jesus' defence. He is the Son of God, and judge of the world. Witness of John, of His Father, of His works, and of Moses.*

S. John v. 19—47.

JESUS therefore answered and said unto them,   19
Jn. 8. 28.   Verily, verily, I say unto you, The Son can do nothing
— 14. 10. of himself, but what he seeth the Father doing : for what
things soever he doeth, these the Son also doeth in like
2 Pet. 1.17. manner. For the Father loveth the Son, and sheweth 20
him all things that himself doeth : and greater works than
these will he shew him, that ye may marvel. For as the 21
Father raiseth the dead and quickeneth them, even so
the Son also quickeneth whom he will. For neither doth 22
the Father judge any man, but he hath given all judge-
Mt. 25. 31. ment unto the Son ; that all may honour the Son, even 23
as they honour the Father. He that honoureth not the
1 Jn. 2. 23. Son honoureth not the Father which sent him. Verily, 24
verily, I say unto you, He that heareth my word, and
Jn. 6. 47. believeth him that sent me, hath eternal life, and cometh
1 Jn. 3. 14. not into judgement, but hath passed out of death into life.
Verily, verily, I say unto you, The hour cometh, and now 25
Eph. 2. 5. is, when the dead shall hear the voice of the Son of
— 5. 14. God ; and they that hear shall live. For as the Father 26
hath life in himself, even so gave he to the Son also to
Acts 10.42. have life in himself : and he gave him authority to execute 27
Dan. 12. 2. judgement, because he is the Son of man. Marvel not 28
at this : for the hour cometh, in which all that are in the
Is. 26. 19. tombs shall hear his voice, and shall come forth ; they that 29
1 Co.15.52. have done good, unto the resurrection of life ; and they
Dan. 12. 2. that have done ill, unto the resurrection of judgement.
I can of myself do nothing : as I hear, I judge : and 30
Mt. 26. 39. my judgement is righteous ; because I seek not mine own
Jn. 6. 38. will, but the will of him that sent me. If I bear witness 31
of myself, my witness is not true. It is another that 32
Jn. 8. 13... beareth witness of me ; and I know that the witness
which he witnesseth of me is true. Ye have sent unto 33
Jn. 1. 19... John, and he hath borne witness unto the truth. But the 34
18. 23   witness which I receive is not from man : howbeit I say
these things, that ye may be saved. He was the lamp 35
2 Pet.1.19. that burneth and shineth : and ye were willing to rejoice

36 for a season in his light.   But the witness which I have
is greater than that of John: for the works which the 1 Jn. 5. 9.
Father hath given me to accomplish, the very works that Jn. 10. 25.
37 I do, bear witness of me, that the Father hath sent me.   89
And the Father which sent me, he hath borne witness of Mt. 3. 17.
me.   Ye have neither heard his voice at any time, nor Deu. 4. 12.
38 seen his form.   And ye have not his word abiding in 1Tim.6.16.
39 you: for whom he sent, him ye believe not.   Ye search
the scriptures, because ye think that in them ye have Is. 34. 16.
eternal life; and these are they which bear witness of Lk. 24. 27.
40 me; and ye will not come to me, that ye may have life. Jn. 3. 19.
41, 42 I receive not glory from men.   But I know you, that ye
43 have not the love of God in yourselves.   I am come in
my Father's name, and ye receive me not: if another
44 shall come in his own name, him ye will receive.   How Mt. 24. 24.
can ye believe, which receive glory one of another, and Mt. 23. 6.
the glory that cometh from the only God ye seek not?
45 Think not that I will accuse you to the Father: there is
one that accuseth you, even Moses, on whom ye have set
46 your hope.   For if ye believed Moses, ye would believe
47 me; for he wrote of me.   But if ye believe not his Deu.18.15.
writings, how shall ye believe my words?

29. *Teaching at Nazareth. Rejected.*

S. Luke iv. 14—30.

AND Jesus returned in the power of the Spirit into 14
Galilee : and a fame went out concerning him through
all the region round about.   And he taught in their 15
synagogues, being glorified of all.

57   And he came to Nazareth, where he had been brought 16
up : and he entered, as his custom was, into the syna-
Acts 13.15. gogue on the sabbath day, and stood up to read.   And 17
there was delivered unto him the book of the prophet
Isaiah.   And he opened the book, and found the place
where it was written,

Is. 61. 1.   The Spirit of the Lord is upon me,   18
Because he anointed me to preach good tidings to
                    the poor :
He hath sent me to proclaim release to the captives,
And recovering of sight to the blind,
To set at liberty them that are bruised,
To proclaim the acceptable year of the Lord.   19
And he closed the book, and gave it back to the attend- 20
ant, and sat down : and the eyes of all in the synagogue
were fastened on him.   And he began to say unto them, 21
To-day hath this scripture been fulfilled in your ears.
And all bare him witness, and wondered at the words 22
of grace which proceeded out of his mouth : and they
Jn. 6. 42. said, Is not this Joseph's son?   And he said unto them, 23
Mk. 6. 3. Doubtless ye will say unto me this parable, Physician,
54   heal thyself : whatsoever we have heard done at Capernaum, do also here in thine own country.   And he said, 24
Verily I say unto you, No prophet is acceptable in his
own country.   But of a truth I say unto you, There were 25
many widows in Israel in the days of Elijah, when the
heaven was shut up three years and six months, when
there came a great famine over all the land ; and unto 26
1 Ki. 17.9. none of them was Elijah sent, but only to Zarephath, in
the land of Sidon, unto a woman that was a widow.
And there were many lepers in Israel in the time of 27
Elisha the prophet ; and none of them was cleansed,
2 Ki. 5. 14. but only Naaman the Syrian.   And they were all filled 28

with wrath in the synagogue, as they heard these things;
29 and they rose up, and cast him forth out of the city, and
led him unto the brow of the hill whereon their city was
30 built, that they might throw him down headlong. But
he passing through the midst of them went his way.

S. Matthew iv. 12.

12 Now when he heard that John was delivered up, he
withdrew into Galilee;

S. Mark 1. 14.

14 Now after that John was put into prison, Jesus came
into Galilee,

30. *Capernaum. Preaching of repentance.*

S. Matthew iv. 13—17.

13 AND leaving Nazareth, he came and dwelt in Caper-
naum, which is by the sea, in the borders of Zebulun and
14 Naphtali : that it might be fulfilled which was spoken by
Isaiah the Prophet, saying,
15   The land of Zebulun and the land of Naphtali,   Is. 9. 1.
Toward the sea, beyond Jordan,
Galilee of the Gentiles,
16   The people which sat in darkness
Saw a great light,
And to them which sat in the region and shadow of
death,
To them did light spring up.
17   From that time began Jesus to preach, and to say,
Repent ye ; for the kingdom of heaven is at hand.

S. Mark 1. 14, 15.

14 preaching the Gospel of God, and saying, the time is
fulfilled, and the kingdom of God is at hand : repent ye,
and believe in the gospel.

J. H. G.   3

31. *Four fishermen called.*

S. Mark 1. 16—20.

19. 35
Mt. 13.47..

AND passing along by the sea of Galilee, he saw 16
Simon and Andrew the brother of Simon casting a net
in the sea: for they were fishers.   And Jesus said unto 17
them, Come ye after me, and I will make you to become
fishers of men.   And straightway they left the nets, and 18
followed him.   And going on a little further, he saw 19
James the son of Zebedee, and John his brother, who
also were in the boat mending the nets.   And straight- 20
way he called them : and they left their father Zebedee
in the boat with the hired servants, and went after him.

S. Matthew iv. 18—22.

Jn. 1. 42.

And walking by the sea of Galilee, he saw two 18
brethren, Simon who is called Peter, and Andrew his
brother, casting a net into the sea; for they were fishers.
And he saith unto them, Come ye after me, and I will 19
make you fishers of men.   And they straightway left 20
the nets, and followed him.   And going on from thence 21
he saw other two brethren, James the son of Zebedee,
and John his brother, in the boat with Zebedee their
father, mending their nets; and he called them.   And 22
they straightway left the boat and their father, and
followed him.

32. *Demoniac at Capernaum.*

S. Mark 1. 21—28.

21 AND they go into Capernaum; and straightway on
the sabbath day he entered into the synagogue and
22 taught.   And they were astonished at his teaching: for
he taught them as having authority, and not as the Mt. 7. 28.
23 scribes.   And straightway there was in their synagogue a
24 man with an unclean spirit; and he cried out, saying,   56. 58
What have we to do with thee, thou Jesus of Nazareth?   73. 91
art thou come to destroy us?   I know thee who thou art, Acts 19.15.
25 the Holy One of God.   And Jesus rebuked him, saying,
26 Hold thy peace, and come out of him.   And the unclean
spirit, tearing him and crying with a loud voice, came
27 out of him.   And they were all amazed, insomuch that
they questioned among themselves, saying, What is this?
a new teaching! with authority he commandeth even
28 the unclean spirits, and they obey him.   And the report
of him went out straightway everywhere into all the region
of Galilee round about.

S. Luke iv. 31—37.

31 And he came down to Capernaum, a city of Galilee.
32 And he was teaching them on the sabbath day: and they
were astonished at his teaching; for his word was with
33 authority.   And in the synagogue there was a man,
which had a spirit of an unclean devil; and he cried out
34 with a loud voice, Ah! what have we to do with thee,
thou Jesus of Nazareth? art thou come to destroy us?
35 I know thee who thou art, the Holy One of God.   And
Jesus rebuked him, saying, Hold thy peace, and come
out of him.   And when the devil had thrown him down
in the midst, he came out of him, having done him no
36 hurt.   And amazement came upon all, and they spake
together, one with another, saying, What is this word?
for with authority and power he commandeth the unclean
37 spirits, and they come out.   And there went forth a
rumour concerning him into every place of the region
round about.

3—2

33. *Peter's wife's mother.   General healing.*

Mark i. 29—34.

AND straightway, when they were come out of the 29
synagogue, they came into the house of Simon and
1 Cor. 9. 5. Andrew, with James and John.   Now Simon's wife's 30
mother lay sick of a fever; and straightway they tell him
of her: and he came and took her by the hand, and 31
raised her up; and the fever left her, and she ministered
unto them.

And at even, when the sun did set, they brought 32
41. 46. unto him all that were sick, and them that were possessed
67 with devils.   And all the city was gathered together at 33
the door.   And he healed many that were sick with 34
Acts 15.17. divers diseases, and cast out many devils; and he suffered
Mk. 3. 12. not the devils to speak, because they knew him.

S. Luke iv. 38—41.

And he rose up from the synagogue, and entered 38
into the house of Simon.   And Simon's wife's mother
was holden with a great fever; and they besought him
for her.   And he stood over her, and rebuked the fever; 39
and it left her: and immediately she rose up and ministered unto them.

And when the sun was setting, all they that had any 40
sick with divers diseases brought them unto him; and
Acts 10.38. he laid his hands on every one of them, and healed
them.   And devils also came out from many, crying out, 41
and saying, Thou art the Son of God.   And rebuking
them, he suffered them not to speak, because they knew
that he was the Christ.

S. Matthew viii. 14—17.

And when Jesus was come into Peter's house, he 14
saw his wife's mother lying sick of a fever.   And he 15
touched her hand, and the fever left her; and she arose,
and ministered unto him.   And when even was come, 16
they brought unto him many possessed with devils: and
he cast out the spirits with a word, and healed all that
were sick: that it might be fulfilled which was spoken 17
Is. 53. 4. by Isaiah the prophet, saying, Himself took our infirmities, and bare our diseases.

34.　*Circuit of Galilee.　Effect.*

S. Mark 1. 35—39.

35　AND in the morning, a great while before day, he rose
　　up and went out, and departed into a desert place, and　　**42**
36 there prayed.　And Simon and they that were with him
37 followed after him ; and they found him, and say unto
38 him, All are seeking thee.　And he saith unto them, Let
　　us go elsewhere into the next towns, that I may preach
39 there also ; for to this end came I forth.　And he went
　　into their synagogues throughout all Galilee, preaching
　　and casting out devils.

S. Luke iv. 42—44.

42　And when it was day, he came out and went into a
　　desert place : and the multitudes sought after him, and
　　came unto him, and would have stayed him, that he
43 should not go from them.　But he said unto them, I
　　must preach the good tidings of the kingdom of God to Is. 61. 1...
　　the other cities also : for therefore was I sent.
44　And he was preaching in the synagogues of Galilee.

S. Matthew iv. 23—25.

23　And Jesus went about in all Galilee, teaching in their
　　synagogues, and preaching the gospel of the kingdom,
　　and healing all manner of disease and all manner of
24 sickness among the people.　And the report of him went
　　forth into all Syria : and they brought unto him all that
　　were sick, holden with divers diseases and torments,
　　possessed with devils, and epileptic, and palsied ; and he
25 healed them.　And there followed him great multitudes
　　from Galilee and Decapolis and Jerusalem and Judæa
　　and from beyond Jordan.

35. *First draught of fishes.*

S. Luke v. 1—11.

Now it came to pass, while the multitude pressed 1 upon him and heard the word of God, that he was standing by the lake of Gennesaret; and he saw two 2 boats standing by the lake: but the fishermen had gone out of them, and were washing their nets. And he 3 entered into one of the boats, which was Simon's, and asked him to put out a little from the land. And he sat down and taught the multitudes out of the boat. And 4 when he had left speaking, he said unto Simon, Put out into the deep, and let down your nets for a draught. And Simon answered and said, Master, we toiled all 5 night, and took nothing: but at thy word I will let down the nets. And when they had this done, they inclosed a 6 great multitude of fishes; and their nets were breaking; and they beckoned unto their partners in the other boat, 7 that they should come and help them. And they came, and filled both the boats, so that they began to sink. But Simon Peter, when he saw it, fell down at Jesus' 8 knees, saying, Depart from me; for I am a sinful man, O Lord. For he was amazed, and all that were with him, 9 at the draught of the fishes which they had taken; and so 10 were also James and John, sons of Zebedee, which were partners with Simon. And Jesus said unto Simon, Fear not; from henceforth thou shalt catch men. And when 11 they had brought their boats to land, they left all, and followed him.

Mk. 4. 1.
49

Jn. 21. 6.

182

2 Sam.6. 9.
Is. 6. 5.

31

2 Ti. 2. 26.
Gr.

36. *The Leper healed.*

S. Mark 1. 40—45.

And there cometh to him a leper, beseeching him, 40 and kneeling down to him, and saying unto him, If thou wilt, thou canst make me clean. And being moved with 41

114

compassion, he stretched forth his hand, and touched
him, and saith unto him, I will: be thou made clean.
42 And straightway the leprosy departed from him, and he
43 was made clean. And he strictly charged him, and
44 straightway sent him out, and saith unto him, See thou
say nothing to any man: but go thy way, shew thyself Le. 13. 2...
to the priest, and offer for thy cleansing the things which — 14. 2...
45 Moses commanded, for a testimony unto them. But he
went out and began to publish it much, and to spread
abroad the matter, insomuch that Jesus could no more   34
openly enter into a city, but was without in desert
places: and they came to him from every quarter.

S. Luke v. 12—16.

12   And it came to pass, while he was in one of the
cities, behold, a man full of leprosy: and when he saw
Jesus, he fell on his face, and besought him, saying,
13 Lord, if thou wilt, thou canst make me clean. And he
stretched forth his hand, and touched him, saying, I will;
be thou made clean. And straightway the leprosy de-
14 parted from him. And he charged him to tell no man:
but go thy way, and shew thyself to the priest, and offer
for thy cleansing, according as Moses commanded, for
15 a testimony unto them. But so much the more went
abroad the report concerning him: and great multitudes
came together to hear, and to be healed of their infirmities.
16 But he withdrew himself in the deserts, and prayed.

S. Matthew viii. 1—4.

1   And when he was come down from the mountain,
2 great multitudes followed him. And behold, there came
to him a leper and worshipped him, saying, Lord, if thou
3 wilt, thou canst make me clean. And he stretched forth
his hand, and touched him, saying, I will; be thou made
clean. And straightway his leprosy was cleansed. And
4 Jesus saith unto him, See thou tell no man; but go thy
way, shew thyself to the priest, and offer the gift that
Moses commanded, for a testimony unto them.

37. *The Paralytic at Capernaum.*

S. Mark ii. 1—12.

AND when he entered again into Capernaum after 1
some days, it was noised that he was in the house. And 2
many were gathered together, so that there was no longer
room for them, no, not even about the door: and he
spake the word unto them. And they come, bringing 3
unto him a man sick of the palsy, borne of four. And 4
when they could not come nigh unto him for the crowd,
they uncovered the roof where he was: and when they
had broken it up, they let down the bed whereon the
sick of the palsy lay. And Jesus seeing their faith saith 5
unto the sick of the palsy, Son, thy sins are forgiven.
47   But there were certain of the scribes sitting there, and 6
Job 14. 4.   reasoning in their hearts, Why doth this man thus speak? 7
Is. 43. 25. he blasphemeth: who can forgive sins but one, even
Ps. 139. 2. God? And straightway Jesus, perceiving in his spirit 8
Acts 1. 24. that they so reasoned within themselves, saith unto them,
Why reason ye these things in your hearts? Whether is 9
easier, to say to the sick of the palsy, Thy sins are for-
given; or to say, Arise, and take up thy bed, and walk?
But that ye may know that the Son of man hath power 10
on earth to forgive sins (he saith to the sick of the
Jn. 5. 8.   palsy), I say unto thee, Arise, take up thy bed, and go 11
27   unto thy house. And he arose, and straightway took 12
up the bed, and went forth before them all; insomuch
that they were all amazed, and glorified God, saying,
We never saw it on this fashion.

S. Luke v. 17—26.

And it came to pass on one of those days, that he 17
was teaching; and there were Pharisees and doctors of
the law sitting by, which were come out of every village
of Galilee and Judæa and Jerusalem: and the power of
the Lord was with him to heal. And behold, men bring 18

on a bed a man that was palsied: and they sought to
19 bring him in, and to lay him before him. And not
finding by what way they might bring him in because of
the multitude, they went up to the housetop, and let Mk. 13. 14.
him down through the tiles with his couch into the
20 midst before Jesus. And seeing their faith, he said,
21 Man, thy sins are forgiven thee. And the scribes and
the Pharisees began to reason, saying, Who is this that
speaketh blasphemies? Who can forgive sins, but God
22 alone? But Jesus perceiving their reasonings, answered
and said unto them, What reason ye in your hearts?
23 Whether is easier, to say, Thy sins are forgiven thee ; or
24 to say, Arise and walk? But that ye may know that the
Son of man hath power on earth to forgive sins (he said
unto him that was palsied), I say unto thee, Arise, and
25 take up thy couch, and go unto thy house. And immediately he rose up before them, and took up that
whereon he lay, and departed to his house, glorifying
26 God. And amazement took hold on all, and they glorified God ; and they were filled with fear, saying, We
have seen strange things to-day.

S. Matthew ix. 1—8.

1   And he entered into a boat, and crossed over, and
2 came into his own city. And behold, they brought to
him a man sick of the palsy, lying on a bed : and Jesus
seeing their faith said unto the sick of the palsy, Son, be
3 of good cheer ; thy sins are forgiven. And behold,
certain of the scribes said within themselves, This man
4 blasphemeth. And Jesus knowing their thoughts said,
5 Wherefore think ye evil in your hearts? For whether is
easier, to say, Thy sins are forgiven ; or to say, Arise,
6 and walk? But that ye may know that the Son of man
hath power on earth to forgive sins (then saith he to the
sick of the palsy), Arise, and take up thy bed, and go
7 unto thy house. And he arose, and departed to his
8 house. But when the multitudes saw it, they were afraid,
and glorified God, which had given such power unto
men.

38. *Levi (or Matthew) called. Of fasting.*

S. Mark ii. 13—22.

AND he went forth again by the sea side; and all 13
the multitude resorted unto him, and he taught them.
Matthew,   And as he passed by, he saw Levi the son of Alphæus 14
Mt.   sitting at the place of toll, and he saith unto him, Follow
me. And he arose and followed him. And it came to 15
pass, that he was sitting at meat in his house, and
Lk. 15. 1... many publicans and sinners sat down with Jesus and
his disciples: for there were many, and they followed
him. And the scribes of the Pharisees, when they saw 16
that he was eating with the sinners and publicans, said
109   unto his disciples, He eateth and drinketh with publicans
and sinners. And when Jesus heard it, he saith unto 17
them, They that are whole have no need of a physician,
1 Tim. 1. 16. but they that are sick: I came not to call the righteous,
Lk. 19. 10. but sinners.

And John's disciples and the Pharisees were fasting: 18
and they come and say unto him, Why do John's
Lk. 18. 12. disciples and the disciples of the Pharisees fast, but thy
disciples fast not? And Jesus said unto them, Can the 19
Jn. 3. 29. sons of the bride-chamber fast, while the bridegroom is
with them? as long as they have the bridegroom with
them, they cannot fast. But the days will come, when 20
Acts 13. 2.. the bridegroom shall be taken away from them, and then
— 14. 23. will they fast in that day. No man seweth a piece of 21
1 Cor. 7. 5. undressed cloth on an old garment: else that which
should fill it up taketh from it, the new from the old,
and a worse rent is made. And no man putteth new 22
Job 32. 19. wine into old wine-skins: else the wine will burst
the skins, and the wine perisheth, and the skins: but
they put new wine into fresh wine-skins.

S. Luke v. 27—39.

And after these things he went forth, and beheld a 27
publican, named Levi, sitting at the place of toll, and
said unto him, Follow me. And he forsook all, and rose 28
up and followed him. And Levi made him a great feast 29
in his house: and there was a great multitude of publicans and of others that were sitting at meat with them.
And the Pharisees and their scribes murmured against 30
his disciples, saying, Why do ye eat and drink with the
publicans and sinners? And Jesus answering said unto 31
them, They that are whole have no need of a physician;

32 but they that are sick. I am not come to call the
33 righteous but sinners to repentance. And they said
unto him, The disciples of John fast often, and make
supplications; likewise also the disciples of the Pharisees;
34 but thine eat and drink. And Jesus said unto them,
Can ye make the sons of the bride-chamber fast, while
35 the bridegroom is with them? But the days will come;
and when the bridegroom shall be taken away from
36 them, then will they fast in those days. And he spake
also a parable unto them ; No man rendeth a piece from
a new garment and putteth it upon an old garment; else
he will rend the new, and also the piece from the new
37 will not agree with the old. And no man putteth new
wine into old wine-skins ; else the new wine will burst
the skins, and itself will be spilled, and the skins will
38 perish. But new wine must be put into fresh wine-
39 skins. And no man having drunk old wine desireth
new : for he saith, The old is good.

S. Matthew ix. 9—17.

9   And as Jesus passed by from thence, he saw a man,
called Matthew, sitting at the place of toll: and he saith
unto him, Follow me. And he arose, and followed him.
10   And it came to pass, as he sat at meat in the house,
behold, many publicans and sinners came and sat down
11 with Jesus and his disciples. And when the Pharisees
saw it, they said unto his disciples, Why eateth your
12 Master with the publicans and sinners? But when he
heard it, he said, They that are whole have no need of a
13 physician, but they that are sick. But go ye and learn
what this meaneth, I desire mercy, and not sacrifice : for Hos. 6. 6.
I came not to call the righteous, but sinners.   Mic. 6. 6...
14   Then come to him the disciples of John, saying,
Why do we and the Pharisees fast oft, but thy disciples
15 fast not? And Jesus said unto them, Can the sons of
the bride-chamber mourn, as long as the bridegroom is
with them? but the days will come, when the bridegroom shall be taken away from them, and then will they
16 fast. And no man putteth a piece of undressed cloth
upon an old garment; for that which should fill it up
taketh from the garment, and a worse rent is made.
17 Neither do men put new wine into old wine-skins : else
the skins burst, and the wine is spilled, and the skins
perish : but they put new wine into fresh wine-skins, and
both are preserved.

39. *Sabbath.   The ears of corn.*

S. Matthew xii. 1—8.

27   AT that season Jesus went on the sabbath day through 1
          the cornfields; and his disciples were an hungred, and
Deu.23.25. began to pluck ears of corn, and to eat.   But the 2
          Pharisees, when they saw it, said unto him, Behold, thy
          disciples do that which it is not lawful to do upon the
Ex.16.22... sabbath.   But he said unto them, Have ye not read what 3
          David did, when he was an hungred, and they that were
1 Sa. 21. 6. with him; how he entered into the house of God, and 4
Lev. 24. 8. did eat the shewbread, which it was not lawful for him
          to eat, neither for them that were with him, but only for
Num.28.9. the priests?   Or have ye not read in the law, how that 5
          on the sabbath day the priests in the temple profane the
          sabbath, and are guiltless?   But I say unto you, that one 6
2 Ch. 6.18. greater than the temple is here.   But if ye had known 7
Hos. 6. 6. what this meaneth, I desire mercy, and not sacrifice, ye
Mic. 6. 6... would not have condemned the guiltless.   For the Son 8
          of man is lord of the sabbath.

S. Mark ii. 23—28.

23 And it came to pass, that he was going on the sabbath
day through the cornfields; and his disciples began, as
24 they went, to pluck the ears of corn.   And the Pharisees
said unto him, Behold, why do they on the sabbath day
25 that which is not lawful?   And he said unto them, Did
ye never read what David did, when he had need, and
26 was an hungred, he, and they that were with him? How
he entered into the house of God when Abiathar was
high priest, and did eat the shewbread, which it is not
lawful to eat save for the priests, and gave also to them
27 that were with him? And he said unto them, The sabbath
28 was made for man, and not man for the sabbath: so
that the Son of man is lord even of the sabbath.

S. Luke vi. 1—5.

1   Now it came to pass on a sabbath, that he was going
through the cornfields; and his disciples plucked the
ears of corn, and did eat, rubbing them in their hands.
2 But certain of the Pharisees said, Why do ye that which
3 it is not lawful to do on the sabbath day? And Jesus
answering them said, Have ye not read even this, what
David did, when he was an hungred, he, and they that
4 were with him; how he entered into the house of God,
and did take and eat the shewbread, and gave also to
them that were with him; which it is not lawful to eat
5 save for the priests alone? And he said unto them, The
Son of man is lord of the sabbath.

40. *Sabbath. The withered hand.*

S. Luke vi. 6—11.

AND it came to pass on another sabbath, that he 6
27 entered into the synagogue and taught : and there was a
man there, and his right hand was withered.   And the 7
scribes and the Pharisees watched him, whether he would
heal on the sabbath ; that they might find how to
Acts 1. 24. accuse him.   But he knew their thoughts ; and he said 8
to the man that had his hand withered, Rise up, and
stand forth in the midst.   And he arose and stood forth.
Lk. 14.3... And Jesus said unto them, I ask you, Is it lawful on the 9
Jas. 4. 17. sabbath to do good, or to do harm ? to save a life, or to
destroy it ? And he looked round about on them all, 10
and said unto him, Stretch forth thy hand.   And he did
so : and his hand was restored.   But they were filled with 11
madness ; and communed one with another what they
might do to Jesus.

S. Mark iii. 1—6.

1 And he entered again into the synagogue ; and there
2 was a man there which had his hand withered.   And
they watched him, whether he would heal him on the
3 sabbath day; that they might accuse him.   And he
saith unto the man that had his hand withered, Stand
4 forth.   And he saith unto them, Is it lawful on the
sabbath day to do good, or to do harm ? to save a life,
5 or to kill ? But they held their peace.   And when he
had looked round about on them with anger, being
grieved at the hardening of their heart, he saith unto
the man, Stretch forth thy hand.   And he stretched it
6 forth : and his hand was restored.   And the Pharisees Mt. 22. 16.
went out, and straightway with the Herodians took
counsel against him, how they might destroy him.

S. Matthew xii. 9—14.

9 And he departed thence, and went into their synagogue : and behold, a man having a withered hand.
10 And they asked him, saying, Is it lawful to heal on the
11 sabbath day ? that they might accuse him.   And he said
unto them, What man shall there be of you, that shall   **105**
have one sheep, and if this fall into a pit on the sabbath
12 day, will he not lay hold on it, and lift it out ?   How Mt. 5. 26.
much then is a man of more value than a sheep ! Where-
13 fore it is lawful to do good on the sabbath day.   Then
saith he to the man, Stretch forth thy hand.   And he
stretched it forth ; and it was restored whole, as the
14 other.   But the Pharisees went out, and took counsel
against him, how they might destroy him.

41. *Jesus withdraws to the sea of Galilee. Many miracles.*

S. Mark iii. 7—12.

AND Jesus with his disciples withdrew to the sea : 7
and a great multitude from Galilee followed: and from
Judæa, and from Jerusalem, and from Idumæa, and 8
beyond Jordan, and about Tyre and Sidon, a great multitude, hearing what great things he did, came unto him.
And he spake to his disciples, that a little boat should 9
wait on him because of the crowd, lest they should
throng him: for he had healed many ; insomuch that as 10
many as had plagues pressed upon him that they might
33   touch him.   And the unclean spirits, whensoever they 11
beheld him, fell down before him, and cried, saying, Thou
art the Son of God.   And he charged them much that 12
they should not make him known.

S. Matthew xii. 15—21.

And Jesus perceiving it withdrew from thence : and 15
many followed him; and he healed them all, and charged 16
them that they should not make him known : that it 17
might be fulfilled which was spoken by Isaiah the
prophet, saying,

Is. 42. 1...   Behold, my servant whom I have chosen ;   18
My beloved in whom my soul is well pleased:
I will put my Spirit upon him,
And he shall declare judgement to the Gentiles.
He shall not strive, nor cry aloud ;   19
Neither shall any one hear his voice in the streets.
A bruised reed shall he not break,   20
And smoking flax shall he not quench,
Till he send forth judgement unto victory.
Gr.   And in his name shall the Gentiles hope.   21

42. *Appointment of twelve Apostles.*

S. Luke vi. 12—19.

12 . AND it came to pass in these days, that he went out Mt. 14. 23.
into the mountain to pray; and he continued all night in Lk. 9. 28.
13 prayer to God. And when it was day, he called his **63. 72.**
disciples: and he chose from them twelve, whom also he Mt. 10. 2...
14 named apostles; Simon, whom he also named Peter, and **59**
Andrew his brother, and James and John, and Philip and Acts 1. 13.
15 Bartholomew, and Matthew and Thomas, and James the Jn. 1. 42.
son of Alphæus, and Simon which was called the Zealot, Acts 22. 3.
16 and Judas the son of James, and Judas Iscariot, which Jos. 15. 25.
17 was the traitor; and he came down with them, and stood
on a level place, and a great multitude of his disciples,
and a great number of the people from all Judæa and
Jerusalem, and the sea coast of Tyre and Sidon, which
came to hear him, and to be healed of their diseases;
18 and they that were troubled with unclean spirits were
19 healed. And all the multitude sought to touch him: Mk. 5. 30.
for power came forth from him, and healed them all.   **57**

S. Mark iii. 13—19.

13 And he goeth up into the mountain, and calleth unto
him whom he himself would: and they went unto him.
14 And he appointed twelve, that they might be with him,
15 and that he might send them forth to preach, and to
16 have authority to cast out devils: and Simon he sur- Jn. 1. 22.
17 named Peter; and James the son of Zebedee, and John
the brother of James; and them he surnamed Boanerges,
18 which is, Sons of thunder: and Andrew, and Philip, and
Bartholomew, and Matthew, and Thomas, and James
the son of Alphæus, and Thaddæus, and Simon the
19 Cananæan, and Judas Iscariot, which also betrayed him.

43. *Sermon on the Mount.*

S. Matthew v. 1—viii. 1.

AND seeing the multitudes, he went up into the 1
mountain : and when he had sat down, his disciples
came unto him : and he opened his mouth and taught 2
them, saying,

Is. 57. 15;   Blessed are the poor in spirit : for theirs is the king- 3
— 66. 2.   dom of heaven.

Is. 61. 2.   Blessed are they that mourn : for they shall be com- 4
forted.

Ps. 37. 11   Blessed are the meek : for they shall inherit the earth. 5

Is. 65. 13.   Blessed are they that hunger and thirst after right- 6
eousness : for they shall be filled.

Jas. 2. 13.   Blessed are the merciful : for they shall obtain mercy. 7

Ps. 24. 4.   Blessed are the pure in heart : for they shall see God. 8

Ps. 34. 14.   Blessed are the peacemakers : for they shall be called 9
sons of God.

1 Pet. 3. 14.   Blessed are they that have been persecuted for right- 10
2 Tim. 2. 12. eousness' sake : for theirs is the kingdom of heaven.
Blessed are ye when men shall reproach you, and per- 11
1 Pet. 4. 14. secute you, and say all manner of evil against you falsely,
for my sake.   Rejoice, and be exceeding glad : for great 12
1 Th. 2. 15. is your reward in heaven : for so persecuted they the
prophets which were before you.

Ye are the salt of the earth : but if the salt have lost 13
Mk. 9. 50. its savour, wherewith shall it be salted? it is thenceforth
75. 108 good for nothing, but to be cast out and trodden under
Pro. 4. 18. foot of men.   Ye are the light of the world.   A city set 14
on a hill cannot be hid.   Neither do men light a lamp, 15
and put it under the bushel, but on the stand; and it
shineth unto all that are in the house.   Even so let your 16
1 Pet. 2. 12. light shine before men, that they may see your good
1 Co. 14. 25. works, and glorify your Father which is in heaven.

Is. 42. 21.   Think not that I came to destroy the law or the 17
prophets : I came not to destroy, but to fulfil.   For 18
verily I say unto you, Till heaven and earth pass away,
one jot or one tittle shall in no wise pass away from the
Jas. 2. 10. law, till all things be accomplished.   Whosoever there- 19
fore shall break one of these least commandments, and
shall teach men so, shall be called least in the kingdom

[T. O.

S. Luke vi. 20—49.

20   And he lifted up his eyes on his disciples, and said,
Blessed are ye poor: for yours is the kingdom of God. Jas. 2. 5. ·
21 Blessed are ye that hunger now: for ye shall be filled. Is. 55. 1...
Blessed are ye that weep now: for ye shall laugh. Is. 61. 3.
22 Blessed are ye, when men shall hate you, and when 1 Pe. 2. 20.
they shall separate you from their company, and reproach Jn. 16. 2;
you, and cast out your name as evil, for the Son of man's — 9. 34.
23 sake.   Rejoice in that day, and leap for joy : for behold, Acts 5. 41.
your reward is great in heaven: for in the same manner Jas. 1. 2...
24 did their fathers unto the prophets. But woe unto you Amos 6.1..
that are rich! for ye have received your consolation. Lk. 16. 25.
25 Woe unto you, ye that are full now! for ye shall hunger. Is. 65. 13.
Woe unto you, ye that laugh now! for ye shall mourn Pro. 14.13.
26 and weep. Woe unto you, when all men shall speak Jn. 15. 19.
well of you! for in the same manner did their fathers to
the false prophets.

xiv. 34, 35.   (108)

34   *Salt therefore is good: but if even the salt have lost*
35 *its savour, wherewith shall it be seasoned? It is fit neither*
for the land nor for the dunghill: men cast it out. He
that hath ears to hear, let him hear.

xi. 33.   (95)

No man, when he hath lighted a lamp, putteth it in a
cellar, neither under the bushel, but on the stand, that they
which enter in may see the light.

xvi. 17.   (110)

But it is easier for heaven and earth to pass away,
than for one tittle of the law to fall.

S. Matthew v.

of heaven: but whosoever shall do and teach them, he
shall be called great in the kingdom of heaven. For I 20

Ro. 9. 31.. say unto you, that except your righteousness shall exceed
— 10. 3. the righteousness of the scribes and Pharisees, ye shall in
no wise enter into the kingdom of heaven.

Ex. 20. 13.   Ye have heard that it was said to them of old time, 21
Deu. 5. 17. Thou shalt not kill; and whosoever shall kill shall be in
danger of the judgement: but I say unto you, that every 22

Jas. 1. 19.. one who is angry with his brother shall be in danger of
the judgement; and whosoever shall say to his brother,
Raca, shall be in danger of the council; and whosoever

probably shall say, Thou fool, shall be in danger of the hell of fire.
מורה If therefore thou art offering thy gift at the altar, and 23
rebel; there rememberest that thy brother hath aught against
Nu. 20. 10. thee, leave there thy gift before the altar, and go thy 24

Mk. 11. 25. way, first be reconciled to thy brother, and then come
and offer thy gift. Agree with thine adversary quickly, 25
whiles thou art with him in the way; lest haply the ad-

Pro. 25. 8. versary deliver thee to the judge, and the judge deliver
thee to the officer, and thou be cast into prison. Verily 26
I say unto thee, Thou shalt by no means come out
thence, till thou have paid the last farthing.

Ex. 20. 14.   Ye have heard that it was said, Thou shalt not com- 27
Deu. 5. 18. mit adultery: but I say unto you, that every one that 28
Job 31. 1. looketh on a woman to lust after her hath committed
Pro. 6. 25. adultery with her already in his heart. And if thy right 29
Mt. 19. 12. eye causeth thee to stumble, pluck it out, and cast it
from thee: for it is profitable for thee that one of thy

75 members should perish, and not thy whole body be cast
into hell. And if thy right hand causeth thee to stumble, 30
cut it off, and cast it from thee: for it is profitable for
thee that one of thy members should perish, and not thy
whole body go into hell. It was said also, Whosoever 31

Deu. 24. 1.. shall put away his wife, let him give her a writing of
divorcement: but I say unto you, that every one that 32

1Co. 7. 10.. putteth away his wife, saving for the cause of fornication,
maketh her an adulteress: and whosoever shall marry
her when she is put away committeth adultery.

Ex. 20. 7.   Again, ye have heard that it was said to them of old 33
Lev. 19. 12. time, Thou shalt not forswear thyself, but shalt perform
Num. 30. 2. unto the Lord thine oaths: but I say unto you, Swear 34
21.   [T. O.

S. Luke xii. 58, 59.   (99)

58   *For as thou art going with thine adversary before the magistrate, on the way give diligence to be quit of him; lest haply he hale thee unto the judge, and the judge shall deliver thee to the officer, and the officer shall cast thee into*
59 *prison.   I say unto thee, Thou shalt by no means come out thence, till thou have paid the very last mite.*

S. Mark ix. 43—48.   (75)

43   *And if thy hand cause thee to stumble, cut it off: it is good for thee to enter into life maimed, rather than having thy two hands to go into hell, into the unquenchable fire.*
45 *And if thy foot cause thee to stumble, cut it off: it is good for thee to enter into life halt, rather than having thy two*
47 *feet to be cast into hell.   And if thine eye cause thee to stumble, cast it out: it is good for thee to enter into the kingdom of God with one eye, rather than having two eyes*
48 *to be cast into hell; where their worm dieth not, and the fire is not quenched.*

S. Luke xvi. 18.   (110)

18   *Every one that putteth away his wife, and marrieth another, committeth adultery: and he that marrieth one that is put away from a husband committeth adultery.*

S. Matthew v.

not at all; neither by the heaven, for it is the throne of
Is. 66. 1. God; nor by the earth, for it is the footstool of his feet; 35
Ps. 48. 2. nor by Jerusalem, for it is the city of the great King.
Neither shalt thou swear by thy head, for thou canst not 36
make one hair white or black. But let your speech be, 37
Jas. 5. 12. Yea, yea; Nay, nay: and whatsoever is more than these
is of the evil one.

Ex. 21. 24.   Ye have heard that it was said, An eye for an eye, 38
Lev. 24. 20. and a tooth for a tooth: but I say unto you, Resist not 39
Deu. 19. 21. him that is evil: but whosoever smiteth thee on thy right
cheek, turn to him the other also. And if any man 40
1 Cor. 6. 7. would go to law with thee, and take away thy coat, let
Mt. 27. 32. him have thy cloke also. And whosoever shall compel 41
thee to go one mile, go with him twain. Give to him 42
Deu. 15. 8. that asketh thee, and from him that would borrow of
thee turn not thou away.

Lev. 19. 18.   Ye have heard that it was said, Thou shalt love thy 43
neighbour, and hate thine enemy: but I say unto you, 44
Acts 7. 60. Love your enemies, and pray for them that persecute
you; that ye may be sons of your Father which is in 45
Job 25. 3. heaven: for he maketh his sun to rise on the evil and
the good, and sendeth rain on the just and the unjust.
For if ye love them that love you, what reward have ye? 46
do not even the publicans the same? And if ye salute 47
your brethren only, what do ye more than others? do not
De. 18. 13. even the Gentiles the same? Ye therefore shall be per- 48
Jas. 1. 4. fect, as your heavenly Father is perfect.

Take heed that ye do not your righteousness before 6.1
men, to be seen of them: else ye have no reward with
your Father which is in heaven.

He. 13. 16.   When therefore thou doest alms, sound not a trumpet 2
before thee, as the hypocrites do in the synagogues and
in the streets, that they may have glory of men. Verily
I say unto you, They have received their reward. But 3
when thou doest alms, let not thy left hand know what
thy right hand doeth: that thine alms may be in secret: 4
2 Co. 9. 6. and thy Father which seeth in secret shall recompense
thee.

And when ye pray, ye shall not be as the hypocrites: 5
for they love to stand and pray in the synagogues and in
the corners of the streets, that they may be seen of men.
[T. O.

S. Luke vi: 27—36.

27   But I say unto you which hear, Love your enemies, Ex. 23. 4.
28 do good to them that hate you, bless them that curse Pro. 25. 21.
29 you, pray for them that despitefully use you.   To him Acts 7. 60.
   that smiteth thee on the one cheek offer also the other;
   and from him that taketh away thy cloke withhold not 1 Cor. 6. 7.
30 thy coat also.   Give to every one that asketh thee; and Pro. 21. 26.
   of him that taketh away thy goods ask them not again.
31 And as ye would that men should do to you, do ye also Tob. 4. 15.
32 to them likewise.   And if ye love them that love you,
   what thank have ye? for even sinners love those that
33 love them.   And if ye do good to them that do good to
   you, what thank have ye? for even sinners do the same.
34 And if ye lend to them of whom ye hope to receive,
   what thank have ye? even sinners lend to sinners, to
35 receive again as much.   But love your enemies, and do
   them good, and lend, never despairing; and your reward Ps. 37. 26.
   shall be great, and ye shall be sons of the Most High:
36 for he is kind toward the unthankful and evil.   Be ye
   merciful, even as your Father is merciful.

S. Matthew vi.

Verily I say unto you, They have received their reward.
Is. 26. 20. But thou, when thou prayest, enter into thine inner 6
2 Ki. 4. 33. chamber, and having shut thy door, pray to thy Father
which is in secret, and thy Father which seeth in secret
shall recompense thee.   And in praying use not vain 7
1 Ki.18.27. repetitions, as the Gentiles do : for they think that they
Ecclus. shall be heard for their much speaking.   Be not there- 8
7. 14. fore like unto them : for your Father knoweth what things
ye have need of, before ye ask him.   After this manner 9
90 therefore pray ye : Our Father which art in heaven,
Hallowed be thy name.   Thy kingdom come.   Thy will 10
Pro. 30. 8. be done, as in heaven, so on earth.   Give us this day 11
Ecclus. our daily bread.   And forgive us our debts, as we also 12
28. 2. have forgiven our debtors.   And bring us not into temp- 13
tation, but deliver us from the evil one.   For if ye forgive 14
Mk.11.25. men their trespasses, your heavenly Father will also for-
Mt. 18. 35. give you.   But if ye forgive not men their trespasses, 15
Jas. 2. 13. neither will your Father forgive your trespasses.
38 Moreover when ye fast, be not, as the hypocrites, of 16
Is. 58. 3... a sad countenance : for they disfigure their faces, that
they may be seen of men to fast.   Verily I say unto
you, They have received their reward.   But thou, when 17
thou fastest, anoint thy head, and wash thy face ; that 18
thou be not seen of men to fast, but of thy Father which
is in secret : and thy Father, which seeth in secret, shall
recompense thee.
Lk. 12. 33. Lay not up for yourselves treasures upon the earth, 19
Jas. 5. 1... where moth and rust doth consume, and where thieves
1Tim.6.19. break through and steal : but lay up for yourselves 20
treasures in heaven, where neither moth nor rust doth
consume, and where thieves do not break through nor
steal : for where thy treasure is, there will thy heart be 21
95 also.   The lamp of the body is the eye : if therefore 22
thine eye be single, thy whole body shall be full of light.
But if thine eye be evil, thy whole body shall be full of 23
darkness.   If therefore the light that is in thee be dark-
110 ness, how great is the darkness !   No man can serve two 24
masters : for either he will hate the one, and love the
other ; or else he will hold to one, and despise the other.
1Co.10.21. Ye cannot serve God and mammon.   Therefore I say 25
[T. O.

S. Luke xi. 1—4. (90)

1 *And it came to pass, as he was praying in a certain place, that when he ceased, one of his disciples said unto him, Lord, teach us to pray, even as John also taught his* 2 *disciples. And he said unto them, When ye pray, say,* 3 *Father, Hallowed be thy name. Thy kingdom come. Give* 4 *us day by day our daily bread. And forgive us our sins; for we ourselves also forgive every one that is indebted to us. And bring us not into temptation.*

xi. 34—36. (95)

34 *The lamp of the body is thine eye: when thine eye is single, thy whole body also is full of light; but when it is* 35 *evil, thy body also is full of darkness. Look therefore* 36 *whether the light that is in thee be not darkness. If therefore thy whole body be full of light, having no part dark, it shall be wholly full of light, as when the lamp with its bright shining doth give thee light.*

xvi. 13. (110)

No servant can serve two masters: for either he will hate the one, and love the other; or else he will hold to one, and despise the other. Ye cannot serve God and mammon.

S. Matthew vi.

98   unto you, Be not anxious for your life, what ye shall eat, or what ye shall drink; nor yet for your body, what ye shall put on. Is not the life more than the food, and
Job 38. 41. the body than the raiment? Behold the birds of the 26
Ps. 147. 9. heaven, that they sow not, neither do they reap, nor gather into barns; and your heavenly Father feedeth them. Are not ye of much more value than they? And 27 which of you by being anxious can add one cubit unto
Lk. 19. 3. his stature? And why are ye anxious concerning rai- 28
Gr. ment? Consider the lilies of the field, how they grow; they toil not, neither do they spin: yet I say unto you, 29 that even Solomon in all his glory was not arrayed like
Ps. 104. 14. one of these. But if God doth so clothe the grass of the 30
Jas. 1. 10. field, which to-day is, and to-morrow is cast into the oven, shall he not much more clothe you, O ye of little
Ps. 55. 22. faith? Be not therefore anxious, saying, What shall we 31
1 Pet. 5. 7. eat? or, What shall we drink? or, Wherewithal shall we
Phil. 4. 6. be clothed? For after all these things do the Gentiles 32 seek; for your heavenly Father knoweth that ye have need of all these things. But seek ye first his kingdom, 33
1 Ki. 3. 13. and his righteousness; and all these things shall be added
1 Tim. 4. 8. unto you. Be not therefore anxious for the morrow: for 34 the morrow will be anxious for itself. Sufficient unto the day is the evil thereof.
Rom. 2. 1.   Judge not, that ye be not judged. For with what 7. 1, 2
Mk. 4. 24. judgement ye judge, ye shall be judged: and with what
Ro. 14. 3... measure ye mete, it shall be measured unto you. And 3
Jas. 2. 13. why beholdest thou the mote that is in thy brother's eye, but considerest not the beam that is in thine own eye? Or how wilt thou say to thy brother, Let me cast 4 out the mote out of thine eye; and lo, the beam is in thine own eye? Thou hypocrite, cast out first the beam 5 out of thine own eye; and then shalt thou see clearly to cast out the mote out of thy brother's eye.
Pro. 9. 7...   Give not that which is holy unto the dogs, neither 6
— 23. 9. cast your pearls before the swine, lest haply they trample them under their feet, and turn and rend you.
90   Ask, and it shall be given you; seek, and ye 7 shall find; knock, and it shall be opened unto you:

[T. O.

S. Luke xii. 22—34. (98)

22   *Therefore I say unto you, Be not anxious for your life,*
    what ye shall eat; nor yet for your body, what ye shall put
23 *on. For the life is more than the food, and the body than the*
24 *raiment. Consider the ravens, that they sow not, neither*
    reap; which have no store-chamber nor barn; and God
    feedeth them: of how much more value are ye than the birds!
25 *And which of you by being anxious can add a cubit unto his*
26 *stature? If then ye are not able to do even that which is least,*
27 *why are ye anxious concerning the rest? Consider the lilies,*
    how they grow: they toil not, neither do they spin; yet I say
    unto you, Even Solomon in all his glory was not arrayed
28 *like one of these. But if God doth so clothe the grass in the*
    field, which to-day is, and to-morrow is cast into the oven;
29 *how much more shall he clothe you, O ye of little faith? And*
    seek not ye what ye shall eat, and what ye shall drink, neither
30 *be ye of doubtful mind. For all these things do the nations of*
    the world seek after: but your Father knoweth that ye have
31 *need of these things. Howbeit seek ye his kingdom, and these*
32 *things shall be added unto you. Fear not, little flock; for it*
    is your Father's good pleasure to give you the kingdom.
33 *Sell that ye have, and give alms; make for yourselves purses*
    which wax not old, a treasure in the heavens that faileth not,
34 *where no thief draweth near, nor moth destroyeth. For*
    where your treasure is, there will your heart be also.

vi. 37—42.

37   And judge not, and ye shall not be judged: and Jas. 4. 11.
condemn not, and ye shall not be condemned: release, Rom. 14. 4.
38 and ye shall be released: give, and it shall be given unto
you; good measure, pressed down, shaken together, Pro. 19. 17.
running over, shall they give into your bosom. For with Ps. 79. 12.
what measure ye mete it shall be measured to you again. Jas. 2. 13.
39   And he spake also a parable unto them, Can the Mt. 15. 14.
blind guide the blind? shall they not both fall into a
40 pit? The disciple is not above his master: but every Mt. 10. 24.
41 one when he is perfected shall be as his master. And
why beholdest thou the mote that is in thy brother's eye,
but considerest not the beam that is in thine own eye?
42 Or how canst thou say to thy brother, Brother, let me
cast out the mote that is in thine eye, when thou thyself
beholdest not the beam that is in thine own eye? Thou
hypocrite, cast out first the beam out of thine own eye,
and then shalt thou see clearly to cast out the mote that
is in thy brother's eye.

xi. 9—13. (90)

9   *And I say unto you, Ask, and it shall be given you; seek,*
and ye shall find; knock, and it shall be opened unto you.

S. Matthew vii.

Jas. 1. 5.   for every one that asketh receiveth ; and he that seeketh 8
1 Jn. 5. 14..   findeth ; and to him that knocketh it shall be opened. Or 9
         what man is there of you, who, if his son shall ask him
         for a loaf, will give him a stone; or if he shall ask for a 10
Gen. 6. 5.   fish, will give him a serpent? If ye then, being evil, know 11
         how to give good gifts unto your children, how much
         more shall your Father which is in heaven give good
         things to them that ask him? All things therefore what- 12
Jas. 2. 8.   soever ye would that men should do unto you, even
133   so do ye also unto them: for this is the law and the
         prophets.

103.   Enter ye in by the narrow gate: for wide is the gate, 13
         and broad is the way, that leadeth to destruction, and
         many be they that enter in thereby. For narrow is the 14
         gate, and straitened the way, that leadeth unto life, and
         few be they that find it.

Deu. 13. 2..   Beware of false prophets, which come to you in 15
Acts 20. 29. sheep's clothing, but inwardly are ravening wolves. By 16
         their fruits ye shall know them. Do men gather grapes
         of thorns, or figs of thistles? Even so every good tree 17
Mt. 12. 33.. bringeth forth good fruit; but the corrupt tree bringeth
91   forth evil fruit. A good tree cannot bring forth evil 18
         fruit, neither can a corrupt tree bring forth good fruit.
Mt. 3. 10. Every tree that bringeth not forth good fruit is hewn 19
Jn. 15. 2... down, and cast into the fire. Therefore by their fruits 20
151   ye shall know them. Not every one that saith unto me, 21
Hos. 8. 2... Lord, Lord, shall enter into the kingdom of heaven; but
Rom. 2. 13. he that doeth the will of my Father which is in heaven.
Jas. 1. 22.. Many will say to me in that day, Lord, Lord, did we not 22
Jer. 27. 15. prophesy by thy name, and by thy name cast out devils,
— 14. 14. and by thy name do many mighty works? And then 23
Lk. 13. 27. will I profess unto them, I never knew you: depart from
Ps. 6. 8.   me, ye that work iniquity. Every one therefore which 24
         heareth these words of mine, and doeth them, shall be
         likened unto a wise man, which built his house upon the
         rock: and the rain descended, and the floods came, and 25
         the winds blew, and beat upon that house; and it fell
         not: for it was founded upon the rock. And every one 26
Jas. 1. 23.. that heareth these words of mine, and doeth them not,
         shall be likened unto a foolish man, which built his house
         upon the sand: and the rain descended, and the floods 27
         came, and the winds blew, and smote upon that house;
         and it fell: and great was the fall thereof.   [T. O.

S. Luke xi.

10 *For every one that asketh receiveth; and he that seeketh findeth;*
11 *and to him that knocketh it shall be opened.   And of which*
of you that is a father shall his son ask a loaf, and he give him
12 *a stone? or a fish, and he for a fish give him a serpent? Or*
13 *if he shall ask an egg, will he give him a scorpion?   If ye*
then, being evil, know how to give good gifts unto your
children, how much more shall your heavenly Father give
the Holy Spirit to them that ask him?

xiii. 24—27.

24   *Strive to enter in by the narrow door: for many, I say*
25 *unto you, shall seek to enter in, and shall not be able.   When*
once the master of the house is risen up, and hath shut to the
door, and ye begin to stand without, and to knock at the door,
saying, Lord, open to us; and he shall answer and say to
you, I know you not whence ye are; then shall ye begin to
26 *say, We did eat and drink in thy presence, and thou didst*
27 *teach in our streets; and he shall say, I tell you, I know*
not whence ye are; depart from me, all ye workers of
iniquity.

vi. 43—49.

43   For there is no good tree that bringeth forth corrupt   Mt. 12. 33.
fruit; nor again a corrupt tree that bringeth forth good   91
44 fruit.   For each tree is known by its own fruit.   For of
thorns men do not gather figs, nor of a bramble bush
45 gather they grapes.   The good man out of the good
treasure of his heart bringeth forth that which is good; Mt. 12. 35.
and the evil man out of the evil treasure bringeth forth
that which is evil: for out of the abundance of the heart
his mouth speaketh.
46   And why call ye me, Lord, Lord, and do not the
47 things which I say?   Every one that cometh unto me,
and heareth my words, and doeth them, I will shew you
48 to whom he is like: he is like a man building a house,
who digged and went deep, and laid a foundation upon
the rock: and when a flood arose, the stream brake
against that house, and could not shake it: because it
49 had been well builded.   But he that heareth, and doeth
not, is like a man that built a house upon the earth
without a foundation; against which the stream brake,
and straightway it fell in; and the ruin of that house was
great.

S. Matthew vii. 28—viii. 1.

And it came to pass, when Jesus ended these words, 28
the multitudes were astonished at his teaching: for he 29
Jn. 7. 46.   taught them as one having authority, and not as their
scribes.

And when he was come down from the mountain, 8.1
great multitudes followed him.

44.   *The centurion's servant healed.*

S. Luke vii. 1—10.

AFTER he had ended all his sayings in the ears of 1
the people, he entered into Capernaum.
Mk. 15. 39.   And a certain centurion's servant, who was dear unto 2
Acts 10. 2.   him, was sick and at the point of death.   And when he 3
heard concerning Jesus, he sent unto him elders of the
Jews, asking him that he would come and save his
servant.   And they, when they came to Jesus, besought 4
him earnestly, saying, He is worthy that thou shouldest
do this for him: for he loveth our nation, and himself 5
built us our synagogue.   And Jesus went with them. 6
And when he was now not far from the house, the centurion sent friends to him, saying unto him, Lord, trouble
not thyself: for I am not worthy that thou shouldest
come under my roof: wherefore neither thought I my- 7
self worthy to come unto thee: but say the word, and
Ps. 107. 20.   my servant shall be healed.   For I also am a man set 8
under authority, having under myself soldiers: and I
say to this one, Go, and he goeth; and to another,
Come, and he cometh; and to my servant, Do this,
and he doeth it.   And when Jesus heard these things, 9
he marvelled at him, and turned and said to the multi-
Mt. 15. 28.   tude that followed him, I say unto you, I have not
68   found so great faith, no, not in Israel.   And they that 10
were sent, returning to the house, found the servant
whole.

S. Matthew viii. 5—13.

5   And when he was entered into Capernaum, there
6 came unto him a centurion, beseeching him, and saying,
Lord, my servant lieth in the house sick of the palsy,
7 grievously tormented. And he saith unto him, I will
8 come and heal him. And the centurion answered and
said, Lord, I am not worthy that thou shouldest come
under my roof: but only say the word, and my servant
9 shall be healed. For I also am a man under authority,
having under myself soldiers: and I say to this one,
Go, and he goeth; and to another, Come, and he
cometh; and to my servant, Do this, and he doeth it.
10 And when Jesus heard it, he marvelled, and said to
them that followed, Verily I say unto you, I have not
11 found so great faith, no, not in Israel. And I say unto
you, that many shall come from the east and the west, Mal. 1. 11.
and shall sit down with Abraham, and Isaac, and Jacob, Is. 59. 19.
12 in the kingdom of heaven: but the sons of the kingdom
shall be cast forth into the outer darkness: there shall Mt. 21. 43.
13 be the weeping and gnashing of teeth. And Jesus 2 Pet. 2. 17.
said unto the centurion, Go thy way; as thou hast Jude 13.
believed, so be it done unto thee. And the servant was
healed in that hour.

45. *The widow's son raised.*

S. Luke vii. 11—17.

AND it came to pass soon afterwards, that he went to 11
a city called Nain; and his disciples went with him, and
a great multitude. Now when he drew near to the gate 12
of the city, behold, there was carried out one that was
dead, the only son of his mother, and she was a widow:
and much people of the city was with her. And when 13
the Lord saw her, he had compassion on her, and said
unto her, Weep not. And he came nigh and touched 14
the bier: and the bearers stood still. And he said,
57. 112. Young man, I say unto thee, Arise. And he that was 15
dead sat up, and began to speak. And he gave him to
his mother. And fear took hold on all: and they glori- 16
fied God, saying, A great prophet is arisen among us:
Lk. i. 68. and, God hath visited his people. And this report went 17
forth concerning him in the whole of Judæa, and all the
region round about.

S. Mark v. 40—43. (57)

*But he, having put them all forth, taketh the father of 40
the child and her mother and them that were with him,
and goeth in where the child was. And taking the child 41
by the hand, he saith unto her, Talitha cumi; which is,
being interpreted, Damsel, I say unto thee, Arise. And 42
straightway the damsel rose up, and walked; for she was
twelve years old. And they were amazed straightway
with a great amazement. And he charged them much 43
that no man should know this: and he commanded that
something should be given her to eat.*

S. John xi. 41—44. (112)

*So they took away the stone. And Jesus lifted up his 41
eyes, and said, Father, I thank thee that thou heardest me.
And I knew that thou hearest me always: but because of 42
the multitude which standeth around I said it, that they
may believe that thou didst send me. And when he had 43
thus spoken, he cried with a loud voice, Lazarus, come forth.
He that was dead came forth, bound hand and foot with 44
grave-clothes; and his face was bound about with a napkin.
Jesus saith unto them, Loose him, and let him go.*

46. *John Baptist's question. Jesus' testimony to him.*

S. Luke vii. 18—35.

18 AND the disciples of John told him of all these things.
19 And John calling unto him two of his disciples sent
them to the Lord, saying, Art thou he that cometh, or
20 look we for another? And when the men were come
unto him, they said, John the Baptist hath sent us unto
thee, saying, Art thou he that cometh, or look we for
21 another? In that hour he cured many of diseases and   33
plagues and evil spirits; and on many that were blind
22 he bestowed sight. And he answered and said unto
them, Go your way, and tell John what things ye have
seen and heard; the blind receive their sight, the lame   Is. 35. 5...
walk, the lepers are cleansed, and the deaf hear, the dead   — 29. 18.
are raised up, and the poor have good tidings preached   Is. 61. 1.
23 unto them. And blessed is he whosoever shall find none   Jas. 2. 5.
occasion of stumbling in me.   [T.O. 1 Pet. 2. 8.

S. Matthew xi. 2—19.

2 Now when John heard in the prison the works of the   Lk. 3. 20.
3 Christ, he sent by his disciples, and said unto him, Art
4 thou he that cometh, or look we for another? And Jesus
answered and said unto them, Go your way and tell
5 John the things which ye do hear and see: the blind
receive their sight, and the lame walk, the lepers are
cleansed, and the deaf hear, and the dead are raised up,
6 and the poor have good tidings preached to them. And
blessed is he, whosoever shall find none occasion of
stumbling in me.   [T. O.

J. H. G.   5

66 THIS IS ELIJAH,

S. Luke vii.

And when the messengers of John were departed, 24
he began to say unto the multitudes concerning John,
What went ye out into the wilderness to behold? a reed
Eph. 4. 14. shaken with the wind? But what went ye out to see? a 25
man clothed in soft raiment? Behold, they which are
gorgeously apparelled, and live delicately, are in kings'
courts. But what went ye out to see? a prophet? 26
Yea, I say unto you, and much more than a prophet.
This is he of whom it is written, 27
Mal. 3. 1. Behold, I send my messenger before thy face,
Who shall prepare thy way before thee.
I say unto you, Among them that are born of women 28
there is none greater than John: yet he that is but
little in the kingdom of God is greater than he. And 29
Mt. 21. 31. all the people when they heard, and the publicans, justi-
128 fied God, being baptized with the baptism of John. But 30
1 Tim. 2. 4. the Pharisees and the lawyers rejected for themselves
the counsel of God, being not baptized of him. Where- 31
unto then shall I liken the men of this generation, and
to what are they like? They are like unto children that 32
Lk. 15. 25. sit in the marketplace, and call one to another; which
Mk. 5. 38. say, We piped unto you, and ye did not dance; we
wailed, and ye did not weep. For John the Baptist is 33
come eating no bread nor drinking wine; and ye say,
Jn. 2. 2. He hath a devil. The Son of man is come eating and 34
Lk. 14. 1. drinking; and ye say, Behold, a gluttonous man, and a
Jn. 12. 2. winebibber, a friend of publicans and sinners! And 35
wisdom is justified of all her children.

S. Matthew xi.

7 And as these went their way, Jesus began to say
unto the multitudes concerning John, What went ye out
into the wilderness to behold? a reed shaken with the
8 wind? But what went ye out for to see? a man clothed
in soft raiment? Behold, they that wear soft raiment are
9 in kings' houses. But wherefore went ye out? to see a
prophet? Yea, I say unto you, and much more than a
10 prophet. This is he, of whom it is written,

    Behold, I send my messenger before thy face,
    Who shall prepare thy way before thee.

11 Verily I say unto you, Among them that are born of
women there hath not arisen a greater than John the
Baptist: yet he that is but little in the kingdom of
12 heaven is greater than he. And from the days of John
the Baptist until now the kingdom of heaven suffereth Lk. 16. 16.
13 violence, and men of violence take it by force. For all **110**
14 the prophets and the law prophesied until John. And if
ye are willing to receive it, this is Elijah, which is to Mal. 4. 5.
15, 16 come. He that hath ears to hear, let him hear. But
whereunto shall I liken this generation? It is like unto
children sitting in the marketplaces, which call unto
17 their fellows, and say, We piped unto you, and ye did
18 not dance; we wailed, and ye did not mourn. For
John came neither eating nor drinking, and they say,
19 He hath a devil. The Son of man came eating and
drinking, and they say, Behold, a gluttonous man, and a
winebibber, a friend of publicans and sinners! And
wisdom is justified by her works.

47. *Jesus' feet anointed.   The sinner forgiven.*

S. Luke vii. 36—50.

AND one of the Pharisees desired him that he would 36
eat with him.   And he entered into the Pharisee's house,
and sat down to meat.   And behold, a woman which 37
was in the city, a sinner; and when she knew that he
was sitting at meat in the Pharisee's house, she brought
Mk. 14. 3. an alabaster cruse of ointment, and standing behind at 38
125   his feet, 'weeping, she began to wet his feet with her
tears, and wiped them with the hair of her head, and
kissed his feet, and anointed them with the ointment.
Now when the Pharisee which had bidden him saw it, 39
Lk. 15. 2. he spake within himself, saying, This man, if he were a
Is. 65. 5. prophet, would have perceived who and what manner of
woman this is which toucheth him, that she is a sinner.
And Jesus answering said unto him, Simon, I have some- 40
what to say unto thee.   And he saith, Master, say on.
A certain lender had two debtors: the one owed five 41
hundred pence, and the other fifty.   When they had not 42
Mt.18.23... wherewith to pay, he forgave them both.   Which of
them therefore will love him most?   Simon answered 43
and said, He, I suppose, to whom he forgave the most.
And he said unto him, Thou hast rightly judged.   And 44
turning to the woman, he said unto Simon, Seest thou
this woman?   I entered into thine house, thou gavest
Gen. 18. 4. me no water for my feet: but she hath wetted my feet
with her tears, and wiped them with her hair.   Thou 45
Ex. 18. 7. gavest me no kiss: but she, since the time I came in,
hath not ceased to kiss my feet.   My head with oil thou 46
Ps. 23. 5. didst not anoint: but she hath anointed my feet with
ointment.   Wherefore I say unto thee, Her sins, which 47
are many, are forgiven; for she loved much: but to
whom little is forgiven, the same loveth little.   And he 48
said unto her, Thy sins are forgiven.   And they that sat 49
Mk. 2. 7. at meat with him began to say within themselves, Who
37   is this that even forgiveth sins?   And he said unto the 50
woman, Thy faith hath saved thee; go in peace.

S. John xii. 1—8. (125)

1 *Jesus therefore six days before the passover came to
Bethany, where Lazarus was, whom Jesus raised from the*
2 *dead. So they made him a supper there: and Martha
served; but Lazarus was one of them that sat at meat with*
3 *him. Mary therefore took a pound of ointment of spikenard,
very precious, and anointed the feet of Jesus, and wiped his
feet with her hair: and the house was filled with the odour*
4 *of the ointment. But Judas Iscariot, one of his disciples,*
5 *which should betray him, saith, Why was not this ointment*
6 *sold for three hundred pence, and given to the poor? Now
this he said, not because he cared for the poor; but because
he was a thief, and having the bag took away what was put*
7 *therein. Jesus therefore said, Suffer her to keep it against*
8 *the day of my burying. For the poor ye have always with
you; but me ye have not always.*

S. Mark xiv. 3—9. (125)

3 *And while he was in Bethany in the house of Simon the
leper, as he sat at meat, there came a woman having an
alabaster cruse of ointment of spikenard very costly; and she*
4 *brake the cruse, and poured it over his head. But there were
some that had indignation among themselves, saying, To
what purpose hath this waste of the ointment been made?*
5 *For this ointment might have been sold for above three
hundred pence, and given to the poor. And they murmured*
6 *against her. But Jesus said, Let her alone; why trouble ye*
7 *her? she hath wrought a good work on me. For ye have
the poor always with you, and whensoever ye will ye can do*
8 *them good: but me ye have not always. She hath done
what she could: she hath anointed my body aforehand for*
9 *the burying. And verily I say unto you, Wheresoever the
gospel shall be preached throughout the whole world, that
also which this woman hath done shall be spoken of for a
memorial of her.*

48. *Circuit in Galilee. Ministering women.*

S. Luke viii. 1—3.

1 AND it came to pass soon afterwards, that he went
about through cities and villages, preaching and bringing
the good tidings of the kingdom of God, and with him
2 the twelve, and certain women which had been healed
of evil spirits and infirmities, Mary that was called Mag-
3 dalene, from whom seven devils had gone out, and Jo- Mk. 16. 9.
anna the wife of Chuza Herod's steward, and Susanna,
and many others, which ministered unto them of their Lk. 23. 55.
substance.

49. *The parable of the sower.*

S. Mark iv. 1—9.

AND again he began to teach by the sea side. And 1
there is gathered unto him a very great multitude, so
Lk. 5. 3. that he entered into a boat, and sat in the sea; and all
35   the multitude were by the sea on the land. And he 2
Ps. 78. 2. taught them many things in parables, and said unto
them in his teaching, Hearken: Behold the sower went 3
forth to sow: and it came to pass, as he sowed, some 4
seed fell by the way side, and the birds came and devoured it. And other fell on the rocky ground, where it 5
had not much earth; and straightway it sprang up, ·
Jas. 1. 11. because it had no deepness of earth: and when the sun 6
was risen, it was scorched; and because it had no root,
Jer. 4. 3. it withered away. And other fell among the thorns, and 7
the thorns grew up, and choked it, and it yielded no fruit.
Jn. 15. 5. And others fell into the good ground, and yielded fruit, 8
Col. 1. 6. growing up and increasing; and brought forth, thirtyfold,
and sixtyfold, and a hundredfold. And he said, Who 9
hath ears to hear, let him hear.

S. Matthew xiii. 1—9

1 On that day went Jesus out of the house, and sat by
2 the sea side. And there were gathered unto him great
multitudes, so that he entered into a boat, and sat; and
3 all the multitude stood on the beach. And he spake to
them many things in parables, saying, Behold, the sower
4 went forth to sow; and as he sowed, some seeds fell by
the way side, and the birds came and devoured them:
5 and others fell upon the rocky places, where they had
not much earth: and straightway they sprang up, because
6 they had no deepness of earth: and when the sun was
risen, they were scorched; and because they had no
7 root, they withered away. And others fell upon the
8 thorns; and the thorns grew up, and choked them: and
others fell upon the good ground, and yielded fruit, some
9 a hundredfold, some sixty, some thirty. He that hath
ears, let him hear.

S. Luke viii. 4—8.

4 And when a great multitude came together, and they
of every city resorted unto him, he spake by a parable:
5 The sower went forth to sow his seed: and as he sowed,
some fell by the way side; and it was trodden under
foot, and the birds of the heaven devoured it. And
6 other fell on the rock; and as soon as it grew, it withered
away, because it had no moisture. And other fell amidst
7 the thorns; and the thorns grew with it, and choked it.
8 And other fell into the good ground, and grew, and
brought forth fruit a hundredfold. As he said these
things, he cried, He that hath ears to hear, let him
hear.

50. *Of teaching by parables. The sower explained.*

S. Matthew xiii. 10—23.

AND the disciples came, and said unto him, Why 10
speakest thou unto them in parables? And he answered 11
Mt. 11. 25. and said unto them, Unto you it is given to know the
mysteries of the kingdom of heaven, but to them it is
Mt. 25. 28.. not given.   For whosoever hath, to him shall be given, 12
and he shall have abundance: but whosoever hath not,
from him shall be taken away even that which he hath.
Lk. 19. 24.. Therefore speak I to them in parables; because seeing 13
they see not, and hearing they hear not, neither do they
understand.   And unto them is fulfilled the prophecy of 14
Isaiah, which saith,

Is. 6. 9.   By hearing ye shall hear, and shall in no wise
Jn. 12. 40.   understand;
Acts 28. 26.   And seeing ye shall see, and shall in no wise perceive:
               For this people's heart is waxed gross,   15
Heb. 5. 11.   And their ears are dull of hearing,
               And their eyes they have closed;
               Lest haply they should perceive with their eyes,
               And hear with their ears,
               And understand with their heart,
               And should turn again,
               And I should heal them.
Lk. 10. 24. But blessed are your eyes, for they see; and your ears, 16
for they hear.   For verily I say unto you, that many 17
Heb. 11. 13. prophets and righteous men desired to see the things
1 Pet. 1. 10. which ye see, and saw them not; and to hear the things
which ye hear, and heard them not.   [T. O.

S. Mark iv. 10—20.

10 And when he was alone, they that were about him
11 with the twelve asked of him the parables. And he said
unto them, Unto you is given the mystery of the kingdom of God: but unto them that are without, all things
12 are done in parables: that seeing they may see, and not
perceive; and hearing they may hear, and not understand; lest haply they should turn again, and it should
be forgiven them.   [T. O.

S. Luke viii. 9—15.

9 And his disciples asked him what this parable might
10 be. And he said, Unto you it is given to know the
mysteries of the kingdom of God: but to the rest in
parables; that seeing they may not see, and hearing
they may not understand.   [T. O.

S. Matthew xiii.

Hear then ye the parable of the sower.   When any 18
one heareth the word of the kingdom, and understandeth 19
Eph. 2. 2. it not, then cometh the evil one, and snatcheth away
that which hath been sown in his heart.   This is he that
was sown by the way side.   And he that was sown upon 20
the rocky places, this is he that heareth the word, and
Eph. 3. 17. straightway with joy receiveth it ; yet hath he not root in 21
himself, but endureth for a while ; and when tribulation
Mt. 24. 12. or persecution ariseth because of the word, straightway
he stumbleth.   And he that was sown among the thorns,
Mt. 6. 25. this is he that heareth the word ; and the care of the
Mk. 10. 23. world, and the deceitfulness of riches, choke the word, 22
1 Tim. 6. 9. and he becometh unfruitful.   And he that was sown 23
upon the good ground, this is he that heareth the word,
and understandeth it ; who verily beareth fruit, and
bringeth forth, some a hundredfold, some sixty, some
thirty.

8. Mark iv.

13 And he saith unto them, Know ye not this parable?
14 and how shall ye know all the parables? The sower
15 soweth the word. And these are they by the way side, 1Cor.3.6...
where the word is sown; and when they have heard,
straightway cometh Satan, and taketh away the word
16 which hath been sown in them. And these in like
manner are they that are sown upon the rocky places,
who, when they have heard the word, straightway receive
17 it with joy; and they have no root in themselves, but
endure for a while; then, when tribulation or persecution
ariseth because of the word, straightway they stumble.
18 And others are they that are sown among the thorns;
19 these are they that have heard the word, and the cares
of the world, and the deceitfulness of riches, and the
lusts of other things entering in, choke the word, and it
20 becometh unfruitful. And those are they that were
sown upon the good ground; such as hear the word,
and accept it, and bear fruit, thirtyfold, and sixtyfold,
and a hundredfold.

8. Luke viii.

11 Now the parable is this: The seed is the word of
12 God. And those by the way side are they that have
heard; then cometh the devil, and taketh away the word
from their heart, that they may not believe and be saved.
13 And those on the rock are they which, when they have
heard, receive the word with joy; and these have no
root, which for a while believe, and in time of temptation
14 fall away. And that which fell among the thorns, these
are they that have heard, and as they go on their way
they are choked with cares and riches and pleasures of
15 this life, and bring no fruit to perfection. And that in
the good ground, these are such as in an honest and Jn. 8. 47.
good heart, having heard the word, hold it fast, and Prov. 16. 1.
bring forth fruit with patience.

51. *Parable of the lamp.   The tares.   The seed.*
The mustard seed.   The leaven.

S. Mark iv. 21—34.

Mt. 5. 16.   AND he said unto them, Is the lamp brought to be 21
Psalm   put under the bushel, or under the bed, and not to be
119.105.   put on the stand? For there is nothing hid, save that it 22
Pro.20.27.   should be manifested; neither was anything made secret,
Mt. 10. 26. but that it should come to light. If any man hath ears 23
Lk. 12. 2.   to hear, let him hear. And he said unto them, Take 24
59. 97   heed what ye hear: with what measure ye mete it shall
Mt. 7. 2.   be measured unto you: and more shall be given unto
43*   you. For he that hath, to him shall be given: and he 25
Mt. 25. 29. that hath not, from him shall be taken away even that
123. 139   which he hath.
             And he said, So is the kingdom of God, as if a man 26
             should cast seed upon the earth; and should sleep and 27
             rise night and day, and the seed should spring up and
             grow, he knoweth not how. The earth beareth fruit of 28
             herself; first the blade, then the ear, then the full corn
Joel 3. 13. in the ear. But when the fruit is ripe, straightway he 29
Rev.14.15.   putteth forth the sickle, because the harvest is come.
             And he said, How shall we liken the kingdom of 30
             God? or in what parable shall we set it forth? It is like 31
103   a grain of mustard seed, which, when it is sown upon the
             earth, though it be less than all the seeds that are upon
             the earth, yet when it is sown, groweth up, and be- 32
             cometh greater than all the herbs, and putteth out
Dan. 4. 12. great branches; so that the birds of the heaven can
Ez.17.22... lodge under the shadow thereof.
             And with many such parables spake he the word unto 33
             them, as they were able to hear it: and without a parable 34
             spake he not unto them: but privately to his own
             disciples he expounded all things.

S. Matthew xiii. 24—35.

             Another parable set he before them, saying, The 24
             kingdom of God is likened unto a man that sowed
Hos. 2. 23. good seed in his field: but while men slept, his enemy 25
             came and sowed tares also among the wheat, and went

26 away. But when the blade sprang up, and brought forth
27 fruit, then appeared the tares also. And the servants of
the householder came and said unto him, Sir, didst thou
not sow good seed in thy field? whence then hath it tares?
28 And he said unto them, An enemy hath done this. And
the servants say unto him, Wilt thou then that we go and
29 gather them up? But he saith, Nay; lest haply while ye
gather up the tares, ye root up the wheat with them.
30 Let both grow together until the harvest: and in the
time of the harvest I will say to the reapers, Gather up
first the tares, and bind them in bundles to burn them: Mt. 3. 12.
but gather the wheat into my barn. Amos 9. 9.
31 Another parable set he before them, saying, The
kingdom of heaven is like unto a grain of mustard seed,
32 which a man took, and sowed in his field: which indeed
is less than all seeds; but when it is grown, it is greater
than the herbs, and becometh a tree, so that the birds
of the heaven come and lodge in the branches thereof.
33 Another parable spake he unto them; The kingdom **102**
of heaven is like unto leaven, which a woman took, and Ex. 16. 36
hid in three measures of meal, till it was all leavened. cp.Gr.&H.
34 All these things spake Jesus in parables unto the
multitudes; and without a parable spake he nothing
35 unto them: that it might be fulfilled which was spoken Ps. 78. 2.
by the prophet, saying,
I will open my mouth in parables;
I will utter things hidden from the foundation of the
world.

8. Luke viii. 16—18.

16 And no man, when he hath lighted a lamp, covereth
it with a vessel, or putteth it under a bed; but putteth it
on a stand, that they which enter in may see the light.
17 For nothing is hid, that shall not be made manifest; nor
anything secret, that shall not be known and come to
18 light. Take heed therefore how ye hear: for whosoever
hath, to him shall be given; and whosoever hath not,
from him shall be taken away even that which he
thinketh he hath.

52. *Parable of the tares explained. The hidden
treasure. The pearl. The net.*

S. Matthew xiii. 36—52.

THEN he left the multitudes, and went into the house: 36
and his disciples came unto him, saying, Explain unto us
the parable of the tares of the field. And he answered 37
and said, He that soweth the good seed is the Son of
Ro. 10. 18. man; and the field is the world; and the good seed, 38
these are the sons of the kingdom; and the tares are the
Jn. 8. 44. sons of the evil one; and the enemy that sowed them is 39
1 Jn. 3. 8. the devil: and the harvest is the end of the world; and
Re.14.15... the reapers are angels. As therefore the tares are 40
gathered up and burned with fire; so shall it be in the
140 end of the world. The Son of man shall send forth his 41
angels, and they shall gather out of his kingdom all
things that cause stumbling, and them that do iniquity,
Is. 66. 24. and shall cast them into the furnace of fire: there shall 42
be the weeping and gnashing of teeth. Then shall the 43
Dan. 12. 3. righteous shine forth as the sun in the kingdom of their
Rev. 7. 9. Father. He that hath ears, let him hear.

The kingdom of heaven is like unto a treasure hidden 44
in the field; which a man found, and hid; and in his
Phil. 3. 7.. joy he goeth and selleth all that he hath, and buyeth that
Is. 55. 1. field.
Rev. 3. 18. Again, the kingdom of heaven is like unto a man that 45
is a merchant seeking goodly pearls: and having found 46
Pro. 3. 13.. one pearl of great price, he went and sold all that he
had, and bought it.

Again, the kingdom of heaven is like unto a net, that 47
Mt. 22. 10. was cast into the sea, and gathered of every kind: which, 48
when it was filled, they drew up on the beach; and they
sat down, and gathered the good into vessels, but the
bad they cast away. So shall it be in the end of the 49
Mt. 25. 32. world: the angels shall come forth, and sever the wicked
140 from among the righteous, and shall cast them into the 50
furnace of fire: there shall be the weeping and gnashing
of teeth.

Have ye understood all these things? They say 51
unto him, Yea. And he said unto them, Therefore 52
every scribe who hath been made a disciple to the
kingdom of heaven is like unto a man that is a householder, which bringeth forth out of his treasure things
new and old.

53.   *His mother and his brethren.*

S. Matthew xii. 46—50.

46   WHILE he was yet speaking to the multitudes, behold,
his mother and his brethren stood without, seeking to   **54**
47 speak to him.   And one said unto him, Behold, thy
mother and thy brethren stand without, seeking to speak
48 to thee.   But he answered and said unto him that told
him, Who is my mother? and who are my brethren?
49 And he stretched forth his hand towards his disciples,
50 and said, Behold, my mother and my brethren! For
whosoever shall do the will of my Father which is in Jn. 15. 10.
heaven, he is my brother, and sister, and mother.

S. Mark iii. 31—35.

31   And there come his mother and his brethren; and,
32 standing without, they sent unto him, calling him.   And
a multitude was sitting about him; and they say unto
him, Behold, thy mother and thy brethren without seek
33 for thee.   And he answereth them, and saith, Who is
34 my mother and my brethren?   And looking round on
them which sat round about him, he saith, Behold, my
35 mother and my brethren! For whosoever shall do the
will of God, the same is my brother, and sister, and
mother.

S. Luke viii. 19—21.

19   And there came to him his mother and brethren, and
20 they could not come at him for the crowd.   And it was
told him, Thy mother and thy brethren stand without,
21 desiring to see thee.   But he answered and said unto
them, My mother and my brethren are these which hear
the word of God, and do it.

54. *His own received him not.*

S. Mark vi. 1—6.

AND he went out from thence; and he cometh into 1
his own country; and his disciples follow him.   And 2
when the sabbath was come, he began to teach in the
Lk. 4.16... synagogue: and many hearing him were astonished,
29   saying, Whence hath this man these things? and, What
is the wisdom that is given unto this man, and what
mean such mighty works wrought by his hands?   Is not 3
this the carpenter, the son of Mary, and brother of
Gal. 1. 19. James, and Joses, and Judas, and Simon? and are not
Jude 1.   his sisters here with us?   And they were offended in
him.   And Jesus said unto them, A prophet is not 4
Jn. 4. 44. without honour, save in his own country, and among his
Gen. 19.22. own kin, and in his own house.   And he could there do 5
Mk. 9. 23.. no mighty work, save that he laid his hands upon a few
Acts 14. 9. sick folk, and healed them.   And he marvelled because 6
of their unbelief.

S. Matthew xiii. 53—58.

And it came to pass, when Jesus had finished these 53
parables, he departed thence.   And coming into his own 54
country he taught them in their synagogue, insomuch
that they were astonished, and said, Whence hath this
man this wisdom, and these mighty works?   Is not this 55
the carpenter's son?   is not his mother called Mary?
and his brethren, James, and Joseph, and Simon, and
Judas?   And his sisters, are they not all with us? 56
Whence then hath this man all these things?   And they 57
were offended in him.   But Jesus said unto them, A
prophet is not without honour, save in his own country,
and in his own house.   And he did not many mighty 58
works there because of their unbelief.

55. *He stilleth the storm.*

S. Mark iv. 35—41.

35 AND on that day, when even was come, he saith
36 unto them, Let us go over unto the other side. And
leaving the multitude, they take him with them, even as
he was, in the boat. And other boats were with him.
37 And there ariseth a great storm of wind, and the waves
beat into the boat, insomuch that the boat was now
38 filling. And he himself was in the stern, asleep on the
cushion : and they awake him, and say unto him, Master,
39 carest thou not that we perish? And he awoke, and rebuked the wind, and said unto the sea, Peace, be still. Ps. 89. 9.
40 And the wind ceased, and there was a great calm. And Ps. 107. 29.
he said unto them, Why are ye fearful? have ye not yet   63
41 faith? And they feared exceedingly, and said one to
another, Who then is this, that even the wind and the
sea obey him?

S. Luke viii. 22—25.

22 Now it came to pass on one of those days, that he
entered into a boat, himself and his disciples ; and he
said unto them, Let us go over unto the other side of
23 the lake : and they launched forth. But as they sailed he
fell asleep : and there came down a storm of wind on
the lake ; and they were filling with water, and were in
24 jeopardy. And they came to him, and awoke him, saying,
Master, master, we perish. And he awoke, and rebuked
the wind and the raging of the water : and they ceased,
25 and there was a calm. And he said unto them, Where
is your faith? And being afraid they marvelled, saying
one to another, Who then is this, that he commandeth
even the winds and the water, and they obey him?

S. Matthew viii. 23—27.

23 And when he was entered into a boat, his disciples
24 followed him. And behold, there arose a great tempest
in the sea, insomuch that the boat was covered with the
25 waves : but he was asleep. And they came to him, and
26 awoke him, saying, Save, Lord; we perish. And he saith
unto them, Why are ye fearful, O ye of little faith? Then
he arose, and rebuked the winds and the sea ; and there
27 was a great calm. And the men marvelled, saying, What
manner of man is this, that even the winds and the sea
obey him?

J. H. G.   6

56. *Demoniacs healed. The swine.*

S. Mark v. 1—20.

AND they came to the other side of the sea, into the 1
country of the Gerasenes. And when he was come out 2
of the boat, straightway there met him out of the tombs
a man with an unclean spirit, who had his dwelling in 3
the tombs: and no man could any more bind him, no,
not with a chain; because that he had been often bound 4
with fetters and chains, and the chains had been rent
asunder by him, and the fetters broken in pieces: and
no man had strength to tame him. And always, night 5
and day, in the tombs and in the mountains, he was
crying out, and cutting himself with stones. And when 6
he saw Jesus from afar, he ran and worshipped him;
Mk. 1. 24. and crying out with a loud voice, he saith, What have I 7
32   to do with thee, Jesus, thou Son of the Most High God?
I adjure thee by God, torment me not. For he said 8
unto him, Come forth, thou unclean spirit, out of the
man. And he asked him, What is thy name? And he 9
saith unto him, My name is Legion; for we are many.
And he besought him much that he would not send 10
them away out of the country. Now there was on the 11
Lev. 11. 7. mountain side a great herd of swine feeding. And they 12
Is. 65. 4. besought him, saying, send us into the swine, that we
may enter into them. And he gave them leave. And 13
the unclean spirits came out, and entered into the swine:
and the herd rushed down the steep into the sea, in
number about two thousand; and they were choked in
the sea. And they that fed them fled, and told it in 14
the city, and in the country. And they came to see
what it was that had come to pass. And they come to 15
[T. O.

S. Luke viii. 26—39.

And they arrived at the country of the Gerasenes, 26
which is over against Galilee. And when he was come 27
forth upon the land, there met him a certain man out of
the city, who had devils; and for a long time he had
worn no clothes, and abode not in any house, but in the
tombs. And when he saw Jesus, he cried out, and fell 28
down before him, and with a loud voice said, What have

I to do with thee, Jesus, thou son of the Most High
29 God? I beseech thee, torment me not. For he commanded the unclean spirit to come out from the man.
For oftentimes it had seized him: and he was kept
under guard, and bound with chains and fetters; and
breaking the bands asunder, he was driven of the devil
30 into the deserts. And Jesus asked him, What is thy
name? And he said, Legion; for many devils were
31 entered into him. And they intreated him that he would
32 not command them to depart into the abyss. Now there Rev. 20. 1..
was there a herd of many swine feeding on the mountain:
and they intreated him that he would give them leave to
33 enter into them. And he gave them leave. And the
devils came out from the man, and entered into the
swine: and the herd rushed down the steep into the
34 lake, and were choked. And when they that fed them
saw what had come to pass, they fled, and told it in the
35 city and in the country. And they went out to see
what had come to pass; and they came to Jesus, and
[T. O.

S. Matthew viii. 28—34.

28   And when he was come to the other side into the
country of the Gadarenes, there met him two possessed
with devils, coming forth out of the tombs, exceeding
29 fierce, so that no man could pass by that way. And
behold, they cried out, saying, What have we to do with
thee, thou Son of God? art thou come hither to torment
30 us before the time? Now there was afar off from them a
31 herd of many swine feeding. And the devils besought
him, saying, If thou cast us out, send us away into the
32 herd of swine. And he said unto them, Go. And they
came out, and went into the swine: and behold, the
whole herd rushed down the steep into the sea, and
33 perished in the waters. And they that fed them fled,
and went away into the city, and told every thing, and
what was befallen to them that were possessed with
[T. O.

S. Mark v.

Jesus, and behold him that was possessed with devils sitting, clothed and in his right mind, even him that had the legion: and they were afraid. And they that saw it 16 declared unto them how it befell him that was possessed with devils, and concerning the swine. And they began 17

Acts 16. 39. to beseech him to depart from their borders. And as 18 he was entering into the boat, he that had been possessed with devils besought him that he might be with him. And he suffered him not, but saith unto him, Go to thy 19 house unto thy friends, and tell them how great things the Lord hath done for thee, and how he had mercy on thee. And he went his way, and began to publish 20 in Decapolis how great things Jesus had done for him: and all men did marvel.

S. Luke viii.

found the man, from whom the devils were gone out,

Lk. 10. 39. sitting, clothed and in his right mind, at the feet of Jesus: and they were afraid. And they that saw it told 36 them how he that was possessed with devils was made whole. And all the people of the country of the Gera- 37 senes round about asked him to depart from them; for they were holden with great fear: and he entered into a boat, and returned. But the man from whom the 38 devils were gone out prayed him that he might be with him: but he sent him away, saying, Return to thy house, 39 and declare how great things God hath done for thee. And he went his way, publishing throughout the whole city how great things Jesus had done for him.

S. Matthew viii.

devils. And behold, all the city came out to meet Jesus: 34 and when they saw him, they besought him that he would depart from their borders.

57. *Jaïrus' daughter. The issue of blood.*

S. Mark v. 21—43.

21 AND when Jesus had crossed over again in the boat
unto the other side, a great multitude was gathered unto
22 him : and he was by the sea. And there cometh one
of the rulers of the synagogue, Jaïrus by name ; and
seeing him, he falleth at his feet, and beseecheth him
23 much, saying, My little daughter is at the point of death :
I pray thee, that thou come and lay thy hands on her,
24 that she may be made whole, and live. And he went
with him ; and a great multitude followed him, and they
thronged him.
25 And a woman, which had an issue of blood twelve Le.15.19...
26 years, and had suffered many things of many physicians,
and had spent all that she had, and was nothing bettered,
27 but rather grew worse, having heard the things concerning
Jesus, came in the crowd behind, and touched his gar-
[T. O.

S. Luke viii. 40—56.

40 And as Jesus returned, the multitude welcomed him ;
41 for they were all waiting for him. And behold, there
came a man named Jaïrus, and he was a ruler of
the synagogue : and he fell down at Jesus' feet, and
42 besought him to come into his house ; for he had an
only daughter, about twelve years of age, and she lay a
dying. But as he went the multitudes thronged him.
43 And a woman having an issue of blood twelve years,
which had spent all her living upon physicians, and
44 could not be healed of any, came behind him, and
[T. O.

S. Matthew ix. 18—26.

18 While he spake these things unto them, behold, there
came a ruler, and worshipped him, saying, My daughter
is even now dead : but come and lay thy hand upon her,
19 and she shall live. And Jesus arose, and followed him,
20 and so did his disciples. And behold, a woman, who
had an issue of blood twelve years, came behind him,
[T. O.

ment. For she said, If I touch but his garments, I shall 28
be made whole. And straightway the fountain of her 29
blood was dried up; and she felt in her body that she
was healed of her plague. And straightway Jesus, per- 30
Lk. 6. 19. ceiving in himself that the power proceeding from him
had gone forth, turned him about in the crowd, and said,
Who touched my garments? And his disciples said unto 31
him, Thou seest the multitude thronging thee, and sayest
thou, Who touched me? And he looked round about to 32
see her that had done this thing. But the woman fearing 33
and trembling, knowing what had been done to her,
came and fell down before him, and told him all the
Mk. 10. 52. truth. And he said unto her, Daughter, thy faith hath 34
Acts 3. 16. made thee whole; go in peace, and be whole of thy
plague.

While he yet spake, they come from the ruler of the 35
synagogue's house, saying, Thy daughter is dead: why
troublest thou the Master any further? But Jesus, not 36
heeding the word spoken, saith unto the ruler of the
synagogue, Fear not, only believe. And he suffered no 37
72. 156 man to follow with him, save Peter, and James, and
John the brother of James. And they come to the 38
house of the ruler of the synagogue; and he beholdeth
Lk. 7. 32. a tumult, and many weeping and wailing greatly. And 39
when he was entered in, he saith unto them, Why make
ye a tumult, and weep? the child is not dead, but
Jn. 11. 11. sleepeth. And they laughed him to scorn. But he, 40
having put them all forth, taketh the father of the child
and her mother and them that were with him, and goeth
in where the child was. And taking the child by the 41
hand, he saith unto her, Talitha cumi; which is, being
45. 112 interpreted, Damsel, I say unto thee, Arise. And straight- 42
way the damsel rose up, and walked; for she was twelve
years old. And they were amazed straightway with a
great amazement. And he charged them much that 43
Mk. 7. 36. no man should know this: and he commanded that
something should be given her to eat.

S. Luke viii.

touched the border of his garment: and immediately the
45 issue of her blood stanched. And Jesus said, Who is it
that touched me? And when all denied, Peter said, and
they that were with him, Master, the multitudes press
46 thee and crush thee. But Jesus said, Some one did
touch me: for I perceived that power had gone forth
47 from me. And when the woman saw that she was not
hid, she came trembling, and falling down before him
declared in the presence of all the people for what cause
she touched him, and how she was healed immediately.
48 And he said unto her, Daughter, thy faith hath made
thee whole; go in peace.
49   While he yet spake, there cometh one from the ruler
of the synagogue's house, saying, Thy daughter is dead;
50 trouble not the Master. But Jesus hearing it, answered
him, Fear not: only believe, and she shall be made
51 whole. And when he came to the house, he suffered
not any man to enter in with him, save Peter, and John,
and James, and the father of the maiden and her mother.
52 And all were weeping, and bewailing her: but he said,
53 Weep not; for she is not dead, but sleepeth. And they
54 laughed him to scorn, knowing that she was dead. But
he, taking her by the hand, called, saying, Maiden, arise.
55 And her spirit returned, and she rose up immediately:
and he commanded that something be given her to eat.
56 And her parents were amazed: but he charged them to
tell no man what had been done.

Nu. 15. 38.
Deu. 22. 12.
Mt. 23. 5.
63

Lk. 7. 11.

S. Matthew ix.

21 and touched the border of his garment: for she said
within herself, If I do but touch his garment, I shall be
22 made whole. But Jesus turning and seeing her said,
Daughter, be of good cheer; thy faith hath made thee
whole. And the woman was made whole from that
23 hour. And when Jesus came into the ruler's house, and
saw the flute-players, and the crowd making a tumult, he
24 said, Give place: for the damsel is not dead, but sleepeth.
25 And they laughed him to scorn. But when the crowd
was put forth, he entered in, and took her by the hand;
26 and the damsel arose. And the fame hereof went forth
into all that land.

58. *Two blind men. A dumb demoniac.*

S. Matthew ix. 27—34.

AND as Jesus passed by from thence, two blind men 27
followed him, crying out, and saying, Have mercy on us,
Mt. 15. 22. thou son of David. And when he was come into the 28
Mk. 10. 47. house, the blind men came to him : and Jesus saith unto
them, Believe ye that I am able to do this? They say
unto him, Yea, Lord. Then touched he their eyes, 29
Acts 14. 9. saying, According to your faith be it done unto you.
And their eyes were opened. And Jesus strictly charged 30
them, saying, See that no man know it. But they went 31
forth, and spread abroad his fame in all that land.

And as they went forth, behold, there was brought to 32
him a dumb man possessed with a devil. And when the 33
73. 91 devil was cast out, the dumb man spake : and the multitudes marvelled, saying, It was never so seen in Israel.
But the Pharisees said, By the prince of the devils casteth 34
he out devils.

59. *Mission of the twelve. Instructions.*

S. Mark vi. 6—13.

AND he went round about the villages teaching.   6
And he called unto him the twelve, and began to 7
send them forth by two and two; and he gave them
authority over the unclean spirits; and he charged them 8
that they should take nothing for their journey, save a
staff only; no bread, no wallet, no money in their purse;
but to go shod with sandals : and, said he, put not on 9
two coats. And he said unto them, Wheresoever ye 10
enter into a house, there abide till ye depart thence.
And whatsoever place shall not receive you, and they 11
hear you not, as ye go forth thence, shake off the dust
that is under your feet for a testimony unto them. And 12
they went out, and preached that men should repent.
Lk. 10. 34. And they cast out many devils, and anointed with oil 13
Jas. 5. 14. many that were sick, and healed them.

S. Luke ix. 1—6.

And he called the twelve together, and gave them 1
power and authority over all devils, and to cure diseases.
And he sent them forth to preach the kingdom of God, 2
and to heal the sick. And he said unto them, Take 3
nothing for your journey, neither staff, nor wallet, nor

4 bread, nor money; neither have two coats. And into
  whatsoever house ye enter, there abide, and thence
5 depart. And as many as receive you not, when ye depart from that city, shake off the dust from your feet for
  a testimony against them. And they departed, and
6 went throughout the villages, preaching the gospel, and
  healing everywhere.

S. Matthew ix. 35—xi. 1.

35   And Jesus went about all the cities and the villages,
  teaching in their synagogues, and preaching the gospel
  of the kingdom, and healing all manner of disease Acts 10. 38.
36 and all manner of sickness. But when he saw the
  multitudes, he was moved with compassion for them,
  because they were distressed and scattered, as sheep not Nu. 27. 17.
37 having a shepherd. Then saith he unto his disciples, Eze. 34. 5.
  The harvest truly is plenteous, but the labourers are few. Jn. 4. 35.
38 Pray ye therefore the Lord of the harvest, that he send
 1 forth labourers into his harvest. And he called unto him Mk. 4. 29.
  his twelve disciples, and gave them authority over unclean spirits, to cast them out, and to heal all manner
  of disease and all manner of sickness.

2   Now the names of the twelve apostles are these : The   42
  first, Simon, who is called Peter, and Andrew his brother; Acts 1. 13...
3 James the son of Zebedee, and John his brother ; Philip, Jn. 1. 42.
  and Bartholomew ; Thomas, and Matthew the publican ;
4 James the son of Alphæus, and Thaddæus ; Simon the
  Cananæan, and Judas Iscariot, who also betrayed him. Acts 22. 3.
5 These twelve Jesus sent forth, and charged them, saying, Jos. 15. 25.
    Go not into any way of the Gentiles, and enter not
6 into any city of the Samaritans : but go rather to the lost Mt. 15. 24.
7 sheep of the house of Israel. And as ye go, preach, Acts 13. 46.
8 saying, The kingdom of heaven is at hand. Heal the
  sick, raise the dead, cleanse the lepers, cast out devils :
9 freely ye received, freely give. Get you no gold, nor Acts 8. 18..
10 silver, nor brass in your purses ; no wallet for your Lk. 10. 4.
  journey, neither two coats, nor shoes, nor staff : for the   83
11 labourer is worthy of his food. And into whatsoever city 1 Cor. 9. 7..
  or village ye shall enter, search out who in it is worthy ; 1 Ti. 5. 18.
12 and there abide till ye go forth. And as ye enter into
13 the house, salute it. And if the house be worthy, let
  your peace come upon it: but if it be not worthy, let your
14 peace return to you. And whosoever shall not receive
  you, nor hear your words, as ye go forth out of that house Neh. 5. 13.
15 or that city, shake off the dust of your feet. Verily I Acts 13. 51.

S. Matthew x.

84   say unto you, It shall be more tolerable for the land of
Sodom and Gomorrah in the day of judgement, than for
that city.

Behold, I send you forth as sheep in the midst of 16
Ro. 16. 19. wolves : be ye therefore wise as serpents, and harm-
1Co.14.20. less as doves.   But beware of men: for they will deliver 17
Acts 22.19. you up to councils, and in their synagogues they will
Mk. 13. 9.. scourge you; yea and before governors and kings shall 18
137   ye be brought for my sake, for a testimony to them and
to the Gentiles.   But when they deliver you up, be not 19
anxious how or what ye shall speak : for it shall be given
you in that hour what ye shall speak.   For it is not ye 20
1 Cor. 2.13. that speak, but the Spirit of your Father that speaketh in
you.   And brother shall deliver up brother to death, and 21
Mic. 7. 6. the father his child : and children shall rise up against
parents, and cause them to be put to death.   And ye 22
shall be hated of all men for my name's sake : but he
Jas. 1. 12. that endureth to the end, the same shall be saved.   But 23
Acts 8. 4. when they persecute you in this city, flee into the next :
for verily I say unto you, Ye shall not have gone through
the cities of Israel, till the Son of man be come.

Lk. 6. 40.   A disciple is not above his master, nor a servant 24
Jn. 13. 16. above his lord.   It is enough for the disciple that he be 25
as his master, and the servant as his lord.   If they have
called the master of the house Beelzebub, how much
more shall they call them of his household !   Fear them 26
Mk. 4. 22. not therefore : for there is nothing covered, that shall not
Lk. 12. 2. be revealed; and hid, that shall not be known.   What I 27
51. 97   tell you in the darkness, speak ye in the light : and what
ye hear in the ear, proclaim upon the housetops.   And 28
Is. 8. 12.. be not afraid of them which kill the body, but are not
Lk.12.4... able to kill the soul : but rather fear him which is able
Jas. 4. 12. to destroy both soul and body in hell.   Are not two 29
sparrows sold for a farthing? and not one of them shall
fall on the ground without your Father : but the very 30
2Sa.14.11. hairs of your head are all numbered.   Fear not there- 31
fore; ye are of more value than many sparrows.   Every one 32
Rev. 3. 5. therefore who shall confess me before men, him will I
also confess before my Father which is in heaven.   But 33
Lk. 9. 26. whosoever shall deny me before men, him will I also
2Tim.2.12. deny before my Father which is in heaven.

34	Think not that I came to send peace on the earth:
35 I came not to send peace, but a sword.   For I came to Lk.12.51...
set a man at variance against his father, and the daughter Mic. 7. 6.
against her mother, and the daughter in law against her
36 mother in law : and a man's foes shall be they of his own
37 household.   He that loveth father or mother more than Lk.14.26...
me is not worthy of me ; and he that loveth son or
38 daughter more than me is not worthy of me.   And he
that doth not take his cross and follow after me, is not Lk. 9. 24.
39 worthy of me.   He that findeth his life shall lose it; **71**
and he that loseth his life for my sake shall find it. Jn. 12. 25.
40	He that receiveth you receiveth me, and he that Mt. 18. 5.
receiveth me receiveth him that sent me.   He that Jn. 13. 20.
41 receiveth a prophet in the name of a prophet shall
receive a prophet's reward; and he that receiveth a 1 Ki.17.10..
righteous man in the name of a righteous man shall re- 2 Ki. 4. 8..
42 ceive a righteous man's reward.   And whosoever shall Mk. 9. 41.
give to drink unto one of these little ones a cup of cold	**75**
water only, in the name of a disciple, verily I say unto Ge. 24. 18..
you, he shall in no wise lose his reward.
1	And it came to pass, when Jesus had made an end of
commanding his twelve disciples, he departed thence to
teach and preach in their cities.

S. Luke x. 3—12. (83)

3	*Go your ways : behold, I send you forth as lambs in*
4 *the midst of wolves.   Carry no purse, no wallet, no shoes :*
5 *and salute no man on the way.   And into whatsoever*
6 *house ye shall enter, first say, Peace be to this house.   And*
if a son of peace be there, your peace shall rest upon him :
7 *but if not, it shall turn to you again.   And in that same*
house remain, eating and drinking such things as they give :
for the labourer is worthy of his hire.   Go not from house
8 *to house.   And into whatsoever city ye enter, and they*
9 *receive you, eat such things as are set before you : and heal*
the sick that are therein, and say unto them, The kingdom
10 *of God is come nigh unto you.   But into whatsoever city*
ye shall enter, and they receive you not, go out into the
11 *streets thereof and say, Even the dust from your city, that*
cleaveth to our feet, we do wipe off against you : howbeit
12 *know this, that the kingdom of God is come nigh.   I say*
unto you, It shall be more tolerable in that day for Sodom,
than for that city.

60. *Herod's opinion of Jesus. His murder of John the Baptist.*

S. Mark vi. 14—29.

AND king Herod heard thereof; for his name had 14
become known : and he said, John the Baptist is risen
from the dead, and therefore do these powers work in
71   him. But others said, It is Elijah. And others said, It is 15
a prophet, even as one of the prophets. But Herod, 16
when he heard thereof, said, John, whom I beheaded, he
Lk. 3. 20.. is risen. For Herod himself had sent forth and laid hold 17
15   upon John, and bound him in prison for the sake of
Ex. 20. 14. Herodias, his brother Philip's wife : for he had married
Le. 18. 16. her. For John said unto Herod, It is not lawful for 18
— 20. 21. thee to have thy brother's wife. And Herodias set 19
herself against him, and desired to kill him; and she
could not; for Herod feared John, knowing that he 20
was a righteous man and a holy, and kept him safe.
And when he heard him, he was much perplexed; and
he heard him gladly. And when a convenient day was 21
Gen.40.20. come, that Herod on his birthday made a supper to his
lords, and the high captains, and the chief men of
Galilee; and when the daughter of Herodias herself 22
came in and danced, she pleased Herod and them that
sat at meat with him ; and the king said unto the
damsel, Ask of me whatsoever thou wilt, and I will give
Est. 5. 3... it thee. And he sware unto her, Whatsoever thou shalt 23
— 7. 2. ask of me, I will give it thee, unto the half of my
kingdom. And she went out, and said unto her mother, 24
What shall I ask? And she said, The head of John the
Baptist. And she came in straightway with haste unto 25
the king, and asked, saying, I will that thou forthwith
give me in a charger the head of John the Baptist. And 26
Jud. 11.35. the king was exceeding sorry; but for the sake of his
cf. 1 Sam. oaths, and of them that sat at meat, he would not reject
25. 22, 33. her. And straightway the king sent forth a soldier of his 27
guard, and commanded to bring his head : and he went
and beheaded him in the prison, and brought his head 28
in a charger, and gave it to the damsel; and the damsel
gave it to her mother. And when his disciples heard 29
Acts 8. 2. thereof, they came and took up his corpse, and laid it
in a tomb.

S. Matthew xiv. 1—12.

1   At that season Herod the tetrarch heard the report
2 concerning Jesus, and said unto his servants, This is
John the Baptist; he is risen from the dead; and there-
3 fore do these powers work in him. For Herod had laid
hold on John, and bound him, and put him in prison for
4 the sake of Herodias, his brother Philip's wife. For
John said unto him, It is not lawful for thee to have her.
5 And when he would have put him to death, he feared
the multitude, because they counted him as a prophet.
6 But when Herod's birthday came, the daughter of Hero-
7 dias danced in the midst, and pleased Herod. Where-
upon he promised with an oath to give her whatsoever
8 she should ask. And she, being put forward by her
mother, saith, Give me here in a charger the head of
9 John the Baptist. And the king was grieved; but for
the sake of his oaths, and of them which sat at meat
10 with him, he commanded it to be given; and he sent,
11 and beheaded John in the prison. And his head was
brought in a charger, and given to the damsel: and she
12 brought it to her mother. And his disciples came, and
took up the corpse, and buried him; and they went
and told Jesus.

S. Luke ix. 7—9.

7   Now Herod the tetrarch heard of all that was done:
and he was much perplexed, because that it was said by
8 some, that John was risen from the dead; and by some,
that Elijah had appeared; and by others, that one of the
9 old prophets was risen again. And Herod said, John I
beheaded: but who is this, about whom I hear such
things? And he sought to see him.

61. *Jesus withdraws.   Passover at hand.*

S. Mark vi. 30—37.

AND the apostles gather themselves together unto 30 Jesus; and they told him all things, whatsoever they had done, and whatsoever they had taught.   And he saith 31 unto them, Come ye yourselves apart into a desert place, and rest a while.   For there were many coming and going, and they had no leisure so much as to eat. And they went away in the boat to a desert place apart. 32 And the people saw them going, and many knew them, 33 and they ran there together on foot from all the cities, and outwent them.   And he came forth and saw a great 34
Nu. 27. 17. multitude, and he had compassion on them, because
Ezek. 34. 5. they were as sheep not having a shepherd : and he began to teach them many things.   And when the day was 35 now far spent, his disciples came unto him, and said, The place is desert, and the day is now far spent : send 36 them away, that they may go into the country and villages round about, and buy themselves somewhat to eat.   But he answered and said unto them, Give ye them 37 to eat.

S. John vi. 1—4.

After these things Jesus went away to the other 1 side of the sea of Galilee, which is the sea of Tiberias. And a great multitude followed him, because they be- 2 held the signs which he did on them that were sick. And Jesus went up into the mountain, and there he sat 3 with his disciples.   Now the passover, the feast of the 4 Jews, was at hand.

S. Luke ix. 10—13.

10 And the apostles, when they were returned, declared unto him what things they had done. And he took them, and withdrew apart to a city called Bethsaida.
11 But the multitudes perceiving it followed him: and he welcomed them, and spake to them of the kingdom of God, and them that had need of healing he healed. Acts 10.38.
12 And the day began to wear away; and the twelve came, and said unto him, Send the multitude away, that they may go into the villages and country round about, and lodge, and get victuals: for we are here in a desert
13 place. But he said unto them, Give ye them to eat.

S. Matthew xiv. 13—16.

13 Now when Jesus heard it, he withdrew from thence in a boat, to a desert place apart: and when the multitudes heard thereof, they followed him on foot from
14 the cities. And he came forth, and saw a great multitude, and he had compassion on them, and healed their sick.
15 And when even was come, the disciples came to him, saying, The place is desert, and the time is already past; send the multitudes away, that they may go into the
16 villages, and buy themselves food. But Jesus said unto them, They have no need to go away; give ye them to eat.

62. *Five thousand men fed.*

S. John vi. 5—14.

JESUS therefore lifting up his eyes, and seeing that 5
68   a great multitude cometh unto him, saith unto Philip,
Whence are we to buy bread, that these may eat? And 6
Jn. 14. 9. this he said to prove him: for he himself knew what he
would do.   Philip answered him, Two hundred penny- 7
worth of bread is not sufficient for them, that every one
Nu. 11. 22. may take a little.   One of his disciples, Andrew, Simon 8
Peter's brother, saith unto him, There is a lad here, 9
which hath five barley loaves, and two fishes: but what
2 Ki. 4. 43. are these among so many? Jesus said, Make the people 10
sit down.   Now there was much grass in the place.
So the men sat down, in number about five thousand.
Jesus therefore took the loaves; and having given 11
thanks, he distributed to them that were set down; likewise also of the fishes as much as they would.   And 12
when they were filled, he saith unto his disciples, Gather
up the broken pieces which remain over, that nothing
be lost.   So they gathered them up, and filled twelve 13
baskets with broken pieces from the five barley loaves,
which remained over unto them that had eaten.   When 14
therefore the people saw the sign which he did, they said,
De. 18. 18.. This is of a truth the prophet that cometh into the
world.

S. Matthew xiv. 17—21.

And they say unto him, We have here but five loaves, 17
and two fishes.   And he said, Bring them hither to me. 18
And he commanded the multitudes to sit down on the 19
grass; and he took the five loaves, and the two fishes,
Lk. 24. 30, and looking up to heaven, he blessed, and brake and
35.   gave the loaves to the disciples, and the disciples to the
multitudes.   And they did all eat, and were filled: and 20
they took up that which remained over of the broken
pieces, twelve baskets full.   And they that did eat were 21
about five thousand men, beside women and children.

S. Mark vi. 37—44.

37 And they say unto him, Shall we go and buy two hundred pennyworth of bread, and give them to eat?
38 And he saith unto them, How many loaves have ye? go and see. And when they knew, they say, Five, and two
39 fishes. And he commanded them that all should sit
40 down by companies upon the green grass. And they sat
41 down in ranks, by hundreds, and by fifties. And he took the five loaves and the two fishes, and looking up to heaven, he blessed, and brake the loaves; and he gave to the disciples to set before them; and the two
42 fishes divided he among them all. And they did all eat,
43 and were filled. And they took up broken pieces,
44 twelve basketfuls, and also of the fishes. And they that ate the loaves were five thousand men.

1 Sa. 9. 13.
Lk. 24. 30..
Rom. 14. 6.

S. Luke ix. 13—17.

13 And they said, We have no more than five loaves and two fishes; except we should go and buy food for all
14 this people. For they were about five thousand men. And he said unto his disciples, Make them sit down in
15 companies, about fifty each. And they did so, and made
16 them all sit down. And he took the five loaves and the two fishes, and looking up to heaven, he blessed them, and brake; and gave to the disciples to set before the
17 multitude. And they did eat, and were all filled: and there was taken up that which remained over to them of broken pieces, twelve baskets.

63. *Jesus walketh on the sea.   Peter.   General healing.*

S. Matthew xiv. 22—36.

AND straightway he constrained the disciples to enter 22
into the boat, and to go before him unto the other side,
till he should send the multitudes away.   And after 23
he had sent the multitudes away, he went up into the

Lk. 6. 12. mountain apart to pray: and when even was come, he
— 9. 28. was there alone.   But the boat was now in the midst of 24
the sea, distressed by the waves; for the wind was contrary.   And in the fourth watch of the night he came 25
unto them, walking upon the sea.   And when the disciples 26

Job 9. 8. saw him walking on the sea, they were troubled, saying,
Lk. 24. 37. It is an apparition; and they cried out for fear.   But 27
180 straightway Jesus spake unto them, saying, Be of good
cheer; it is I; be not afraid.   And Peter answered him 28

Jn. 21. 7. and said, Lord, if it be thou, bid me come unto thee
upon the waters.   And he said, Come.   And Peter went 29
down from the boat, and walked upon the waters, to
come to Jesus.   But when he saw the wind, he was 30
afraid; and beginning to sink, he cried out, saying,

Mt. 8. 25. Lord, save me.   And immediately Jesus stretched forth 31
his hand, and took hold of him, and saith unto him, O
thou of little faith, wherefore didst thou doubt?   And 32
55 when they were gone up into the boat, the wind ceased.

Ps. 89. 9. And they that were in the boat worshipped him, saying, 33
Mt. 16. 16. Of a truth thou art the Son of God.

And when they had crossed over, they came to the 34
land, unto Gennesaret.   And when the men of that 35
place knew him, they sent into all that region round
about, and brought unto him all that were sick; and they 36

Acts 19.12. besought him that they might only touch the border of
— 10.38. his garment: and as many as touched were made whole.
57

S. Mark vi. 45—56.

And straightway he constrained his disciples to enter 45
into the boat, and to go before him unto the other side
to Bethsaida, while he himself sendeth the multitude
away.   And after he had taken leave of them, he de- 46

47 parted into the mountain to pray. And when even was
come, the boat was in the midst of the sea, and he alone
48 on the land. And seeing them distressed in rowing, for
the wind was contrary unto them, about the fourth
watch of the night he cometh unto them, walking on the
49 sea; and he would have passed by them: but they,
when they saw him walking on the sea, supposed that
50 it was an apparition, and cried out: for they all saw
him, and were troubled. But he straightway spake with
them, and saith unto them, Be of good cheer: it is I;
51 be not afraid. And he went up unto them into the
boat; and the wind ceased: and they were sore amazed
52 in themselves; for they understood not concerning the
loaves, but their heart was hardened.
53 And when they had crossed over, they came to the
54 land unto Gennesaret, and moored to the shore. And
when they were come out of the boat, straightway the
55 people knew him, and ran round about that whole
region, and began to carry about on their beds those
56 that were sick, where they heard he was. And wheresoever he entered, into villages, or into cities, or into the
country, they laid the sick in the marketplaces, and Acts 5. 15...
besought him that they might touch if it were but the
border of his garment: and as many as touched him
were made whole.

S. John vi. 15—21.

15 Jesus therefore perceiving that they were about to Jn. 18. 36.
come and take him by force, to make him king, withdrew
again into the mountain himself alone.
16 And when evening came, his disciples went down
17 unto the sea; and they entered into a boat, and were
going over the sea unto Capernaum. And it was now
18 dark, and Jesus had not yet come to them. And the
sea was rising by reason of a great wind that blew.
19 When therefore they had rowed about five and twenty
or thirty furlongs, they behold Jesus walking on the
sea, and drawing nigh unto the boat: and they were
20 afraid. But he saith unto them, It is I; be not afraid.
21 They were willing therefore to receive him into the
boat: and straightway the boat was at the land whither Ps. 107. 30.
they were going.

7—2

64. *The bread of life.*

S. John vi. 22—71.

On the morrow, the multitude which stood on the 22
other side of the sea saw that there was none other boat
there, save one, and that Jesus entered not with his
disciples into the boat, but that his disciples went away
alone (howbeit there came boats from Tiberias nigh unto 23
the place where they ate the bread after the Lord had
given thanks): when the multitude therefore saw that 24
Jesus was not there, neither his disciples, they themselves
got into the boats, and came to Capernaum, seeking
Jesus. And when they found him on the other side of 25
the sea, they said unto him, Rabbi, when camest thou
hither? Jesus answered them and said, Verily, verily, I 26
say unto you, Ye seek me, not because ye saw signs, but
Is. 55. 1... because ye ate of the loaves, and were filled. Work not 27
for the meat which perisheth, but for the meat which
Mt. 5. 6. abideth unto eternal life, which the Son of man shall
give unto you: for him the Father, even God, hath
Jn. 3. 33. sealed. They said therefore unto him, What must we 28
do, that we may work the works of God? Jesus 29
answered and said unto them, This is the work of God,
1 Jn. 3. 23. that ye believe on him whom he hath sent. They said 30
therefore unto him, What then doest thou for a sign, that
we may see, and believe thee? what workest thou? Our 31
Ex. 16. 4... fathers ate the manna in the wilderness; as it is written,
Ps. 78. 24. He gave them bread out of heaven to eat. Jesus there- 32
fore said unto them, Verily, verily, I say unto you, It was
not Moses that gave you the bread out of heaven; but
Deu. 8. 3. my Father giveth you the true bread out of heaven. For 33
the bread of God is that which cometh down out of
heaven, and giveth life unto the world. They said there- 34
fore unto him, Lord, evermore give us this bread. Jesus 35
said unto them, I am the bread of life: he that cometh
Jn. 4. 14. to me shall not hunger, and he that believeth on me
shall never thirst. But I said unto you, that ye have 36

S. John vi.

37 seen me, and yet believe not. All that which the Father
giveth me shall come unto me ; and him that cometh to Ro. 10. 11..
38 me I will in no wise cast out. For I am come down 1 Jn. 2. 19.
from heaven, not to do mine own will, but the will of
39 him that sent me. And this is the will of him that sent
me, that of all that which he hath given me I should lose Jn. 17. 12.
40 nothing, but should raise it up at the last day. For this
is the will of my Father, that every one that beholdeth
the Son, and believeth on him, should have eternal life ; Jn. 5. 24.
and I will raise him up at the last day.
41   The Jews therefore murmured concerning him,
because he said, I am the bread which came down out
42 of heaven. And they said, Is not this Jesus, the son Lk. 4. 22.
of Joseph, whose father and mother we know? how Mt. 13. 55.
doth he now say, I am come down out of heaven ? **29. 54**
43 Jesus answered and said unto them, Murmur not among
44 yourselves. No man can come to me, except the Father
which sent me draw him : and I will raise him up in the
45 last day. It is written in the prophets, And they shall Is. 54. 13.
all be taught of God. Every one that hath heard from Jer. 31. 33...
46 the Father, and hath learned, cometh unto me. Not Heb. 8. 10..
that any man hath seen the Father, save he which is Jn. 1. 18.
47 from God, he hath seen the Father. Verily, verily, I say
48 unto you, He that believeth hath eternal life. I am the Jn. 3. 16
49 bread of life. Your fathers did eat the manna in the
50 wilderness, and they died. This is the bread which
cometh down out of heaven, that a man may eat thereof, Rev. 2. 17.
51 and not die. I am the living bread which came down out Jn. 3. 13.
of heaven : if any man eat of this bread, he shall live for Jn. 8. 51...
ever : yea and the bread which I will give is my flesh, for
the life of the world.
52   The Jews therefore strove one with another, saying,
53 How can this man give us his flesh to eat? Jesus there- 1Co. 11. 24.
fore said unto them, Verily, verily, I say unto you, Mt. 26. 26..
Except ye eat the flesh of the Son of man and drink his **148**
54 blood, ye have not life in yourselves. He that eateth my
flesh and drinketh my blood hath eternal life ; and I will
55 raise him up at the last day. For my flesh is meat 1Co. 10. 16.
56 indeed, and my blood is drink indeed. He that eateth
my flesh and drinketh my blood abideth in me, and I in 1 Jn. 3. 24.

S. John vi.

him.   As the living Father sent me, and I live because 57
of the Father; so he that eateth me, he also shall live
because of me.   This is the bread which came down out 58
of heaven : not as the fathers did eat, and died : he that
Rev. 2. 17. eateth this bread shall live for ever.   These things said 59
he in the synagogue, as he taught in Capernaum.

Many therefore of his disciples, when they heard this, 60
said, This is a hard saying; who can hear it?   But Jesus 61
knowing in himself that his disciples murmured at this,
Mt. 11. 6. said unto them, Doth this cause you to stumble?   What 62
then if ye should behold the Son of man ascending where
2 Cor. 3. 6. he was before?   It is the spirit that quickeneth; the 63
flesh profiteth nothing : the words that I have spoken
unto you are spirit, and are life.   But there are some of 64
Jn. 2. 24... you that believe not.   For Jesus knew from the beginning
who they were that believed not, and who it was that
Jn. 13. 11. should betray him.   And he said, For this cause have I 65
said unto you, that no man can come unto me, except it
be given unto him of the Father.

Upon this many of his disciples went back, and 66
walked no more with him.   Jesus said therefore unto the 67
twelve, Would ye also go away?   Simon Peter answered 68
him, Lord,˙to whom shall we go?   thou hast the words of
Mt. 16. 16. eternal life.   And we have believed and know that thou 69
71   art the Holy One of God.   Jesus answered them, Did 70
not I choose you the twelve, and one of you is a devil?
Jn. 13. 27. Now he spake of Judas the son of Simon Iscariot, for he 71
Jos. 15. 25. it was that should betray him, being one of the twelve.

65. *The unwashen hands.*

S. Mark vii. 1—23.

1 AND there are gathered together unto him the Pharisees, and certain of the scribes, which had come from
2 Jerusalem, and had seen that some of his disciples ate
3 their bread with defiled, that is, unwashen, hands. For
the Pharisees, and all the Jews, except they wash their
hands diligently, eat not, holding the tradition of the Col. 2. 8.
4 elders: and when they come from the marketplace,
except they wash themselves, they eat not: and many
other things there be, which they have received to hold,
5 washings of cups, and pots, and brasen vessels. And the Jn. 2. 6.
Pharisees and the scribes ask him, Why walk not thy
disciples according to the tradition of the elders, but
6 eat their bread with defiled hands? And he said unto
them, Well did Isaiah prophesy of you hypocrites, as it
is written,

> This people honoureth me with their lips,   Is. 29. 13.
> But their heart is far from me.   Gr.
>   Eze. 33. 31.
7   But in vain do they worship me,
> Teaching as their doctrines the precepts of men.   Tit. 1. 14.
8 Ye leave the commandment of God, and hold fast the
9 tradition of men. And he said unto them, Full well do 2 Cor. 11.4.
ye reject the commandment of God, that ye may keep (ironical.)

> [T. O.

S. Matthew xv. 1—20.

1 Then there come to Jesus from Jerusalem Pharisees
2 and scribes, saying, Why do thy disciples transgress the
tradition of the elders? for they wash not their hands
3 when they eat bread. And he answered and said unto
them, Why do ye also transgress the commandment of

> [T. O.

S. Mark vii.

Ex. 20. 12.
Deu. 5. 16.
Ex. 21. 17.
Lev. 20. 9.
Pro. 20. 20.

your tradition.   For Moses said, Honour thy father and 10
thy mother; and, He that speaketh evil of father or
mother, let him die the death: but ye say, If a man 11
shall say to his father or his mother, That wherewith thou
mightest have been profited by me is Corban, that is to
say, Given to God; ye no longer suffer him to do aught 12
for his father or his mother; making void the word of 13
God by your tradition, which ye have delivered: and
many such like things ye do.   And he called to him the 14
multitude again, and said unto them, Hear me all of

Acts 10. 15.
Ro. 14. 14.
1 Tim. 4. 4.

you, and understand: there is nothing from without the 15
man, that going into him can defile him: but the things
which proceed out of the man are those that defile the
man.   And when he was entered into the house from 17
the multitude, his disciples asked of him the parable.
And he saith unto them, Are ye so without understanding 18
also?   Perceive ye not, that whatsoever from without

1 Cor. 6. 13.

goeth into the man, it cannot defile him; because it 19
goeth not into his heart, but into his belly, and goeth

Acts 10. 15.
Jas. 3. 6.
Gen. 6. 5;
— 8. 21.
Gal. 5. 19...

out into the draught? This he said, making all meats
clean.   And he said, That which proceedeth out of the 20
man, that defileth the man.   For from within, out of the 21
heart of men, evil thoughts proceed, fornications, thefts, 22
murders, adulteries, covetings, wickednesses, deceit, las-
civiousness, an evil eye, railing, pride, foolishness: all 23
these evil things proceed from within, and defile the
man.

S. Matthew xv.

4 God because of your tradition? For God said, Honour
thy father and thy mother: and, He that speaketh evil
5 of father or mother, let him die the death.   But ye say,
Whosoever shall say to his father or his mother, That
wherewith thou mightest have been profited by me is
6 given to God; he shall not honour his father.   And ye
have made void the word of God because of your
7 tradition.   Ye hypocrites, well did Isaiah prophesy of
you, saying,

8   This people honoureth me with their lips;
       But their heart is far from me.
9   But in vain do they worship me,
       Teaching as their doctrines the precepts of men.
10 And he called to him the multitude, and said unto them,
11 Hear, and understand: Not that which entereth into the
mouth defileth the man; but that which proceedeth out
12 of the mouth, this defileth the man.   Then came the
disciples, and said unto him, Knowest thou that the
Pharisees were offended, when they heard this saying?
13 But he answered and said, Every plant which my heavenly Jn. 15 2.
14 Father planted not, shall be rooted up.   Let them alone:
they are blind guides.   And if the blind guide the blind, Is. 9. 16.
15 both shall fall into a pit.   And Peter answered and said
16 unto him, Declare unto us the parable.   And he said,
17 Are ye also even yet without understanding? Perceive
ye not, that whatsoever goeth into the mouth passeth
18 into the belly, and is cast out into the draught?   But the
things which proceed out of the mouth come forth out
19 of the heart; and they defile the man.   For out of the
heart come forth evil thoughts, murders, adulteries,
20 fornications, thefts, false witness, railings: these are the
things which defile the man: but to eat with unwashen
hands defileth not the man.

66. *The Syrophœnician woman.*

S. Mark vii. 24—30.

AND from thence he arose, and went away into the 24 borders of Tyre and Sidon. And he entered into a house, and would have no man know it: and he could not be hid. But straightway a woman, whose little 25 daughter had an unclean spirit, having heard of him, came and fell down at his feet. Now the woman was a 26 Ro. 10. 12. Greek, a Syrophœnician by race. And she besought him that he would cast forth the devil out of her daughter. And he said unto her, Let the children first 27 be filled: for it is not meet to take the children's bread Mt. 7. 6. and cast it to the dogs. But she answered and saith 28 unto him, Yea, Lord: even the dogs under the table eat of the children's crumbs. And he said unto her, For 29 Lk. 7. 9. this saying go thy way; the devil is gone out of thy 44 daughter. And she went away unto her house, and found 30 the child laid upon the bed, and the devil gone out.

S. Matthew xv. 21—28.

And Jesus went out thence, and withdrew into the 21 parts of Tyre and Sidon. And behold, a Canaanitish 22 woman came out from those borders, and cried, saying, Have mercy on me, O Lord, thou son of David; my daughter is grievously vexed with a devil. But he an- 23 swered her not a word. And his disciples came and besought him, saying, Send her away; for she crieth after Mt. 10. 6. us. But he answered and said, I was not sent but unto 24 Acts 3. 26. the lost sheep of the house of Israel. But she came 25 and worshipped him, saying, Lord, help me. And he 26 answered and said, It is not meet to take the children's bread and cast it to the dogs. But she said, Yea, Lord: 27 for even the dogs eat of the crumbs which fall from their masters' table. Then Jesus answered and said unto her, 28 O woman, great is thy faith: be it done unto thee even as thou wilt. And her daughter was healed from that hour.

67. *A deaf and dumb man, and many others, healed.*

S. Mark vii. 31—37.

31   AND again he went out from the borders of Tyre, and came through Sidon unto the sea of Galilee, through
32 the midst of the borders of Decapolis.   And they bring unto him one that was deaf, and had an impediment in his speech ; and they beseech him to lay his hand upon
33 him.   And he took him aside from the multitude Mk. 8. 23. privately, and put his fingers into his ears, and he spat, Jn. 9. 6.
34 and touched his tongue ; and looking up to heaven, he   **70. 80** sighed, and saith unto him, Ephphatha, that is, Be Jn. 11. 33..
35 opened.   And his ears were opened, and the bond of
36 his tongue was loosed, and he spake plain.   And he charged them that they should tell no man : but the Mk. 5. 43. more he charged them, so much the more a great deal
37 they published it.   And they were beyond measure astonished, saying, He hath done all things well : he maketh even the deaf to hear, and the dumb to speak.   Is. 35. 5...

S. Matthew xv. 29—31.

29   And Jesus departed thence, and came nigh unto the sea of Galilee ; and he went up into the mountain, and
30 sat there.   And there came unto him great multitudes, having with them the lame, blind, dumb, maimed, and   **33** many others, and they cast them down at his feet ; and
31 he healed them : insomuch that the multitude wondered, when they saw the dumb speaking, the maimed whole, and the lame walking, and the blind seeing : and they glorified the God of Israel.

68. *Four thousand men fed.*

S. Mark viii. 1—10.

62   IN those days, when there was again a great multitude, 1
and they had nothing to eat, he called unto him his
disciples, and saith unto them, I have compassion on 2
the multitude, because they continue with me now three
days, and have nothing to eat : and if I send them away 3
fasting to their home, they will faint in the way; and
some of them are come from far. And his disciples 4
2 Ki. 4. 43. answered him, Whence shall one be able to fill these
men with bread here in a desert place? And he asked 5
Mt. 14. 17.. them, How many loaves have ye? And they said,
Seven. And he commandeth the multitude to sit down 6
on the ground : and he took the seven loaves, and
1 Sa. 9. 13. having given thanks, he brake, and gave to his disciples,
Lk. 22. 19. to set before them; and they set them before the multitude. And they had a few small fishes : and having 7
blessed them, he commanded to set these also before
Acts 9. 25. them. And they did eat, and were filled : and they took 8
Gr. up, of broken pieces that remained over, seven baskets.
And they were about four thousand : and he sent them 9
away. And straightway he entered into the boat with 10
his disciples, and came into the parts of Dalmanutha.

S. Matthew xv. 32—39.

32 And Jesus called unto him his disciples, and said, I
have compassion on the multitude, because they continue
with me now three days and have nothing to eat : and I
would not send them away fasting, lest haply they faint
33 in the way. And the disciples say unto him, Whence
should we have so many loaves in a desert place, as to
34 fill so great a multitude? And Jesus saith unto them,
How many loaves have ye? And they said, Seven, and a
35 few small fishes. And he commanded the multitude to sit
36 down on the ground ; and he took the seven loaves and
the fishes ; and he gave thanks and brake, and gave to
37 the disciples, and the disciples to the multitudes. And
they did all eat, and were filled : and they took up that
which remained over of the broken pieces, seven baskets
38 full. And they that did eat were four thousand men,
39 beside women and children. And he sent away the
multitudes, and entered into the boat, and came into the
borders of Magadan.

69. *A sign from heaven.   The leaven of the Pharisees.*

S. Matthew xvi. 1—12.

Jn. 6. 30.   AND the Pharisees and Sadducees came, and tempting 1
1 Cor.1.22. him asked him to shew them a sign from heaven.   But 2
Mt. 12. 38. he answered and said unto them, When it is evening, ye
    94   say, It will be fair weather: for the heaven is red.   And 3
in the morning, It will be foul weather to-day: for the
Lk. 12. 56. heaven is red and lowring.   Ye know how to discern the
    99   face of the heaven; but ye cannot discern the signs of
the times.   An evil and adulterous generation seeketh 4
after a sign; and there shall no sign be given unto it,
but the sign of Jonah.   And he left them, and departed.
And the disciples came to the other side and forgot to 5
Lk. 12. 1. take bread.   And Jesus said unto them, Take heed and 6
beware of the leaven of the Pharisees and Sadducees.
And they reasoned among themselves, saying, We took 7
no bread.   And Jesus perceiving it said, O ye of little 8
faith, why reason ye among yourselves, because ye have
no bread? Do ye not yet perceive, neither remember the 9
    62   five loaves of the five thousand, and how many baskets
ye took up? Neither the seven loaves of the four 10
    68   thousand, and how many baskets ye took up?   How is 11
it that ye do not perceive that I spake not to you concerning bread? But beware of the leaven of the Pharisees
and Sadducees.   Then understood they how that he bade 12
1Cor.5.6... them not beware of the leaven of bread, but of the
teaching of the Pharisees and Sadducees.

S. Mark viii. 11—21.

11 And the Pharisees came forth, and began to question with him, seeking of him a sign from heaven, tempting
12 him. And he sighed deeply in his spirit, and saith, Why doth this generation seek a sign? verily I say unto you,
13 There shall no sign be given unto this generation. And he left them, and again entering into the boat departed to the other side.
14 And they forgot to take bread; and they had not in
15 the boat with them more than one loaf. And he charged them, saying, Take heed, beware of the leaven of the
16 Pharisees and the leaven of Herod. And they reasoned
17 one with another, saying, We have no bread. And Jesus perceiving it saith unto them, Why reason ye, because ye have no bread? do ye not yet perceive, neither
18 understand? have ye your heart hardened? Having Jer. 5. 21. eyes, see ye not? and having ears, hear ye not? and do Ezek. 12. 2.
19 ye not remember? When I brake the five loaves among the five thousand, how many baskets full of broken
20 pieces took ye up? They say unto him, Twelve. And when the seven among the four thousand, how many basketfuls of broken pieces took ye up? And they say
21 unto him, Seven. And he said unto them, Do ye not yet understand?

70. *A blind man healed gradually.*

S. Mark viii. 22—26.

22 AND they come unto Bethsaida. And they bring to
23 him a blind man, and beseech him to touch him. And he took hold of the blind man by the hand, and brought him out of the village; and when he had spit on his eyes, Mk. 7. 33. and laid his hands upon him, he asked him, Seest thou Jn. 9. 6.
24 aught? And he looked up, and said, I see men; for I
25 behold them as trees, walking. Then again he laid his 67. 80 hands upon his eyes; and he looked stedfastly, and was
26 restored, and saw all things clearly. And he sent him away to his home, saying, Do not even enter into the village.

71.   *The great confession.   The passion foretold.*

S. Matthew xvi. 13—28.

Now when Jesus came into the parts of Cæsarea 13
Philippi, he asked his disciples, saying, Who do men say
that the Son of man is?   And they said, Some say John 14
60   the Baptist; some, Elijah: and others, Jeremiah, or one
of the prophets.   He saith unto them, But who say ye 15
that I am?   And Simon Peter answered and said, Thou 16
Jn. 6. 69.   art the Christ, the Son of the living God.   And Jesus 17
— 11. 27.   answered and said unto him, Blessed art thou, Simon
1Cor. 2. 10.   Bar-Jonah: for flesh and blood hath not revealed it unto
thee, but my Father which is in heaven.   And I also 18
Jn. 1. 42.   say unto thee, that thou art Peter, and upon this rock
Eph. 2. 20.   I will build my church; and the gates of Hades shall
Rev. 21. 14.   not prevail against it.   I will give unto thee the keys 19
Is. 22. 22.   of the kingdom of heaven: and whatsoever thou shalt
Mt. 18. 18.   bind on earth shall be bound in heaven: and whatsoever
76   thou shalt loose on earth shall be loosed in heaven.
Then charged he the disciples that they should tell no 20
man that he was the Christ.
Mt. 20. 17.   From that time began Jesus to shew unto his dis- 21
121   ciples, how that he must go unto Jerusalem, and suffer
many things of the elders and chief priests and scribes,
and be killed, and the third day be raised up.   And 22
Peter took him, and began to rebuke him, saying, Be it
Gen. 43. 22.   far from thee, Lord: this shall never be unto thee.   But 23
Gr.   he turned, and said unto Peter, Get thee behind me,
Mt. 4. 10.   Satan: thou art a stumblingblock unto me: for thou
mindest not the things of God, but the things of men.
[T. O.

S. Mark viii. 27—ix. 1.

27 And Jesus went forth, and his disciples, into the
villages of Cæsarea Philippi: and in the way he asked
his disciples, saying unto them, Who do men say that I
28 am? And they told him, saying, John the Baptist: and
29 others, Elijah; but others, One of the prophets. And he
asked them, But who say ye that I am? Peter answereth
30 and saith unto him, Thou art the Christ. And he
31 charged them that they should tell no man of him. And
he began to teach them, that the Son of man must
suffer many things, and be rejected by the elders, and
the chief priests, and the scribes, and be killed, and
32 after three days rise again. And he spake the saying
openly. And Peter took him, and began to rebuke
33 him. But he turning about, and seeing his disciples,
rebuked Peter, and saith, Get thee behind me, Satan:
for thou mindest not the things of God, but the things
of men.   [T. O.

S. Luke ix. 18—27.

18 And it came to pass, as he was praying alone, the
disciples were with him: and he asked them, saying,
19 Who do the multitudes say that I am? And they answering said, John the Baptist; but others say, Elijah;
and others, that one of the old prophets is risen again.
20 And he said unto them, But who say ye that I am?
21 And Peter answering said, The Christ of God. But he
charged them, and commanded them to tell this to no
22 man; saying, The Son of man must suffer many things,
and be rejected of the elders and chief priests and
scribes, and be killed, and the third day be raised up.
                                                 [T. O.

S. Matthew xvi.

Then said Jesus unto his disciples, If any man would 24
come after me, let him deny himself, and take up his
cross, and follow me. For whosoever would save his 25
life shall lose it: and whosoever shall lose his life for
my sake shall find it. For what shall a man be profited, 26
if he shall gain the whole world, and forfeit his life? or
what shall a man give in exchange for his life? For the 27
Son of man shall come in the glory of his Father with
his angels; and then shall he render unto every man
according to his deeds. Verily I say unto you, There be 28
some of them that stand here, which shall in no wise
taste of death, till they see the Son of man coming in
his kingdom.

Mt. 10. 38.
59. 71
Jn. 12. 25.
Ps. 49. 7..
140
Ps. 62. 12.
Rom. 2. 6.
Pro. 24. 12.
Jn. 21. 22.
Mt. 24. 30.
137

S. Mark viii.

And he called unto him the multitude with his 34
disciples, and said unto them, If any man would come
after me, let him deny himself, and take up his cross,
and follow me. For whosoever would save his life shall 35
lose it; and whosoever shall lose his life for my sake
and the gospel's shall save it. For what doth it profit a 36
man, to gain the whole world, and forfeit his life? For 37
what should a man give in exchange for his life? For 38
whosoever shall be ashamed of me and of my words in
this adulterous and sinful generation, the Son of man
also shall be ashamed of him, when he cometh in the
glory of his Father with the holy angels. And he said 19
unto them, Verily I say unto you, There be some here
of them that stand by, which shall in no wise taste of
death, till they see the kingdom of God come with
power.

Ro. 1. 16.
2 Tim. 1.8.
— 2. 12.

S. Luke ix.

And he said unto all, If any man would come after 23
me, let him deny himself, and take up his cross daily,
and follow me. For whosoever would save his life shall 24
lose it; but whosoever shall lose his life for my sake, the
same shall save it. For what is a man profited, if he 25
gain the whole world, and lose or forfeit his own self?
For whosoever shall be ashamed of me and of my 26

words, of him shall the Son of man be ashamed, when
he cometh in his own glory, and the glory of the Father,
27 and of the holy angels. But I tell you of a truth, There
be some of them that stand here, which shall in no wise
taste of death, till they see the kingdom of God.

S. Matthew xxv. 31—46. (140)

31 *But when the Son of man shall come in his glory, and
all the angels with him, then shall he sit on the throne of*
32 *his glory: and before him shall be gathered all the nations:
and he shall separate them one from another, as the*
33 *shepherd separateth the sheep from the goats: and he shall
set the sheep on his right hand, but the goats on the left.*
34 *Then shall the King say unto them on his right hand,
Come, ye blessed of my Father, inherit the kingdom pre-*
35 *pared for you from the foundation of the world: for I was
an hungred, and ye gave me meat : I was thirsty, and ye
gave me drink: I was a stranger, and ye took me in ;*
36 *naked, and ye clothed me: I was sick, and ye visited me:*
37 *I was in prison, and ye came unto me. Then shall the
righteous answer him, saying, Lord, when saw we thee an
hungred, and fed thee? or athirst, and gave thee drink?*
38 *And when saw we thee a stranger, and took thee in? or*
39 *naked, and clothed thee? And when saw we thee sick, or*
40 *in prison, and came unto thee? And the King shall
answer and say unto them, Verily I say unto you, Inasmuch as ye did it unto one of these my brethren, even these*
41 *least, ye did it unto me. Then shall he say also unto
them on the left hand, Depart from me, ye cursed, into the
eternal fire which is prepared for the devil and his angels:*
42 *for I was an hungred, and ye gave me no meat: I was*
43 *thirsty, and ye gave me no drink: I was a stranger, and
ye took me not in ; naked, and ye clothed me not ; sick, and*
44 *in prison, and ye visited me not. Then shall they also
answer, saying, Lord, when saw we thee an hungred, or
athirst, or a stranger, or naked, or sick, or in prison, and*
45 *did not minister unto thee? Then shall he answer them,
saying, Verily I say unto you, Inasmuch as ye did it not*
46 *unto one of these least, ye did it not unto me. And these
shall go away into eternal punishment: but the righteous
into eternal life.*

72. *The Transfiguration. Elijah.*

S. Mark ix. 2—13.

Mk. 5. 37.   AND after six days Jesus taketh with him Peter, and 2
Mt. 26. 37. James, and John, and bringeth them up into a high
57. 156 mountain apart by themselves: and he was transfigured
Dan. 7. 9. before them: and his garments became glistering, ex- 3
ceeding white; so as no fuller on earth can whiten them.
And there appeared unto them Elijah with Moses: and 4
they were talking with Jesus. And Peter answereth and 5
saith to Jesus, Rabbi, it is good for us to be here: and
let us make three tabernacles; one for thee, and one
for Moses, and one for Elijah. For he wist not what to 6
answer; for they became sore afraid. And there came 7
a cloud overshadowing them: and there came a voice
2 Pet. 1. 17. out of the cloud, This is my beloved Son: hear ye him.
Mt. 3. 17. And suddenly looking round about, they saw no one any 8
16   more, save Jesus only with themselves.

    And as they were coming down from the mountain, 9
he charged them that they should tell no man what
things they had seen, save when the Son of man should
have risen again from the dead. And they kept the 10
saying, questioning among themselves what the rising
again from the dead should mean. And they asked 11
Mal. 4. 5. him, saying, The scribes say that Elijah must first come.
And he said unto them, Elijah indeed cometh first, and 12
Acts 3. 21. restoreth all things: and how is it written of the Son
Is. 53. 2... of man, that he should suffer many things and be set at
Ps. 22. 6.. nought? But I say unto you, that Elijah is come, and 13
they have also done unto him whatsoever they listed,
Mt. 14. 3... even as it is written of him.
60

S. Matthew xvii. 1—13.

    And after six days Jesus taketh with him Peter, and 1
James, and John his brother, and bringeth them up into
a high mountain apart: and he was transfigured before 2
Rev. 1. 13.. them: and his face did shine as the sun, and his
garments became white as the light. And behold, there 3
appeared unto them Moses and Elijah talking with him.
And Peter answered, and said unto Jesus, Lord, it is 4
good for us to be here: if thou wilt, I will make here
three tabernacles; one for thee, and one for Moses, and

5 one for Elijah. While he was yet speaking, behold, a bright cloud overshadowed them: and behold, a voice out of the cloud, saying, This is my beloved Son, in 6 whom I am well pleased; hear ye him. And when the disciples heard it, they fell on their face, and were sore 7 afraid. And Jesus came and touched them and said, Dan. 10.18. 8 Arise, and be not afraid. And lifting up their eyes, they saw no one, save Jesus only.

9 And as they were coming down from the mountain, Jesus commanded them, saying, Tell the vision to no 10 man, until the Son of man be risen from the dead. And his disciples asked him, saying, Why then say the scribes 11 that Elijah must first come? And he answered and said, 12 Elijah indeed cometh, and shall restore all things: but I say unto you, that Elijah is come already, and they knew him not, but did unto him whatsoever they listed. 13 Even so shall the Son of man also suffer of them. Then understood the disciples that he spake unto them of John the Baptist.

8. Luke ix. 28—36.

28 And it came to pass about eight days after these sayings, he took with him Peter and John and James, 29 and went up into the mountain to pray. And as he was praying, the fashion of his countenance was altered, and 30 his raiment became white and dazzling. And behold, there talked with him two men, which were Moses and 31 Elijah; who appeared in glory, and spake of his decease 32 which he was about to accomplish at Jerusalem. Now Peter and they that were with him were heavy with sleep: Mt. 26. 43. but when they were fully awake, they saw his glory, and Jn. 1. 14. 33 the two men that stood with him. And it came to pass, 1 Jn. 1. 1... as they were parting from him, Peter said unto Jesus, Master, it is good for us to be here: and let us make three tabernacles; one for thee, and one for Moses, and 34 one for Elijah: not knowing what he said. And while he said these things, there came a cloud, and overshadowed them: and they feared as they entered into 35 the cloud. And a voice came out of the cloud, saying, 36 This is my Son, my chosen: hear ye him. And when the voice came, Jesus was found alone. And they held their peace, and told no man in those days any of the things which they had seen.

73. *The boy with a deaf and dumb spirit.*
The passion foretold.

S. Mark ix. 14—32.

AND when they came to the disciples, they saw a 14
great multitude about them, and scribes questioning with
them.   And straightway all the multitude, when they saw 15
him, were greatly amazed, and running to him saluted
him.   And he asked them, What question ye with them? 16
And one of the multitude answered him, Master, I 17
brought unto thee my son, which hath a dumb spirit;
and wheresoever it taketh him, it dasheth him down: and 18
he foameth, and grindeth his teeth, and pineth away:
and I spake to thy disciples that they should cast it out;
and they were not able.   And he answereth them and 19
saith, O faithless generation, how long shall I be with
you? how long shall I bear with you? bring him unto
me.   And they brought him unto him: and when he 20

Mk. i. 26.   saw him, straightway the spirit tare him grievously; and
he fell on the ground, and wallowed foaming.   And he 21
asked his father, How long time is it since this hath
come unto him?   And he said, From a child.   And oft- 22
times it hath cast him both into the fire and into the
waters, to destroy him: but if thou canst do anything,
have compassion on us, and help us.   And Jesus said 23

Mk. 11. 23.   unto him, If thou canst!   All things are possible to him
Jn. 11. 40.   that believeth.   Straightway the father of the child cried 24
out, and said, I believe; help thou mine unbelief.   And 25
when Jesus saw that a multitude came running together,

58. 91   he rebuked the unclean spirit, saying unto him, Thou
dumb and deaf spirit, I command thee, come out of him,
and enter no more into him.   And having cried out, and 26
torn him much, he came out: and the child became as
one dead; insomuch that the more part said, He is
dead.   But Jesus took him by the hand, and raised him 27
up; and he arose.   [T. O.

S. Luke ix. 37—45.

37 And it came pass, on the next day, when they were come down from the mountain, a great multitude met
38 him. And behold, a man from the multitude cried, saying, Master, I beseech thee to look upon my son; for
39 he is mine only child: and behold, a spirit taketh him, and he suddenly crieth out; and it teareth him that he foameth, and it hardly departeth from him, bruising him
40 sorely. And I besought thy disciples to cast it out;
41 and they could not. And Jesus answered and said, O faithless and perverse generation, how long shall I be with you, and bear with you? bring hither thy son.
42 And as he was yet a coming, the devil dashed him down, and tare him grievously. But Jesus rebuked the unclean spirit, and healed the boy, and gave him back to his Lk. 7. 15.
43 father. And they were all astonished at the majesty of God. [T. O.

S. Matthew xvii. 14—23.

14 And when they were come to the multitude, there
15 came to him a man, kneeling to him, and saying, Lord, have mercy on my son: for he is epileptic, and suffereth grievously: for oft-times he falleth into the fire, and
16 oft-times into the water. And I brought him to thy
17 disciples, and they could not cure him. And Jesus answered and said, O faithless and perverse generation, how long shall I be with you? how long shall I bear
18 with you? bring him hither to me. And Jesus rebuked him; and the devil went out from him: and the boy was cured from that hour. [T. O.

S. Mark ix.

And when he was come into the house, his disciples 28
asked him privately, saying, We could not cast it out.
And he said unto them, This kind can come out by 29
2Cor.12.8. nothing, save by prayer.

And they went forth from thence, and passed through 30
Galilee; and he would not that any man should know it.
Lk. 24. 6. For he taught his disciples, and said unto them, The Son 31
175 of man is delivered up into the hands of men, and they
shall kill him; and when he is killed, after three days
Lk. 18. 34. he shall rise again. But they understood not the saying, 32
121 and were afraid to ask him.

S. Luke ix.

But while all were marvelling at all the things which
he did, he said unto his disciples, Let these words sink 44
into your ears: for the Son of man shall be delivered up
into the hands of men. But they understood not this 45
saying, and it was concealed from them, that they should
not perceive it: and they were afraid to ask him about
this saying.

S. Matthew xvii.

Then came the disciples to Jesus apart, and said, 19
Why could not we cast it out? And he saith unto them, 20
Mt. 21. 21. Because of your little faith: for verily I say unto you, If
127 ye have faith as a grain of mustard seed, ye shall say
1 Cor.13.2. unto this mountain, Remove hence to yonder place; and
it shall remove; and nothing shall be impossible unto you.

And while they abode in Galilee, Jesus said unto 22
them, The Son of man shall be delivered up into the
hands of men; and they shall kill him, and the third 23
day he shall be raised up. And they were exceeding
sorry.

74. *The temple tax supplied.*

S. Matthew xvii. 24—27.

24 AND when they were come to Capernaum, they that Ex.30.12...
received the half-shekel came to Peter, and said, Doth — 38. 26.
not your master pay the half-shekel? He saith, Yea.
25 And when he came into the house, Jesus spake first to
him, saying, What thinkest thou, Simon? the kings of
the earth, from whom do they receive toll or tribute? Rom.13.6.
26 from their sons, or from strangers? And when he said,
From strangers, Jesus said unto him, Therefore the sons
27 are free. But, lest we cause them to stumble, go thou
to the sea, and cast a hook, and take up the fish that Hab. 1.15.
first cometh up; and when thou hast opened his mouth,
thou shalt find a shekel: that take, and give unto them
for me and thee.

Exodus xxx. 11—16.

11, 12 *And the LORD spake unto Moses, saying, When thou
takest the sum of the children of Israel, according to those
that are numbered of them, then shall they give every man
a ransom for his soul unto the LORD, when thou numberest
them; that there be no plague among them, when thou
13 numberest them. This they shall give, every one that
passeth over unto them that are numbered, half a shekel
after the shekel of the sanctuary: (the shekel is twenty
gerahs:) half a shekel for an offering to the LORD.
14 Every one that passeth over unto them that are numbered,
from twenty years old and upward, shall give the offering
15 of the LORD. The rich shall not give more, and the poor
shall not give less, than the half shekel, when they give the
offering of the LORD, to make atonement for your souls.
16 And thou shalt take the atonement money from the children
of Israel, and shalt appoint it for the service of the tent of
meeting; that it may be a memorial for the children of
Israel before the LORD, to make atonement for your souls.*

75. *Of little children.   Our duties towards them.*

S. Mark ix. 33—50.

AND they came to Capernaum : and when he was in 33
the house he asked them, What were ye reasoning in
the way ?   But they held their peace : for they had dis- 34
Lk. 22. 24. puted one with another in the way, who was the greatest.
145   And he sat down, and called the twelve ; and he saith 35
Mt. 20. 21. unto them, If any man would be first, he shall be last
121   of all, and minister of all.   And he took a little child, and 36
set him in the midst of them : and taking him in his arms,
Mt. 10. 40.. he said unto them, Whosoever shall receive one of such 37
59   little children in my name, receiveth me : and whosoever
Jn. 13. 20. receiveth me, receiveth not me, but him that sent me.
Nu. 11. 28.   John said unto him, Master, we saw one casting out 38
Mt. 12. 27. devils in thy name : and we forbade him, because he
Acts 19.13. followed not us.   But Jesus said, Forbid him not : for 39
Phil. i. 18. there is no man which shall do a mighty work in my
Cp.   name, and be able quickly to speak evil of me.   For 40
Mt. 12. 30. he that is not against us is for us.   For whosoever shall 41
Mt. 10. 42. give you a cup of water to drink, because ye are Christ's,
59   verily I say unto you, he shall in no wise lose his reward.
Lk. 17. 1... And whosoever shall cause one of these little ones that 42
113   believe on me to stumble, it were better for him if a
great millstone were hanged about his neck, and he were
Mt. 5. 29... cast into the sea.   And if thy hand cause thee to 43
43*   stumble, cut it off : it is good for thee to enter into life
Deu. 13. 6. maimed, rather than having thy two hands to go into
hell, into the unquenchable fire.   And if thy foot cause 45
thee to stumble, cut it off : it is good for thee to enter
into life halt, rather than having thy two feet to be cast
into hell.   And if thine eye cause thee to stumble, cast 47
it out : it is good for thee to enter into the kingdom of
God with one eye, rather than having two eyes to be cast
Is. 66. 24. into hell ; where their worm dieth not, and the fire is not 48
Lev. 2. 13. quenched.   For every one shall be salted with fire. 49
Mt. 5. 13. Salt is good : but if the salt have lost its saltness, 50
Lk. 14. 34. wherewith will ye season it ?   Have salt in yourselves,
43*. 108 and be at peace one with another.
Col. 4. 6.

S. Matthew xviii. 1—14.

In that hour came the disciples unto Jesus, saying, 1
Who then is greatest in the kingdom of heaven ?   And he 2
called to him a little child, and set him in the midst of 3
Mk. 10. 15. them, and said, Verily I say unto you, Except ye turn,

and become as little children, ye shall in no wise enter Mt. 19. 14.
4 into the kingdom of heaven.   Whosoever therefore shall   **118**
humble himself as this little child, the same is the greatest Ps. 131. 2.
5 in the kingdom of heaven.   And whoso shall receive one 1Co.14.20.
6 such little child in my name receiveth me : but whoso
shall cause one of these little ones which believe on me
to stumble, it is profitable for him that a great millstone
should be hanged about his neck, and that he should be
7 sunk in the depth of the sea.   Woe unto the world because of occasions of stumbling ! for it must needs be
that the occasions come ; but woe to that man through 1Co.11.19.
8 whom the occasion cometh !   And if thy hand or thy
foot causeth thee to stumble, cut it off, and cast it from
thee : it is good for thee to enter into life maimed or
halt, rather than having two hands or two feet to be cast
9 into the eternal fire.   And if thine eye causeth thee to
stumble, pluck it out, and cast it from thee : it is good
for thee to enter into life with one eye, rather than
10 having two eyes to be cast into the hell of fire.   See
that ye despise not one of these little ones ; for I say
unto you, that in heaven their angels do always behold Ps. 91. 11.
12 the face of my Father which is in heaven.   How think Heb. 1.13.
ye ? if any man have a hundred sheep, and one of them Lk.15. 3...
be gone astray, doth he not leave the ninety and nine,   **109**
and go unto the mountains, and seek that which goeth Ezek.34.6.
13 astray ?   And if so be that he find it, verily I say unto Ps. 119.
you, he rejoiceth over it more than over the ninety and 176.
14 nine which have not gone astray.   Even so it is not the 2 Pet. 3. 9.
will of your Father which is in heaven, that one of these 1 Tim. 2.4.
little ones should perish.

S. Luke ix. 46—50.

46   And there arose a reasoning among them, which of
47 them should be greatest.   But when Jesus saw the
reasoning of their heart, he took a little child, and set
48 him by his side, and said unto them, Whosoever shall
receive this little child in my name receiveth me : and
whosoever shall receive me receiveth him that sent me :
for he that is least among you all, the same is great.
49   And John answered and said, Master, we saw one
casting out devils in thy name ; and we forbade him,
50 because he followeth not with us.   But Jesus said unto
him, Forbid him not : for he that is not against you is
for you.

76. *Of offences against ourselves. The unmerciful servant.*

S. Matthew xviii. 15—35.

Lev.19.17.   AND if thy brother sin against thee, go, shew him his 15
Lk. 17. 3.. fault between thee and him alone : if he hear thee, thou
  113   hast gained thy brother. But if he hear thee not, take 16
Deu.19.15. with thee one or two more, that at the mouth of two
    witnesses or three every word may be established. And 17
2 Cor.13.1. if he refuse to hear them, tell it unto the church : and if
1 Cor.5.11. he refuse to hear the church also, let him be unto thee
2 Th. 3. 14. as the Gentile and the publican. Verily I say unto you, 18
    What things soever ye shall bind on earth shall be bound
Mt. 16. 19. in heaven: and what things soever ye shall loose on earth
  71   shall be loosed in heaven. Again I say unto you, that if 19
    two of you shall agree on earth as touching anything that
1 Jn. 3. 22; they shall ask, it shall be done for them of my Father
— 5. 14. which is in heaven. For where two or three are gathered 20
1 Cor. 5. 4. together in my name, there am I in the midst of them.
       Then came Peter, and said to him, Lord, how oft 21
    shall my brother sin against me, and I forgive him?
Amo.1.3... until seven times? Jesus saith unto him, I say not unto 22
Gen. 4. 24. thee, Until seven times ; but, Until seventy times seven.
  ·Gr.   Therefore is the kingdom of heaven likened unto a 23
    certain king, which would make a reckoning with his
    servants. And when he had begun to reckon, one was 24
    brought unto him, which owed him ten thousand talents.
    But forasmuch as he had not wherewith to pay, his lord 25
Le.25.39... commanded him to be sold, and his wife, and children,
Deu.15.12. and all that he had, and payment to be made. The 26
2 Ki. 4. 1. servant therefore fell down and worshipped him, saying,
    Lord, have patience with me, and I will pay thee all.
Lk. 7. 42. And the lord of that servant, being moved with com- 27
  47   passion, released him, and forgave him the debt. But 28
    that servant went out, and found one of his fellow-
    servants, which owed him a hundred pence : and he
    laid hold on him, and took him by the throat, saying,
    Pay what thou owest. So his fellow-servant fell down 29
    and besought him, saying, Have patience with me, and
Ecclus.   I will pay thee. And he would not: but went and cast 30
  28. 4. him into prison, till he should pay that which was due.

31 So when his fellow-servants saw what was done, they
were exceeding sorry, and came and told unto their lord
32 all that was done.   Then his lord called him unto him,
and saith to him, Thou wicked servant, I forgave thee
33 all that debt, because thou besoughtest me: shouldest Mt. 6. 12...
not thou also have had mercy on thy fellow-servant, even Eph. 4. 32.
34 as I had mercy on thee?   And his lord was wroth, and Col. 3. 13.
delivered him to the tormentors, till he should pay all
35 that was due.   So shall also my heavenly Father do unto Jas. 2. 13.
you, if ye forgive not every one his brother from your Mk. 11. 25.
hearts.

77. *The feast of tabernacles.*

S. John vii. 1—52.

1   AND after these things Jesus walked in Galilee: for
he would not walk in Judæa, because the Jews sought Jn. 5. 16.
2 to kill him.   Now the feast of the Jews, the feast of
3 tabernacles, was at hand.   His brethren therefore said Le. 23. 34..
unto him, Depart hence, and go into Judæa, that thy
disciples also may behold thy works which thou doest.
4 For no man doeth anything in secret, and himself
seeketh to be known openly.   If thou doest these things,
5 manifest thyself to the world.   For even his brethren did
6 not believe on him.   Jesus therefore saith unto them,
My time is not yet come; but your time is alway ready. Jn. 8. 20.
7 The world cannot hate you; but me it hateth, because I Jn. 15. 19.
8 testify of it, that its works are evil.   Go ye up unto the
feast: I go not up yet unto this feast; because my time
9 is not yet fulfilled.   And having said these things unto
them, he abode still in Galilee.
10   But when his brethren were gone up unto the feast,
then went he also up, not publicly, but as it were in
11 secret.   The Jews therefore sought him at the feast, and Jn. 11. 56.
12 said, Where is he?   And there was much murmuring   **124**
among the multitudes concerning him: some said, He
is a good man: others said, Not so, but he leadeth the
13 multitude astray.   Howbeit no man spake openly of him
for fear of the Jews.   Jn. 9. 22.
14   But when it was now the midst of the feast Jesus
15 went up into the temple, and taught.   The Jews therefore marvelled, saying, How knoweth this man letters,
16 having never learned?   Jesus therefore answered them, Acts 4. 13.
and said, My teaching is not mine, but his that sent me. Jn. 8. 28.

If any man willeth to do his will, he shall know of the 17
teaching, whether it be of God, or whether I speak from
Jn. 5. 41; myself. He that speaketh from himself seeketh his own 18
— 8. 50. glory : but he that seeketh the glory of him that sent
him, the same is true, and no unrighteousness is in him.
Acts 7. 38. Did not Moses give you the law, and yet none of you 19
doeth the law? Why seek ye to kill me? The multi- 20
tude answered, Thou hast a devil : who seeketh to kill
Jn. 5. 8... thee? Jesus answered and said unto them, I did one 21
27 work, and ye all marvel. For this cause hath Moses 22
Lev. 12. 3. given you circumcision (not that it is of Moses, but of
Gen.17.10. the fathers); and on the sabbath ye circumcise a man.
If a man receiveth circumcision on the sabbath, that the 23
law of Moses may not be broken; are ye wroth with me,
because I made a man every whit whole on the sabbath?
Deu.1.16.. Judge not according to appearance, but judge righteous 24
Is. 11. 3.. judgement.
Some therefore of them of Jerusalem said, Is not 25
this he whom they seek to kill? And lo, he speaketh 26
openly, and they say nothing unto him. Can it be that
the rulers indeed know that this is the Christ? How- 27
Mt. 13. 55. beit we know this man whence he is : but when the
Christ cometh, no one knoweth whence he is. Jesus 28
therefore cried in the temple, teaching and saying, Ye
Jn. 8. 14. both know me, and know whence I am; and I am not
come of myself, but he that sent me is true, whom ye
know not. I know him; because I am from him, and 29
Jn. 8. 42. he sent me. They sought therefore to take him : and 30
Lk. 22. 53. no man laid his hand on him, because his hour was not
Jn. 8. 20. yet come. But of the multitude many believed on him; 31
and they said, When the Christ shall come, will he do
more signs than those which this man hath done? The 32
Pharisees heard the multitude murmuring these things
concerning him; and the chief priests and the Pharisees
Jn. 13. 33. sent officers to take him. Jesus therefore said, Yet a 33
Jn. 16. 16. little while am I with you, and I go unto him that sent
Lk. 17. 22. me. Ye shall seek me, and shall not find me : and 34
Jn. 8. 21. where I am, ye cannot come. The Jews therefore said 35
79 among themselves, Whither will this man go that we
Jas. 1. 1. shall not find him? will he go unto the Dispersion
among the Greeks, and teach the Greeks? What is this 36
word that he said, Ye shall seek me, and shall not find
me : and where I am, ye cannot come?

37   Now on the last day, the great day of the feast, Jesus Lev.23.36.
stood and cried, saying, If any man thirst, let him come
38 unto me, and drink. He that believeth on me, as the Is. 12. 3;
scripture hath said, out of his belly shall flow rivers of — 58. 11.
39 living water. But this spake he of the Spirit, which they Zech. 14.8.
that believed on him were to receive : for the Spirit was Is. 44. 3.
40 not yet given; because Jesus was not yet glorified. Some Joel 2. 28.
of the multitude therefore, when they heard these words,
41 said, This is of a truth the prophet. Others said, This is
the Christ. But some said, What, doth the Christ come
42 out of Galilee? Hath not the scripture said that the Ps. 89. 3.
Christ cometh of the seed of David, and from Bethlehem, Is. 11. 1.
43 the village where David was? So there arose a division Mic. 5. 2.
44 in the multitude because of him. And some of them
would have taken him ; but no man laid hands on him.
45   The officers therefore came to the chief priests and
Pharisees ; and they said unto them, Why did ye not
46 bring him? The officers answered, Never man so spake.
47 The Pharisees therefore answered them, Are ye also led
48 astray? Hath any of the rulers believed on him, or of
49 the Pharisees? But this multitude which knoweth not
50 the law are accursed. Nicodemus saith unto them (he Jn. 3. 1.
51 that came to him before, being one of them), Doth our
law judge a man, except it first hear from himself and Deu.1. 17.
52 know what he doeth? They answered and said unto — 19.15.
him, Art thou also of Galilee? Search, and see that out
of Galilee ariseth no prophet.   Jn. 1. 45.

78. *The adulteress.*

S. John vii. 53—viii. 11.

53   [AND they went every man unto his own house: but
8. 1, 2 Jesus went unto the mount of Olives. And early in the Lk. 21. 37.
morning he came again into the temple, and all the
people came unto him ; and he sat down, and taught
3 them. And the scribes and the Pharisees bring a woman
4 taken in adultery ; and having set her in the midst, they
say unto him, Master, this woman hath been taken in
5 adultery, in the very act. Now in the law Moses com- Lev.20.10.
manded us to stone such: what then sayest thou of her? De. 22. 22;
6 And this they said, tempting him, that they might have   24.
whereof to accuse him. But Jesus stooped down, and Mt. 22. 18.

with his finger wrote on the ground. But when they 7
continued asking him, he lifted up himself, and said unto
Deu. 17.7. them, He that is without sin among you, let him first
Ro. 2. 22. cast a stone at her. And again he stooped down, and 8
with his finger wrote on the ground. And they, when 9
they heard it, went out one by one, beginning from the
eldest, even unto the last: and Jesus was left alone, and
the woman, where she was, in the midst. And Jesus 10
lifted up himself, and said unto her, Woman, where are
they? did no man condemn thee? And she said, No 11
Jn. 3. 17. man, Lord. And Jesus said, Neither do I condemn
Lk. 12. 14. thee: go thy way; from henceforth sin no more.]
Ro. 5. 20...
1 Tim. 1. 15..

79. *Jesus the Son of God, himself God.*

S. John viii. 12—59.

Jn. 1. 9;   AGAIN therefore Jesus spake unto them, saying, I am 12
— 9. 5;   the light of the world: he that followeth me shall not
—12. 35... walk in the darkness, but shall have the light of life.
141   The Pharisees therefore said unto him, Thou bearest 13
Jn. 5. 31. witness of thyself; thy witness is not true. Jesus an- 14
28   swered and said unto them, Even if I bear witness of
myself, my witness is true; for I know whence I came,
Jn. 9. 29... and whither I go; but ye know not whence I come, or
Jn. 8. 11. whither I go. Ye judge after the flesh; I judge no man. 15
— 12. 47. Yea and if I judge, my judgement is true; for I am not 16
alone, but I and the Father that sent me. Yea and in 17
Deu. 17. 6. your law it is written, that the witness of two men is
true. I am he that beareth witness of myself, and the 18
Mt. 3. 17; Father that sent me beareth witness of me. They said 19
— 17. 5. therefore unto him, Where is thy Father? Jesus an-
16. 72 swered, Ye know neither me, nor my Father: if ye knew
Jn. 14. 7... me, ye would know my Father also. These words spake 20
he in the treasury, as he taught in the temple: and no
Jn. 7. 30; man took him; because his hour was not yet come.
44.   He said therefore again unto them, I go away, and 21
Jn. 7. 34... ye shall seek me, and shall die in your sin: whither I go,
77 ye cannot come. The Jews therefore said, Will he kill 22
himself, that he saith, Whither I go, ye cannot come?
And he said unto them, Ye are from beneath; I am from 23
above: ye are of this world; I am not of this world.

24 I said therefore unto you, that ye shall die in your sins:
for except ye believe that I am he, ye shall die in your Mk. 16. 16.
25 sins. They said therefore unto him, Who art thou? Heb. 2. 3.
Jesus said unto them, Even that which I have also spoken
26 unto you from the beginning. I have many things to
speak and to judge concerning you: howbeit he that
sent me is true; and the things which I heard from him,
27 these speak I unto the world. They perceived not that Jn. 1. 18.
28 he spake to them of the Father. Jesus therefore said,
When ye have lifted up the Son of man, then shall ye Jn. 3. 14.
know that I am he, and that I do nothing of myself, but Jn. 5. 30.
29 as the Father taught me, I speak these things. And he
that sent me is with me; he hath not left me alone; Jn. 14. 11.
for I do always the things that are pleasing to him. Jn. 4. 34;
30 As he spake these things, many believed on him. — 6. 38.
31 Jesus therefore said to those Jews which had believed
him, If ye abide in my word, then are ye truly my Jn. 15. 10.
32 disciples; and ye shall know the truth, and the truth
33 shall make you free. They answered unto him, We be Jas. 1. 25.
Abraham's seed, and have never yet been in bondage to
any man: how sayest thou, Ye shall be made free?
34 Jesus answered them, Verily, verily, I say unto you, Ro. 6. 16...
Every one that committeth sin is the bondservant of sin. Gal. 4. 3...
35 And the bondservant abideth not in the house for ever: 2 Pet. 2. 19.
36 the son abideth for ever. If therefore the Son shall make Rom. 8. 2.
37 you free, ye shall be free indeed. I know that ye are Gal. 5. 1.
Abraham's seed; yet ye seek to kill me, because my word Jn. 5. 18.
38 hath not free course in you. I speak the things which I
have seen with my Father: and ye also do the things which Jn. 14. 10.
39 ye heard from your father. They answered and said
unto him, Our father is Abraham. Jesus saith unto Mt. 3. 9.
them, If ye were Abraham's children, ye would do the Gal. 3. 7;
40 works of Abraham. But now ye seek to kill me, a man 29.
that hath told you the truth, which I heard from God:
41 this did not Abraham. Ye do the works of your father.
They said unto him, We were not born of fornication;
42 we have one Father, even God. Jesus said unto them,
If God were your Father, ye would love me: for I came 1 Jn. 5. 1.
forth and am come from God; for neither have I come
43 of myself, but he sent me. Why do ye not understand
my speech? Even because ye cannot hear my word. Jn. 7. 17.
44 Ye are of your father the devil, and the lusts of your 1 Jn. 3. 8.
father it is your will to do. He was a murderer from the

J. H. G. 9

beginning, and stood not in the truth, because there is
no truth in him. When he speaketh a lie, he speaketh
of his own : for he is a liar, and the father thereof. But 45
because I say the truth, ye believe me not. Which of 46
you convicteth me of sin? If I say truth, why do ye
1 Jn. 4. 6. not believe me? He that is of God heareth the words 47
of God : for this cause ye hear them not, because ye are
not of God. The Jews answered and said unto him, 48
Jn. 4. 9. Say we not well that thou art a Samaritan, and hast a
devil? Jesus answered, I have not a devil; but I honour 49
Jn. 5. 41; my Father, and ye dishonour me. But I seek not mine 50
— 7. 18. own glory: there is one that seeketh and judgeth.
Jn. 5. 24; Verily, verily, I say unto you, If a man keep my word, 51
— 11. 26. he shall never see death. The Jews said unto him, Now 52
Zech. 1. 5. we know that thou hast a devil. Abraham is dead, and
the prophets; and thou sayest, If a man keep my word,
he shall never taste of death. Art thou greater than our 53
father Abraham, which is dead? and the prophets are
dead : whom makest thou thyself? Jesus answered, If 54
Jn. 12. 28. I glorify myself, my glory is nothing: it is my Father
that glorifieth me ; of whom ye say, that he is your God;
and ye have not known him : but I know him; and if I 55
should say, I know him not, I shall be like unto you, a
Lk. 10. 24. liar : but I know him, and keep his word. Your father 56
He. 11. 13. Abraham rejoiced to see my day ; and he saw it, and was
glad. The Jews therefore said unto him, Thou art not 57
yet fifty years old, and hast thou seen Abraham? Jesus 58
Is. 43. 13. said unto them, Verily, verily, I say unto you, Before
Jn. 10. 30. Abraham was, I am. They took up stones therefore to 59
cast at him : but Jesus hid himself, and went out of the
Lk. 4. 30. temple.

80. *The man blind from his birth.*

S. John ix. 1—41.

AND as he passed by, he saw a man blind from his 1
birth. And his disciples asked him, saying, Rabbi, who 2
did sin, this man, or his parents, that he should be born
blind? Jesus answered, Neither did this man sin, nor 3
Jn. 11. 4. his parents : but that the works of God should be made
manifest in him. We must work the works of him that 4

sent me, while it is day: the night cometh, when no man Jn. 12. 35.
5 can work.   When I am in the world, I am the light of Jn. 1. 9.
6 the world.   When he had thus spoken, he spat on the Mk. 7. 33;
ground, and made clay of the spittle, and anointed his — 8. 23.
7 eyes with the clay, and said unto him, Go, wash in the   67. 70
pool of Siloam (which is by interpretation, Sent).   He Is. 8. 6.
went away therefore, and washed, and came seeing. Neh. 3. 15.
8 The neighbours therefore, and they which saw him aforetime, that he was a beggar, said, Is not this he that sat
9 and begged?   Others said, It is he: others said, No,
10 but he is like him.   He said, I am he.   They said there-
11 fore unto him, How then were thine eyes opened?   He
answered, The man that is called Jesus made clay, and
anointed mine eyes, and said unto me, Go to Siloam,
and wash: so I went away and washed, and I received
12 sight.   And they said unto him, Where is he?   He saith, ·
I know not.
13   They bring to the Pharisees him that aforetime was
14 blind.   Now it was the sabbath on the day when Jesus Jn. 5. 10.
15 made the clay, and opened his eyes.   Again therefore   27
the Pharisees also asked him how he received his sight.
And he said unto them, He put clay upon mine eyes,
16 and I washed, and do see.   Some therefore of the
Pharisees said, This man is not from God, because he
keepeth not the sabbath.   But others said, How can a
17 man that is a sinner do such signs?   And there was a Jn. 3. 2.
division among them.   They say therefore unto the blind Jn. 7. 33.
man again, What sayest thou of him, in that he opened
18 thine eyes?   And he said, He is a prophet.   The Jews Jn. 4. 19;
therefore did not believe concerning him, that he had — 6. 14.
been blind, and had received his sight, until they called
19 the parents of him that had received his sight, and asked
them, saying, Is this your son, who ye say was born
20 blind?   how then doth he now see?   His parents answered and said, We know that this is our son, and that
21 he was born blind: but how he now seeth, we know not;
or who opened his eyes, we know not: ask him; he is
22 of age; he shall speak for himself.   These things said
his parents, because they feared the Jews: for the Jews
had agreed already, that if any man should confess him
to be Christ, he should be put out of the synagogue. Jn. 12. 42;
23, 24 Therefore said his parents, He is of age; ask him.   So — 16. 2.
they called a second time the man that was blind, and

9—2

Jos. 7. 19. said unto him, Give glory to God: we know that this
man is a sinner. He therefore answered, Whether he be 25
a sinner, I know not: one thing I know, that, whereas I
was blind, now I see. They said therefore unto him, 26
What did he to thee? how opened he thine eyes? He 27
answered them, I told you even now, and ye did not
hear: wherefore would ye hear it again? would ye also
become his disciples? And they reviled him, and said, 28
Thou art his disciple; but we are disciples of Moses.
We know that God hath spoken unto Moses: but as for 29
Jn. 8. 14. this man, we know not whence he is. The man an- 30
swered and said unto them, Why, herein is the marvel,
that ye know not whence he is, and yet he opened mine
Ps. 66. 18. eyes. We know that God heareth not sinners: but if 31
Is. 1. 15. any man be a worshipper of God, and do his will, him
Ps. 34. 15. he heareth. Since the world began it was never heard 32
that any one opened the eyes of a man born blind. If 33
this man were not from God, he could do nothing.
They answered and said unto him, Thou wast altogether 34
born in sins, and dost thou teach us? And they cast
him out.

Jesus heard that they had cast him out; and finding 35
him, he said, Dost thou believe on the Son of God?
He answered and said, And who is he, Lord, that I may 36
believe on him? Jesus said unto him, Thou hast both 37
Jn. 4. 26. seen him, and he it is that speaketh with thee. And he 38
said, Lord, I believe. And he worshipped him. And 39
Jn. 5. 27. Jesus said, For judgement came I into this world, that
Lk. 10. 21. they which see not may see; and that they which see
86 may become blind. Those of the Pharisees which were 40
with him heard these things, and said unto him, Are we
also blind? Jesus said unto them, If ye were blind, ye 41
Jn. 15. 24. would have no sin: but now ye say, We see: your sin
remaineth.

81. *Jesus the good shepherd.*

S. John x. 1—21.

VERILY, verily, I say unto you, He that entereth not 1
by the door into the fold of the sheep, but climbeth up
some other way, the same is a thief and a robber. But 2

he that entereth in by the door is the shepherd of the
3 sheep.   To him the porter openeth ; and the sheep hear
his voice : and he calleth his own sheep by name, and
4 leadeth them out.   When he hath put forth all his own,
he goeth before them, and the sheep follow him : for
5 they know his voice.   And a stranger will they not
follow, but will flee from him : for they know not the
6 voice of strangers.   This parable spake Jesus unto them :
but they understood not what things they were which he
spake unto them.

7   Jesus therefore said unto them again, Verily, verily, I
8 say unto you, I am the door of the sheep.   All that Eph. 2. 18.
came before me are thieves and robbers : but the sheep Eze. 34. 2..
9 did not hear them.   I am the door : by me if any man Jer. 23. 1..
enter in, he shall be saved, and shall go in and go out, Zec. 11. 3..
10 and shall find pasture.   The thief cometh not, but that
he may steal, and kill, and destroy : I came that they
11 may have life, and may have it abundantly.   I am the Is. 40. 11.
good shepherd : the good shepherd layeth down his life Eze. 34. 23.
12 for the sheep.   He that is a hireling, and not a shepherd,
whose own the sheep are not, beholdeth the wolf coming,
and leaveth the sheep, and fleeth, and the wolf snatcheth Zec. 11. 16.
13 them, and scattereth them : he fleeth because he is a
14 hireling, and careth not for the sheep.   I am the good
shepherd ; and I know mine own, and mine own know 2 Ti. 2. 19.
15 me, even as the Father knoweth me, and I know the
16 Father ; and I lay down my life for the sheep.   And Jn. 15. 13.
other sheep I have, which are not of this fold : them also Is. 56. 8.
I must bring, and they shall hear my voice ; and they Ez. 34. 23;
17 shall become one flock, one shepherd.   Therefore doth — 37. 24.
the Father love me, because I lay down my life, that I Is. 53. 12.
18 may take it again.   No one taketh it away from me, but
I lay it down of myself.   I have power to lay it down,
and I have power to take it again.   This commandment Jn. 12. 49..;
received I from my Father.   — 14. 31.
19   There arose a division again among the Jews because
20 of these words.   And many of them said, He hath a
21 devil, and is mad ; why hear ye him ?   Others said,
These are not the sayings of one possessed with a devil.
Can a devil open the eyes of the blind ?   **80**

82. *The Samaritan villagers.   Three answers to disciples.*

S. Luke ix. 51—62.

AND it came to pass, when the days were well-nigh 51
Acts 1. 2. come that he should be received up, he stedfastly set his
face to go to Jerusalem, and sent messengers before his
face: and they went, and entered into a village of the 52
Samaritans, to make ready for him.   And they did not 53
Jn. 4. 9. receive him, because his face was as though he were
going to Jerusalem.   And when his disciples James and 54
John saw this, they said, Lord, wilt thou that we bid fire
2 Ki. 1. 10. to come down from heaven, and consume them?   But 55
he turned, and rebuked them.   And they went to another 56
village.

And as they went in the way, a certain man said unto 57
him, I will follow thee whithersoever thou goest.   And 58
Jesus said unto him, The foxes have holes, and the birds
1 Co. 4. 11. of the heaven have nests; but the Son of man hath not
where to lay his head.   And he said unto another, 59
Follow me.   But he said, Lord, suffer me first to go and
bury my father.   But he said unto him, Leave the dead 60
to bury their own dead; but go thou and publish abroad
the kingdom of God.   And another also said, I will 61
1 Ki. 19. 20. follow thee, Lord; but first suffer me to bid farewell to
them that are at my house.   But Jesus said unto him, 62
No man, having put his hand to the plough, and looking
back, is fit for the kingdom of God.

S. Matthew viii. 19—22.

And there came a scribe, and said unto him, Master, 19
I will follow thee whithersoever thou goest.   And Jesus 20
saith unto him, The foxes have holes, and the birds of
the heaven have nests; but the Son of man hath not
where to lay his head.   And another of the disciples 21
said unto him, Lord, suffer me first to go and bury my
father.   But Jesus saith unto him, Follow me; and leave 22
the dead to bury their own dead.

83. *Mission of the seventy.*

S. Luke x. 1—12.

1   Now after these things the Lord appointed seventy
others, and sent them two and two before his face into
every city and place, whither he himself was about to
2 come. And he said unto them, The harvest is plenteous, Mt. 9. 37...
but the labourers are few : pray ye therefore the Lord of   59
the harvest, that he send forth labourers into his harvest.
3 Go your ways : behold, I send you forth as lambs in the
4 midst of wolves. Carry no purse, no wallet, no shoes :
5 and salute no man on the way. And into whatsoever 2 Ki. 4. 29.
house ye shall enter, first say, Peace be to this house.
6 And if a son of peace be there, your peace shall rest upon
7 him : but if not, it shall turn to you again. And in that
same house remain, eating and drinking such things as 1 Co. 9. 7.
they give : for the labourer is worthy of his hire. Go not 1 Tim. 5. 18.
8 from house to house. And into whatsoever city ye enter,
and they receive you, eat such things as are set before
9 you : and heal the sick that are therein, and say unto
10 them, The kingdom of God is come nigh unto you. But Mt. 4. 17.
into whatsoever city ye shall enter, and they receive you
11 not, go out into the streets thereof and say, Even the
dust from your city, that cleaveth to our feet, we do wipe Acts 13. 51.
off against you : howbeit know this, that the kingdom of
12 God is come nigh. I say unto you, It shall be more
tolerable in that day for Sodom, than for that city.

84. *Of those who reject him.*

S. Matthew xi. 20—24.

THEN began he to upbraid the cities wherein most 20
of his mighty works were done, because they repented
not. Woe unto thee, Chorazin! woe unto thee, Beth- 21
saida! for if the mighty works had been done in Tyre and
Ezek. 3. 6. Sidon which were done in you, they would have repented
Is. 23. long ago in sackcloth and ashes. Howbeit I say unto 22
Ezek. 27, you, it shall be more tolerable for Tyre and Sidon in the
& 28. day of judgement, than for you. And thou, Capernaum, 23
Is. 14. 13.· shalt thou be exalted unto heaven? thou shalt go down
unto Hades: for if the mighty works had been done in
Sodom which were done in thee, it would have remained
until this day. Howbeit I say unto you, that it shall 24
Gen. 19. be more tolerable for the land of Sodom in the day of
judgement, than for thee.

S. Luke x. 13—16.

Woe unto thee, Chorazin! woe unto thee, Bethsaida! 13
for if the mighty works had been done in Tyre and
Sidon, which were done in you, they would have repented long ago, sitting in sackcloth and ashes. Howbeit 14
it shall be more tolerable for Tyre and Sidon in the
judgement, than for you. And thou, Capernaum, shalt 15
thou be exalted unto heaven? thou shalt be brought
Jn. 13. 20. down unto Hades. He that heareth you heareth me; 16
and he that rejecteth you rejecteth me; and he that re-
Jn. 5. 23. jecteth me rejecteth him that sent me.

85. *Return of the seventy.*

S. Luke x. 17—20.

AND the seventy returned with joy, saying, Lord, 17
even the devils are subject unto us in thy name. And 18
Rev. 12. 9. he said unto them, I beheld Satan fallen as lightning
from heaven. Behold, I have given you authority to 19
Ps. 91. 13. tread upon serpents and scorpions, and over all the
Mk. 16. 18. power of the enemy: and nothing shall in any wise hurt
you. Howbeit in this rejoice not, that the spirits are 20
Phil. 4. 3. subject unto you; but rejoice that your names are
Rev. 20. 12. written in heaven.

86. *Of those who receive him.*

S. Luke x. 21—24.

21 IN that same hour he rejoiced in the Holy Spirit, and
said, I thank thee, O Father, Lord of heaven and earth,
that thou didst hide these things from the wise and un- Rom.6.17.
derstanding, and didst reveal them unto babes : yea, (constr.)
22 Father; for so it was well-pleasing in thy sight. All things 1 Co. 1.26..
have been delivered unto me of my Father : and no one Mt. 28. 18;
knoweth who the Son is, save the Father; and who the — 16. 17.
Father is, save the Son, and he to whomsoever the Son Jn. 6. 46.
23 willeth to reveal him. And turning to the disciples, he
said privately, Blessed are the eyes which see the things Mt. 13. 16.
24 that ye see : for I say unto you, that many prophets and   50
kings desired to see the things which ye see, and saw
them not; and to hear the things which ye hear, and He. 11. 13.
heard them not.

S. Matthew xi. 25—30.

25 At that season Jesus answered and said, I thank thee,
O Father, Lord of heaven and earth, that thou didst
hide these things from the wise and understanding, and
26 didst reveal them unto babes : yea, Father, for so it was
27 well-pleasing in thy sight. All things have been delivered
unto me of my Father : and no one knoweth the Son,
save the Father; neither doth any know the Father, save
the Son, and he to whomsoever the Son willeth to reveal
28 him. Come unto me, all ye that labour and are heavy
29 laden, and I will give you rest. Take my yoke upon
you, and learn of me ; for I am meek and lowly in Zec. 9. 9.
30 heart: and ye shall find rest unto your souls. For my Jer. 6. 16.
yoke is easy, and my burden is light.

87. *The good Samaritan.*
S. Luke x. 25—37.

AND behold, a certain lawyer stood up and tempted 25
Lk. 18.18.. him, saying, Master, what shall I do to inherit eternal
119 life? And he said unto him, What is written in the law? 26
how readest thou? And he answering said, Thou shalt 27
Deut. 6. 5. love the Lord thy God with all thy heart, and with all
133 thy soul, and with all thy strength, and with all thy mind;
Lev. 19.18. and thy neighbour as thyself. And he said unto him, 28
Lev. 18. 5. Thou hast answered right : this do, and thou shalt live.
Lk. 16. 15. But he, desiring to justify himself, said unto Jesus, And 29
who is my neighbour? Jesus made answer and said, A 30
certain man was going down from Jerusalem to Jericho ;
and he fell among robbers, which both stripped him and
. beat him, and departed, leaving him half dead. And 31
by chance a certain priest was going down that way :
Ps. 38. 11. and when he saw him, he passed by on the other side.
And in like manner a Levite also, when he came to the 32
place, and saw him, passed by on the other side. But a 33
Jn. 4. 9. certain Samaritan, as he journeyed, came where he was :
and when he saw him, he was moved with compassion,
Is. 1. 6. and came to him, and bound up his wounds, pouring on 34
Mk. 6. 13. them oil and wine ; and he set him on his own beast,
Jas. 5. 14. and brought him to an inn, and took care of him. And 35
Mt. 20. 2. on the morrow he took out two pence, and gave them to
the host, and said, Take care of him ; and whatsoever
thou spendest more, I, when I come back again, will
repay thee. Which of these three, thinkest thou, proved 36
neighbour unto him that fell among the robbers? And 37
he said, He that shewed mercy on him. And Jesus said
unto him, Go, and do thou likewise.

88. *Martha and Mary. The good part.*
S. Luke x. 38—42.

Now as they went on their way, he entered into a 38
certain village : and a certain woman named Martha
Jn. 11.20... received him into her house. And she had a sister 39
89 called Mary, which also sat at the Lord's feet, and heard
Jn. 12. 2... his word. But Martha was cumbered about much serv- 40
125 ing ; and she came up to him, and said, Lord, dost thou
not care that my sister did leave me to serve alone? bid
her therefore that she help me. But the Lord answered 41

and said unto her, Martha, Martha, thou art anxious and
42 troubled about many things : but one thing is needful : Ps. 27. 4.
for Mary hath chosen the good part, which shall not be
taken away from her.

89.   *The feast of dedication.   Jesus one with the Father.*

S. John x. 22—42.

22   AND it was the feast of the dedication at Jerusalem : 1Mac.4.59.
23 it was winter ; and Jesus was walking in the temple in
24 Solomon's porch.   The Jews therefore came round about Acts 3. 11 ;
him, and said unto him, How long dost thou hold us in — 5. 12.
25 suspense?   If thou art the Christ, tell us plainly.   Jesus
answered them, I told you, and ye believe not : the Jn. 8. 42.
works that I do in my Father's name, these bear witness Jn. 5. 36.
26 of me.   But ye believe not, because ye are not of my   **28**
27 sheep.   My sheep hear my voice, and I know them, and
28 they follow me : and I give unto them eternal life ; and
they shall never perish, and no one shall snatch them out Jn. 18. 9.
29 of my hand.   My Father, which hath given them unto
me, is greater than all ; and no one is able to snatch
30 them out of the Father's hand.   I and the Father are
31 one.   The Jews took up stones again to stone him. Jn. 8. 59.
32 Jesus answered them, Many good works have I shewed
you from the Father ; for which of those works do ye
33 stone me?   The Jews answered him, For a good work
we stone thee not, but for blasphemy ; and because that Jn. 5. 18.
34 thou, being a man, makest thyself God.   Jesus answered
them, Is it not written in your law, I said, Ye are gods? Ps. 82. 6.
35 If he called them gods, unto whom the word of God
36 came (and the scripture cannot be broken), say ye of Mt. 5. 18.
him, whom the Father sanctified and sent into the world,
Thou blasphemest ; because I said, I am the Son of
37 God?   If I do not the works of my Father, believe me Jn. 15. 24.
38 not.   But if I do them, though ye believe not me,   **150**
believe the works : that ye may know and understand
39 that the Father is in me, and I in the Father.   They
sought again to take him : and he went forth out of their Jn. 7. 30;
hand.   — 8. 59.
40   And he went away again beyond Jordan into the Mk. 10. 1.
place where John was at the first baptizing ; and there   **117**
41 he abode.   And many came unto him ; and they said,
John indeed did no sign : but all things whatsoever John
42 spake of this man were true.   And many believed on him
. there.

90. *The Lord's prayer. The importunate friend. The father.*

S. Luke xi. 1—13.

AND it came to pass, as he was praying in a certain 1 place, that when he ceased, one of his disciples said unto him, Lord, teach us to pray, even as John also taught his disciples.   And he said unto them, When ye pray, say, 2

Mt. 6. 9...
43*

Father, Hallowed be thy name. Thy kingdom come. Give us day by day our daily bread.   And forgive us our 3, 4 sins; for we ourselves also forgive every one that is indebted to us.   And bring us not into temptation.

And he said unto them, Which of you shall have a 5 friend, and shall go unto him at midnight, and say to him, Friend, lend me three loaves; for a friend of mine 6 is come to me from a journey, and I have nothing to set before him; and he from within shall answer and say, 7 Trouble me not: the door is now shut, and my children are with me in bed; I cannot rise and give thee?   I say 8 unto you, Though he will not rise and give him, because

Lk. 18. 1...
116

he is his friend, yet because of his importunity he will arise and give him as many as he needeth.   And I say 9 unto you, Ask, and it shall be given you; seek, and ye

Mt. 7. 7...
43*
1 Jn. 3. 22.

shall find; knock, and it shall be opened unto you. For every one that asketh receiveth; and he that seeketh 10 findeth; and to him that knocketh it shall be opened. And of which of you that is a father shall his son ask 11 a loaf, and he give him a stone? or a fish, and he for a fish give him a serpent?   Or if he shall ask an egg, 12 will he give him a scorpion?   If ye then, being evil, 13 know how to give good gifts unto your children, how

Jas. 1. 5.

much more shall your heavenly Father give the Holy Spirit to them that ask him?

S. Matthew vi. 5—15. (43*)

5 *And when ye pray, ye shall not be as the hypocrites:
for they love to stand and pray in the synagogues and in
the corners of the streets, that they may be seen of men.
Verily I say unto you, They have received their reward.*
6 *But thou, when thou prayest, enter into thine inner
chamber, and having shut thy door, pray to thy Father
which is in secret, and thy Father which seeth in secret*
7 *shall recompense thee. And in praying use not vain
repetitions, as the Gentiles do: for they think that they*
8 *shall be heard for their much speaking. Be not therefore
like unto them: for your Father knoweth what things*
9 *ye have need of, before ye ask him. After this manner
therefore pray ye: Our Father which art in heaven,*
10 *Hallowed be thy name. Thy kingdom come. Thy will*
11 *be done, as in heaven, so on earth. Give us this day our*
12 *daily bread. And forgive us our debts, as we also have*
13 *forgiven our debtors. And bring us not into temptation,*
14 *but deliver us from the evil one. For if ye forgive men
their trespasses, your heavenly Father will also forgive you.*
15 *But if ye forgive not men their trespasses, neither will your
Father forgive your trespasses.*

S. Matthew vii. 7—11. (43*)

7 *Ask, and it shall be given you; seek, and ye shall find;*
8 *knock, and it shall be opened unto you: for every one that
asketh receiveth; and he that seeketh findeth; and to him*
9 *that knocketh it shall be opened. Or what man is there of
you, who, if his son shall ask him for a loaf, will give him*
10 *a stone; or if he shall ask for a fish, will give him a*
11 *serpent? If ye then, being evil, know how to give good
gifts unto your children, how much more shall your Father
which is in heaven give good things to them that ask him?*
12 *All things therefore whatsoever ye would that men should
do unto you, even so do ye also unto them: for this is the
law and the prophets.*

91. *Beelzebub. Of blasphemy, and of words.*

S. Matthew xii. 22—37.

THEN was brought unto him one possessed with a 22
58. 73 devil, blind and dumb: and he healed him, insomuch
that the dumb man spake and saw. And all the mul- 23
titudes were amazed, and said, Is this the son of David?
But when the Pharisees heard it, they said, This man 24
Mt. 9. 34. doth not cast out devils, but by Beelzebub the prince
of the devils. And knowing their thoughts he said 25
unto them, Every kingdom divided against itself is
brought to desolation; and every city or house divided
against itself shall not stand: and if Satan casteth out 26
Satan, he is divided against himself; how then shall his
Lk. 9. 49. kingdom stand? And if I by Beelzebub cast out devils, 27
Acts 19.13. by whom do your sons cast them out? therefore shall
Ex. 8. 19. they be your judges. But if I by the Spirit of God cast 28
out devils, then is the kingdom of God come upon you.
Or how can one enter into the house of the strong man, 29
and spoil his goods, except he first bind the strong man?
cp. and then he will spoil his house. He that is not with 30
Mk. 9. 40. me is against me; and he that gathereth not with me
scattereth. Therefore I say unto you, Every sin and 31
blasphemy shall be forgiven unto men; but the blasphemy against the Spirit shall not be forgiven. And 32
1 Tim.1.13. whosoever shall speak a word against the Son of man,
it shall be forgiven him; but whosoever shall speak
Heb.6.4... against the Holy Spirit, it shall not be forgiven him,
1 Jn. 5. 16. neither in this world, nor in that which is to come.
Lk. 6. 43. Either make the tree good, and its fruit good; or make 33
Mt.7.16... the tree corrupt, and its fruit corrupt: for the tree is
43. 43* known by its fruit. Ye offspring of vipers, how can ye, 34
Mt. 23. 33. being evil, speak good things? for out of the abundance
Lk. 6. 45. of the heart the mouth speaketh. The good man out 35
of his good treasure bringeth forth good things: and the
evil man out of his evil treasure bringeth forth evil
things. And I say unto you, that every idle word that 36
men shall speak, they shall give account thereof in the
day of judgement. For by thy words thou shalt be 37
justified, and by thy words thou shalt be condemned.

S. Mark iii. 20—30.

20 And he cometh into a house. And the multitude cometh together again, so that they could not so much 21 as eat bread. And when his friends heard it, they went out to lay hold on him : for they said, He is beside him- 22 self. And the scribes which came down from Jerusalem said, He hath Beelzebub, and, By the prince of the 23 devils casteth he out the devils. And he called them unto him, and said unto them in parables, How can 24 Satan cast out Satan? And if a kingdom be divided 25 against itself, that kingdom cannot stand. And if a house be divided against itself, that house will not be 26 able to stand. And if Satan hath risen up against himself, and is divided, he cannot stand, but hath an 27 end. But no one can enter into the house of the strong man, and spoil his goods, except he first bind the strong 28 man ; and then he will spoil his house. Verily I say unto you, All their sins shall be forgiven unto the sons of men, and their blasphemies wherewith soever they shall 29 blaspheme : but whosoever shall blaspheme against the Holy Spirit hath never forgiveness, but he is guilty of an 30 eternal sin : because they said, He hath an unclean spirit.

S. Luke xi. 14—23.

14 And he was casting out a devil which was dumb. And it came to pass, when the devil was gone out, the 15 dumb man spake ; and the multitudes marvelled. But some of them said, By Beelzebub the prince of the 16 devils casteth he out devils. And others, tempting him, 17 sought of him a sign from heaven. But he, knowing their thoughts, said unto them, Every kingdom divided against itself is brought to desolation ; and a house 18 divided against a house falleth. And if Satan also is divided against himself, how shall his kingdom stand? 19 because ye say that I cast out devils by Beelzebub. And if I by Beelzebub cast out devils, by whom do your sons 20 cast them out? therefore shall they be your judges. But if I by the finger of God cast out devils, then is the 21 kingdom of God come upon you. When the strong man fully armed guardeth his own court, his goods are in 22 peace : but when a stronger than he shall come upon him, and overcome him, he taketh from him his whole 23 armour wherein he trusted, and divideth his spoils. He that is not with me is against me ; and he that gathereth not with me scattereth.

92. *The unclean spirit returning.*

S. Matthew xii. 43—45.

But the unclean spirit, when he is gone out of the 43
Job i. 7.   man, passeth through waterless places, seeking rest, and
1 Pet. 5. 8. findeth it not.   Then he saith, I will return to my house 44
whence I came out; and when he is come, he findeth it
empty, swept, and garnished.   Then goeth he and taketh 45
Mk. 16. 9. with himself seven other spirits more evil than himself,
and they enter in and dwell there: and the last state of
2 Pet. 2. 20. that man becometh worse than the first.   Even so shall
it be also unto this evil generation.

S. Luke xi. 24—26.

The unclean spirit when he is gone out of the 24
man, passeth through waterless places, seeking rest; and
finding none, he saith, I will turn back unto my house
whence I came out.   And when he is come, he findeth 25
it swept and garnished.   Then goeth he, and taketh to 26
him seven other spirits more evil than himself; and they
enter in and dwell there: and the last state of that man
becometh worse than the first.

93. *Who are blessed.*

S. Luke xi. 27, 28.

And it came to pass, as he said these things, a 27
certain woman out of the multitude lifted up her voice,
and said unto him, Blessed is the womb that bare thee,
Mt. 12. 49.. and the breasts which thou didst suck.   But he said, 28
53   Yea rather, blessed are they that hear the word of God,
and keep it.

94. *The sign of Jonah. Nineveh. The queen of the south.*

S. Matthew xii. 38—42.

38   Then certain of the scribes and Pharisees answered   **69**
him, saying, Master, we would see a sign from thee. 1 Cor.1.22.
39 But he answered and said unto them, An evil and
adulterous generation seeketh after a sign; and there
shall no sign be given to it but the sign of Jonah the
40 prophet: for as Jonah was three days and three nights Jon. 1. 17.
in the belly of the whale; so shall the Son of man be
three days and three nights in the heart of the earth.
41 The men of Nineveh shall stand up in the judgement
with this generation, and shall condemn it: for they
repented at the preaching of Jonah; and behold a greater Jon. 3. 10.
42 than Jonah is here. The queen of the south shall rise
up in the judgement with this generation, and shall
condemn it: for she came from the ends of the earth to
hear the wisdom of Solomon; and behold a greater than 1 Ki. 10.
Solomon is here.

S. Luke xi. 29—32.

29   And when the multitudes were gathering together
unto him, he began to say, This generation is an evil
generation: it seeketh after a sign; and there shall no
30 sign be given to it but the sign of Jonah. For even as
Jonah became a sign unto the Ninevites, so shall also
31 the Son of man be to this generation. The queen of the
south shall rise up in the judgement with the men of this
generation, and shall condemn them: for she came from
the ends of the earth to hear the wisdom of Solomon;
32 and behold, a greater than Solomon is here. The men
of Nineveh shall stand up in the judgement with this
generation, and shall condemn it: for they repented at
the preaching of Jonah; and behold, a greater than
Jonah is here.

95. *The light in a man.*

S. Luke xi. 33—36.

No man, when he hath lighted a lamp, putteth it in 33
Mt. 5. 15. a cellar, neither under the bushel, but on the stand, that
43*   they which enter in may see the light.   The lamp of thy 34
Mt. 6. 22. body is thine eye: when thine eye is single, thy whole
body also is full of light; but when it is evil, thy body
also is full of darkness.   Look therefore whether the 35
light that is in thee be not darkness.   If therefore thy 36
whole body be full of light, having no part dark, it shall
be wholly full of light, as when the lamp with its bright
shining doth give thee light.

96. *The Pharisees and lawyers.*

S. Luke xi. 37—54.

Now as he spake, a Pharisee asketh him to dine with 37
him: and he went in, and sat down to meat.   And when 38
the Pharisee saw it, he marvelled that he had not first
washed before dinner.   And the Lord said unto him, 39
Mt. 23. 25.. Now do ye Pharisees cleanse the outside of the cup and
135   of the platter; but your inward part is full of extortion
and wickedness.   Ye foolish ones, did not he that made 40
the outside make the inside also?   Howbeit give for alms 41
Lk. 12. 33. those things which are within; and behold, all things are
clean unto you.
Mt. 23. 23..   But woe unto you Pharisees! for ye tithe mint and 42
rue and every herb, and pass over judgement and the
love of God: but these ought ye to have done, and not
to leave the other undone.   Woe unto you Pharisees! 43
Mt. 23. 5. for ye love the chief seats in the synagogues, and the
salutations in the marketplaces.   Woe unto you! for ye 44
Mt. 23. 27. are as the tombs which appear not, and the men that
walk over them know it not.
And one of the lawyers answering saith unto him, 45
Master, in saying this thou reproachest us also.   And he 46
said, Woe unto you lawyers also! for ye lade men with
Mt. 23. 4. burdens grievous to be borne, and ye yourselves touch
not the burdens with one of your fingers.   Woe unto 47
Mt. 23. 29.. you! for ye build the tombs of the prophets, and your
fathers killed them.   So ye are witnesses and consent 48

unto the works of your fathers : for they killed them, and
49 ye build their tombs. Therefore also said the wisdom of
God, I will send unto them prophets and apostles; and Mt. 23. 34.
50 some of them they shall kill and persecute; that the
blood of . all the prophets, which was shed from the
foundation of the world, may be required of this genera-
51 tion; from the blood of Abel unto the blood of Zachariah, Gen. 4. 8.
who perished between the altar and the sanctuary: yea, 2Ch.24.22.
I say unto you, it shall be required of this generation.
52 Woe unto you lawyers ! for ye took away the key of
knowledge : ye entered not in yourselves, and them that Mt. 23. 13.
were entering in ye hindered.
53 And when he was come out from thence, the scribes
and the Pharisees began to press upon him vehemently,
54 and to provoke him to speak of many things; laying
wait for him, to catch something out of his mouth.

97. *Whom to fear. Of confessing Christ.*

S. Luke xii. 1—12.

1 In the mean time, when the many thousands of the
multitude were gathered together, insomuch that they
trode one upon another, he began to say unto his
disciples first of all, Beware ye of the leaven of the Mt. 16. 6.
2 Pharisees, which is hypocrisy. But there is nothing Mk. 4. 22.
covered up, that shall not be revealed: and hid, that Mt.10.26..
3 shall not be known. Wherefore whatsoever ye have said **51. 59**
in the darkness shall be heard in the light; and what ye
have spoken in the ear in the inner chambers shall be
4 proclaimed upon the housetops. And I say unto you
my friends, Be not afraid of them which kill the body, Is. 51. 12..
5 and after that have no more that they can do. But I Jas. 4. 12.
- will warn you whom ye shall fear: Fear him, which after
he hath killed hath power to cast into hell ; yea, I say
6 unto you, Fear him. Are not five sparrows sold for two
farthings? and not one of them is forgotten in the sight
7 of God. But the very hairs of your head are all numbered.
Fear not : ye are of more value than many sparrows.
8 And I say unto you, Every one who shall confess me
before men, him shall the Son of man also confess before
9 the angels of God : but he that denieth me in the 2Tim.2.12.

presence of men shall be denied in the presence of the
angels of God.   And every one who shall speak a word 10
Mt. 12. 31. against the Son of man, it shall be forgiven him: but
   91   unto him that blasphemeth against the Holy Spirit it
shall not be forgiven.   And when they bring you before 11
the synagogues, and the rulers, and the authorities, be
Mt. 10. 19. not anxious how or what ye shall answer, or what ye shall
Lk. 21. 14. say: for the Holy Spirit shall teach you in that very hour 12
59. 137 what ye ought to say.

98. *Of covetousness.   The rich fool.   Of anxiety.*

S. Luke xii. 13—34.

AND one out of the multitude said unto him, Master, 13
bid my brother divide the inheritance with me.   But he 14
Jn. 8. 11. said unto him, Man, who made me a judge or a divider
over you?   And he said unto them, Take heed, and 15
1 Tim. 6. 9. keep yourselves from all covetousness: for a man's life
consisteth not in the abundance of the things which he
possesseth.   And he spake a parable unto them, saying, 16
The ground of a certain rich man brought forth plenti-
Ecclus. fully: and he reasoned within himself, saying, What shall 17
11. 19. I do, because I have not where to bestow my fruits?
Ps. 49. 16.. And he said, This will I do: I will pull down my barns, 18
and build greater; and there will I bestow all my corn
and my goods.   And I will say to my soul, Soul, thou 19
hast much goods laid up for many years; take thine
ease, eat, drink, be merry.   But God said unto him, 20
Job 27. 8. Thou foolish one, this night is thy soul required of thee;
Jas. 4. 14. and the things which thou hast prepared, whose shall
Ps. 39. 6. they be?   So is he that layeth up treasure for himself, 21
1Tim.6.18. and is not rich toward God.
     And he said unto his disciples, Therefore I say unto 22
Mt. 6. 25... you, Be not anxious for your life, what ye shall eat; nor
   43*   yet for your body, what ye shall put on.   For the life is 23
more than the food, and the body than the raiment.
Consider the ravens, that they sow not, neither reap; 24
Job 38. 41. which have no store-chamber nor barn; and God feedeth
Ps. 147. 9. them: of how much more value are ye than the birds!
     And which of you by being anxious can add a cubit unto 25
Lk. 19. 3. his stature?   If then ye are not able to do even that which 26
   Gr.   is least, why are ye anxious concerning the rest?   Con- 27

sider the lilies, how they grow: they toil not, neither do
they spin; yet I say unto you, Even Solomon in all his
28 glory was not arrayed like one of these. But if God
doth so clothe the grass in the field, which to-day is, and Ps. 104. 14.
to-morrow is cast into the oven; how much more shall Jas. 1. 10.
29 he clothe you, O ye of little faith? And seek not ye
what ye shall eat, and what ye shall drink, neither be ye Ps. 55. 22.
30 of doubtful mind. For all these things do the nations of 1 Pet. 5. 7.
the world seek after: but your Father knoweth that ye Phil. 4. 6.
31 have need of these things. Howbeit seek ye his kingdom,
32 and these things shall be added unto you. Fear not, 1 Ki. 3. 13.
little flock; for it is your Father's good pleasure to give 1 Tim. 4. 8.
33 you the kingdom. Sell that ye have, and give alms; Acts 4. 34.
make for yourselves purses which wax not old, a treasure Mt. 6. 20.
in the heavens that faileth not, where no thief draweth **43*. 119**
34 near, neither moth destroyeth. For where your treasure
is, there will your heart be also.

99. *Of watchfulness, stripes, division. Make peace
betimes.*

S. Luke xii. 35—59.

35   LET your loins be girded about, and your lamps Eph. 6. 14.
36 burning; and be ye yourselves like unto men looking for 1 Pet. 1. 13.
their lord, when he shall return from the marriage feast; Mt. 25. 1...
that, when he cometh and knocketh, they may straight-
37 way open unto him. Blessed are those servants, whom Mt. 24. 46.
the lord when he cometh shall find watching: verily I **137**
say unto you, that he shall gird himself, and make them
38 sit down to meat, and shall come and serve them. And Rev. 3. 20.
if he shall come in the second watch, and if in the third,
39 and find them so, blessed are those servants. But know
this, that if the master of the house had known in what Mt. 24. 43.
hour the thief was coming, he would have watched, and 1 Th. 5. 2.
40 not have left his house to be broken through. Be ye 2 Pet. 3. 10.
also ready: for in an hour that ye think not the Son of Rev. 3. 3.
man cometh.
41   And Peter said, Lord, speakest thou this parable
42 unto us, or even unto all? And the Lord said, Who Mt. 24. 44..
then is the faithful and wise steward, whom his lord 1 Cor. 4. 2.
shall set over his household, to give them their portion of
43 food in due season? Blessed is that servant, whom his

lord when he cometh shall find so doing. Of a truth I 44
say unto you, that he will set him over all that he hath.
But if that servant shall say in his heart, My lord 45
2 Pet. 3. 4. delayeth his coming; and shall begin to beat the men-
servants and the maidservants, and to eat and drink, and
to be drunken; the lord of that servant shall come in a 46
day when he expecteth not, and in an hour when he
knoweth not, and shall cut him asunder, and appoint his
Ro. 2. 12... portion with the unfaithful. And that servant, which 47
Nu. 15. 30. knew his lord's will, and made not ready, nor did ac-
Jas. 4. 17. cording to his will, shall be beaten with many stripes;
Lev. 5. 17.. but he that knew not, and did things worthy of stripes, 48
1 Tim.1.13. shall be beaten with few stripes. And to whomsoever
much is given, of him shall much be required: and to
whom they commit much, of him will they ask the more.

    I came to cast fire upon the earth; and what will I, 49
Mt. 20. 22. if it is already kindled? But I have a baptism to be 50
baptized with; and how am I straitened till it be accomplished! Think ye that I am come to give peace in 51
Mt. 10. 34.. the earth? I tell you, Nay; but rather division: for 52
  59   there shall be from henceforth five in one house divided,
three against two, and two against three. They shall be 53
Mic. 7. 6. divided, father against son, and son against father;
mother against daughter, and daughter against her
mother; mother in law against her daughter in law, and
daughter in law against her mother in law.

Mt. 16. 2...   And he said to the multitudes also, When ye see a 54
  69   cloud rising in the west, straightway ye say, There cometh
a shower; and so it cometh to pass. And when ye see 55
Mt. 20. 12. a south wind blowing, ye say, There will be a scorching
Jas. 1. 11. heat; and it cometh to pass. Ye hypocrites, ye know 56
Gr. how to interpret the face of the earth and the heaven;
but how is it that ye know not how to interpret this
time? And why even of yourselves judge ye not what 57
Pro. 25. 8.. is right? For as thou art going with thine adversary 58
Mt. 5. 25... before the magistrate, on the way give diligence to be
43* quit of him; lest haply he hale thee unto the judge, and
the judge shall deliver thee to the officer, and the officer
shall cast thee into prison. I say unto thee, Thou shalt 59
by no means come out thence, till thou have paid the
very last mite.

100. *Of sudden judgements.   The fig-tree in the vineyard.*

S. Luke xiii. 1—9.

1   Now there were some present at that very season which told him of the Galilæans, whose blood Pilate had
2 mingled with their sacrifices.   And he answered and said unto them, Think ye that these Galilæans were sinners above all the Galilæans, because they have suf-
3 fered these things?   I tell you, Nay : but, except ye
4 repent, ye shall all in like manner perish.   Or those eighteen, upon whom the tower in Siloam fell, and killed them, think ye that they were offenders above all the
5 men that dwell in Jerusalem?   I tell you, Nay : but, except ye repent, ye shall all likewise perish.
6   And he spake this parable ; A certain man had a fig tree planted in his vineyard ; and he came seeking fruit Mt. 21. 19.
7 thereon, and found none.   And he said unto the vine-   **127**
dresser, Behold, these three years I come seeking fruit on this fig tree, and find none : cut it down ; why doth
8 it also cumber the ground?   And he answering saith unto him, Lord, let it alone this year also, till I shall
9 dig about it, and dung it : and if it bear fruit thence-forth, well ; but if not, thou shalt cut it down.

101. *The infirm woman healed on the sabbath.*

S. Luke xiii. 10—17.

10   AND he was teaching in one of the synagogues on **27. 40**
11 the sabbath day.   And behold, a woman which had a **77. 105**
spirit of infirmity eighteen years ; and she was bowed
12 together, and could in no wise lift herself up.   And when Jesus saw her, he called her, and said to her,
13 Woman, thou art loosed from thine infirmity.   And he laid his hands upon her : and immediately she was made Mk. 10. 16.
14 straight, and glorified God.   And the ruler of the syna-gogue, being moved with indignation because Jesus had healed on the sabbath, answered and said to the multi-tude, There are six days in which men ought to work : Ex. 20. 9.
in them therefore come and be healed, and not on the
15 day of the sabbath.   But the Lord answered him, and said, Ye hypocrites, doth not each one of you on the Lk. 14. 5.

sabbath loose his ox or his ass from the stall, and lead
him away to watering? And ought not this woman, 16
Lk. 19. 9. being a daughter of Abraham, whom Satan had bound,
. lo, these eighteen years, to have been loosed from this
bond on the day of the sabbath? And as he said these 17
things, all his adversaries were put to shame : and all the
multitude rejoiced for all the glorious things that were
done by him.

102. *Parable of the mustard-seed, and of the leaven.*

S. Luke xiii. 18—21.

HE said therefore, Unto what is the kingdom of God 18
Mt. 13. 31.. like? and whereunto shall I liken it? It is like unto a 19
51 grain of mustard seed, which a man took, and cast into
his own garden ; and it grew, and became a tree ; and
Dan. 4. 12. the birds of the heaven lodged in the branches thereof.
And again he said, Whereunto shall I liken the kingdom 20
Mt. 13. 33. of God? It is like unto leaven, which a woman took and 21
Ex. 16. 36. hid in three measures of meal, till it was all leavened.
cp.Gr.&H.

103. *Are they few that be saved?*

S. Luke xiii. 22—30.

AND he went on his way through cities and villages, 22
teaching, and journeying on unto Jerusalem. And one 23
said unto him, Lord, are they few that be saved? And
Mt. 7. 13... he said unto them, Strive to enter in by the narrow door: 24
43* for many, I say unto you, shall seek to enter in, and
shall not be able. When once the master of the house 25
Mt. 25. 10.. is risen up, and hath shut to the door, and ye begin to
138 stand without, and to knock at the door, saying, Lord,
open to us ; and he shall answer and say to you, I know
you not whence ye are ; then shall ye begin to say, We 26
Mt. 7. 21... did eat and drink in thy presence, and thou didst teach
in our streets ; and he shall say, I tell you, I know not 27
Ps. 6. 8. whence ye are ; depart from me, all ye workers of iniquity. There shall be the weeping and gnashing of 28
Lk. 16. 23.. teeth, when ye shall see Abraham, and Isaac, and Jacob,
111 and all the prophets, in the kingdom of God, and your-
Mal. 1. 11. selves cast forth without. And they shall come from the 29
Is. 59. 19. east and west, and from the north and south, and shall

30 sit down in the kingdom of God. And behold, there are
last which shall be first, and there are first which shall be Mt. 19. 30.
last.

104. *Answer to Herod's threats.*

S. Luke xiii. 31—35.

31 In that very hour there came certain Pharisees, saying to him, Get thee out, and go hence: for Herod would
32 fain kill thee. And he said unto them, Go and say to
that fox, Behold, I cast out devils and perform cures to-
day and to-morrow, and the third day I am perfected. Heb. 2. 10.
33 Howbeit I must go on my way to-day and to-morrow and
the day following : for it cannot be that a prophet perish
34 out of Jerusalem. O Jerusalem, Jerusalem, which kill- Mt. 23. 37..
eth the prophets, and stoneth them that are sent unto **135**
her! how often would I have gathered thy children together, even as a hen gathereth her own brood under
35 her wings, and ye would not! Behold, your house is Jer. 22. 5;
left unto you desolate : and I say unto you, Ye shall not — 12. 7.
see me, until ye shall say, Blessed is he that cometh in Ps. 118. 26.
the name of the Lord.

105. *Dinner on the sabbath. The dropsy healed.*

S. Luke xiv. 1—6.

1 And it came to pass, when he went into the house
of one of the rulers of the Pharisees on a sabbath to eat
2 bread, that they were watching him. And behold, there
was before him a certain man which had the dropsy.
3 And Jesus answering spake unto the lawyers and Pharisees, saying, Is it lawful to heal on the sabbath, or not? 27. 40
4 But they held their peace. And he took him, and healed 77. 101
5 him, and let him go. And he said unto them, Which of
you shall have an ass or an ox fallen into a well, and
will not straightway draw him up on a sabbath day?
6 And they could not answer again unto these things.

106. *The guests reproved. Of true hospitality.*

S. Luke xiv. 7—14.

7 And he spake a parable unto those which were bidden, when he marked how they chose out the chief seats;
8 saying unto them, When thou art bidden of any man to

Pro. 25.6.. a marriage feast, sit not down in the chief seat; lest
haply a more honourable man than thou be bidden of
him, and he that bade thee and him shall come and say 9
to thee, Give this man place; and then thou shalt begin
with shame to take the lowest place. But when thou 10
art bidden, go and sit down in the lowest place; that
when he that hath bidden thee cometh, he may say to
thee, Friend, go up higher: then shalt thou have glory
Mt. 23.12. in the presence of all that sit at meat with thee. For 11
Pro. 29. 23. every one that exalteth himself shall be humbled; and
Lk. 1. 52. he that humbleth himself shall be exalted.

And he said to him also that had bidden him, When 12
thou makest a dinner or a supper, call not thy friends,
nor thy brethren, nor thy kinsmen, nor rich neighbours;
lest haply they also bid thee again, and a recompense be
Neh. 8. 10. made thee. But when thou makest a feast, bid the poor, 13
Tob. 4.7... the maimed, the lame, the blind: and thou shalt be 14
blessed; because they have not wherewith to recompense thee: for thou shalt be recompensed in the resurrection of the just.

107. *The great supper.*

S. Luke xiv. 15—24.

AND when one of them that sat at meat with him 15
Rev. 19. 9. heard these things, he said unto him, Blessed is he that
shall eat bread in the kingdom of God. But he said 16
unto him, A certain man made a great supper; and he
Esth. 6. 14. bade many: and he sent forth his servant at supper time 17
Pro. 9. 2.. to say to them that were bidden, Come; for all things
Mt. 22. 1... are now ready. And they all with one consent began to 18
130   make excuse. The first said unto him, I have bought
Mt. 13. 34. a field, and I must needs go out and see it: I pray thee
have me excused. And another said, I have bought five 19
Lk. 9. 62. yoke of oxen, and I go to prove them: I pray thee have
me excused. And another said, I have married a wife, 20
1 Cor. 7. 33. and therefore I cannot come. And the servant came, 21
and told his lord these things. Then the master of the
house being angry said to his servant, Go out quickly
into the streets and lanes of the city, and bring in hither
the poor and maimed and blind and lame. And the 22
servant said, Lord, what thou didst command is done,
and yet there is room. And the lord said unto the 23

servant, Go out into the highways and hedges, and constrain them to come in, that my house may be filled.
24 For I say unto you, that none of those men which were Acts 13. 46.
bidden shall taste of my supper.

108. *Of bearing the cross, and counting the cost.*

S. Luke xiv. 25—35.

25   Now there went with him great multitudes : and he
26 turned, and said unto them, If any man cometh unto Mt. 10. 37..
me, and hateth not his own father, and mother, and   **59**
wife, and children, and brethren, and sisters, yea, and Deu. 33. 9.
27 his own life also, he cannot be my disciple. Whosoever Rev. 12. 11.
doth not bear his own cross, and come after me, cannot Mt. 16. 24.
28 be my disciple. For which of you, desiring to build a   **71**
tower, doth not first sit down and count the cost, whether
29 he have wherewith to complete it? Lest haply, when he
hath laid a foundation, and is not able to finish, all that
30 behold begin to mock him, saying, This man began to
31 build, and was not able to finish. Or what king, as he
goeth to encounter another king in war, will not sit down
first and take counsel whether he is able with ten thousand to meet him that cometh against him with twenty
32 thousand? Or else, while the other is yet a great way
off, he sendeth an ambassage, and asketh conditions of
33 peace. So therefore whosoever he be of you that re-
nounceth not all that he hath, he cannot be my disciple.
34 Salt therefore is good: but if even the salt have lost its Mt. 5. 13.
35 savour, wherewith shall it be seasoned? It is fit neither   **43***
for the land nor for the dunghill: men cast it out. He Mk. 9. 50.
that hath ears to hear, let him hear.   **75**

109. *Joy in heaven over sinners that repent.*
The lost sheep. The piece of silver. The prodigal son.

S. Luke xv. 1—32.

1   Now all the publicans and sinners were drawing near
2 unto him for to hear him. And both the Pharisees and
the scribes murmured, saying, This man receiveth Lk. 19. 7.
sinners, and eateth with them.   **122**
3, 4   And he spake unto them this parable, saying, What
man of you, having a hundred sheep, and having lost one Mt. 18. 12.
of them, doth not leave the ninety and nine in the   **75**
wilderness, and go after that which is lost, until he find Psalm
119. 176.

it?   And when he hath found it, he layeth it on his 5
shoulders, rejoicing.   And when he cometh home, he 6
calleth together his friends and his neighbours, saying
unto them, Rejoice with me, for I have found my sheep
which was lost.   I say unto you, that even so there shall 7
be joy in heaven over one sinner that repenteth, more
Lk. 5. 32. than over ninety and nine righteous persons, which need
no repentance.

Or what woman having ten pieces of silver, if she 8
lose one piece, doth not light a lamp, and sweep the
house, and seek diligently until she find it?   And when 9
she hath found it, she calleth together her friends and
neighbours, saying, Rejoice with me, for I have found the
piece which I had lost.   Even so, I say unto you, there 10
is joy in the presence of the angels of God over one
sinner that repenteth.

And he said, A certain man had two sons : and the 11,12
younger of them said to his father, Father, give me the
De.21.16... portion of thy substance that falleth to me.   And he
divided unto them his living.   And not many days after 13
the younger son gathered all together, and took his
journey into a far country ; and there he wasted his
substance with riotous living.   And when he had spent 14
Amos 8.11. all, there arose a mighty famine in that country ; and he
began to be in want.   And he went and joined himself 15
to one of the citizens of that country ; and he sent him
into his fields to feed swine.   And he would fain have 16
been filled with the husks that the swine did eat : and no
man gave unto him.   But when he came to himself he 17
said, How many hired servants of my father's have bread
enough and to spare, and I perish here with hunger !   I 18
will arise and go to my father, and will say unto him,
Father, I have sinned against heaven, and in thy sight :
I am no more worthy to be called thy son : make me as 19
one of thy hired servants.   And he arose, and came to 20
Acts 2. 39. his father.   But while he was yet afar off, his father saw
Eph. 2. 17. him, and was moved with compassion, and ran, and
fell on his neck, and kissed him.   And the son said unto 21
Ps. 51. 4. him, Father, I have sinned against heaven, and in thy
sight : I am no more worthy to be called thy son.   But 22
the father said to his servants, Bring forth quickly the
best robe, and put it on him ; and put a ring on his
hand, and shoes on his feet : and bring the fatted calf, 23

and kill it, and let us eat, and make merry: for this my
son was dead, and is alive again; he was lost, and is Eph. 2. 1.
25 found. And they began to be merry. Now his elder Rev. 3. 1.
son was in the field: and as he came and drew nigh to
26 the house, he heard music and dancing. And he called
to him one of the servants, and inquired what these
27 things might be. And he said unto him, Thy brother is
come; and thy father hath killed the fatted calf, because
28 he hath received him safe and sound. But he was angry,
and would not go in: and his father came out, and
29 intreated him. But he answered and said to his father,
Lo, these many years do I serve thee, and I never
transgressed a commandment of thine: and yet thou
never gavest me a kid, that I might make merry with my
30 friends: but when this thy son came, which hath devoured
thy living with harlots, thou killedst for him the fatted
31 calf. And he said unto him, Son, thou art ever with me,
32 and all that is mine is thine. But it was meet to make
merry and be glad: for this thy brother was dead, and is Eph. 5. 14.
alive again; and was lost, and is found.

110. *Of the right use of riches. The unjust steward.*

S. Luke xvi. 1—18.

1 AND he said also unto the disciples, There was a
certain rich man, which had a steward; and the same
was accused unto him that he was wasting his goods.
2 And he called him, and said unto him, What is this that
I hear of thee? render the account of thy stewardship; 1 Cor. 4. 2.
3 for thou canst be no longer steward. And the steward
said within himself, What shall I do, seeing that my
lord taketh away the stewardship from me? I have not
4 strength to dig; to beg I am ashamed. I am resolved
what to do, that, when I am put out of the stewardship,
5 they may receive me into their houses. And calling to
him each one of his lord's debtors, he said to the first,
6 How much owest thou unto my lord? And he said, A
hundred measures of oil. And he said unto him, Take
7 thy bond, and sit down quickly and write fifty. Then
said he to another, And how much owest thou? And he
said, A hundred measures of wheat. He saith unto him,
8 Take thy bond, and write fourscore. And his lord
commended the unrighteous steward because he had

done wisely: for the sons of this world are for their own
generation wiser than the sons of the light.   And I say 9
unto you, Make to yourselves friends by means of the
mammon of unrighteousness; that, when it shall fail, they
may receive you into the eternal tabernacles.   He that 10
is faithful in a very little is faithful also in much: and he
that is unrighteous in a very little is unrighteous also in
much.   If therefore ye have not been faithful in the 11
unrighteous mammon, who will commit to your trust the
true riches?   And if ye have not been faithful in that 12
which is another's, who will give you that which is your
own?   No servant can serve two masters: for either he 13
will hate the one, and love the other; or else he will hold
to one, and despise the other.   Ye cannot serve God and
mammon.

And the Pharisees, who were lovers of money, heard 14
all these things; and they scoffed at him.   And he said 15
unto them, Ye are they that justify yourselves in the
sight of men; but God knoweth your hearts: for that
which is exalted among men is an abomination in the
sight of God.   The law and the prophets were until 16
John: from that time the gospel of the kingdom of God
is preached, and every man entereth violently into it.
But it is easier for heaven and earth to pass away, than 17
for one tittle of the law to fall.   Every one that putteth 18
away his wife, and marrieth another, committeth adultery:
and he that marrieth one that is put away from a husband
committeth adultery.

The marginal references:
1 The. 5. 5.
Dan. 4. 27.
1 Tim. 6. 18.
Mt. 25. 21.
139
Lk. 19. 17.
123
Rev. 3. 18.
Mt. 6. 24.
43*
Lk. 10. 29.
1 Sa. 16. 7.
Mt. 11. 12.
46
Mt. 5. 18.
Mt. 5. 32.
43*
Mt. 19. 9.
117

111.   *Of the wrong use of riches.   Dives and Lazarus.*

S. Luke xvi. 19—31.

Now there was a certain rich man, and he was 19
clothed in purple and fine linen, faring sumptuously
every day: and a certain beggar named Lazarus was 20
laid at his gate, full of sores, and desiring to be fed with 21
the crumbs that fell from the rich man's table; yea, even
the dogs came and licked his sores.   And it came to 22
pass, that the beggar died, and that he was carried away
by the angels into Abraham's bosom: and the rich man
also died, and was buried.   And in Hades he lifted up 23
his eyes, being in torments, and seeth Abraham afar off,
and Lazarus in his bosom.   And he cried and said, 24

Marginal references:
Mt. 15. 27.
Ps. 22. 16.
Lk. 23. 43.

Father Abraham, have mercy on me, and send Lazarus,
that he may dip the tip of his finger in water, and cool
25 my tongue; for I am in anguish in this flame. But Mk. 9. 48.
Abraham said, Son, remember that thou in thy lifetime
receivedst thy good things, and Lazarus in like manner Lk. 6. 24.
evil things : but now here he is comforted, and thou art in — 6. 20.
26 anguish. And beside all this, between us and you there
is a great gulf fixed, that they which would pass from
hence to you may not be able, and that none may cross
27 over from thence to us. And he said, I pray thee therefore, father, that thou wouldest send him to my father's
28 house; for I have five brethren; that he may testify
unto them, lest they also come into this place of torment.
29 But Abraham saith, They have Moses and the prophets; Is. 34. 16.
30 let them hear them. And he said, Nay, father Abraham:
but if one go to them from the dead, they will repent.
31 And he said unto him, If they hear not Moses and the Jn. 5. 47.
prophets, neither will they be persuaded, if one rise from Jn. 11.46..;
the dead. — 12. 10.

112. *The raising of Lazarus.*

S. John xi. 1—54.

1   Now a certain man was sick, Lazarus of Bethany, of
2 the village of Mary and her sister Martha. And it was
that Mary which anointed the Lord with ointment, and Jn. 12. 3.
wiped his feet with her hair, whose brother Lazarus was   **125**
3 sick. The sisters therefore sent unto him, saying, Lord,
4 behold, he whom thou lovest is sick. But when Jesus
heard it, he said, This sickness is not unto death, but for Jn. 9. 3.
the glory of God, that the Son of God may be glorified Jn. 12. 23;
5 thereby. Now Jesus loved Martha, and her sister, and — 13. 31.
6 Lazarus. When therefore he heard that he was sick, he
abode at that time two days in the place where he was.
7 Then after this he saith to the disciples, Let us go into
8 Judæa again. The disciples say unto him, Rabbi, the Jn. 10. 33.
Jews were but now seeking to stone thee; and goest thou   **89**
9 thither again? Jesus answered, Are there not twelve
hours in the day? If a man walk in the day, he
stumbleth not, because he seeth the light of this world.
10 But if a man walk in the night, he stumbleth, because Jn. 12. 35.
11 the light is not in him. These things spake he : and
after this he saith unto them, Our friend Lazarus is
fallen asleep ; but I go, that I may awake him out of sleep. 1 Th. 4. 13.

The disciples therefore said unto him, Lord, if he is 12
fallen asleep, he will recover. Now Jesus had spoken of 13
his death : but they thought that he spake of taking rest
in sleep. Then Jesus therefore said unto them plainly, 14
Lazarus is dead. And I am glad for your sakes that I 15
was not there, to the intent ye may believe; nevertheless
let us go unto him. Thomas therefore, who is called 16
Didymus, said unto his fellow-disciples, Let us also go,

Lk. 22. 33. that we may die with him.

So when Jesus came, he found that he had been in 17
the tomb four days already. Now Bethany was nigh 18
unto Jerusalem, about fifteen furlongs off; and many of 19

Job 2. 11.. the Jews had come to Martha and Mary, to console them
concerning their brother. Martha therefore, when she 20

Lk.10.38.. heard that Jesus was coming, went and met him : but
88 Mary still sat in the house. Martha therefore said unto 21
Jesus, Lord, if thou hadst been here, my brother had not
died. And even now I know that, whatsoever thou 22
shalt ask of God, God will give thee. Jesus saith unto 23
her, Thy brother shall rise again. Martha saith unto 24

Acts 24.15. him, I know that he shall rise again in the resurrection
Jn. 5. 28... at the last day. Jesus said unto her, I am the resur- 25
rection, and the life : he that believeth on me, though he

Jn. 6. 39. die, yet shall he live : and whosoever liveth and believeth 26
on me shall never die. Believest thou this? She saith 27

Mt. 16. 16. unto him, Yea, Lord : I have believed that thou art the
Jn. 6. 69. Christ, the Son of God, even he that cometh into the
world. And when she had said this, she went away, and 28
called Mary her sister secretly, saying, The Master is
here, and calleth thee. And she, when she heard it, 29
arose quickly, and went unto him. (Now Jesus was not 30
yet come into the village, but was still in the place where
Martha met him.) The Jews then which were with her 31
in the house, and were comforting her, when they saw
Mary, that she rose up quickly and went out, followed

Mt. 28. 1. her, supposing that she was going unto the tomb to weep
there. Mary therefore, when she came where Jesus was, 32
and saw him, fell down at his feet, saying unto him,
Lord, if thou hadst been here, my brother had not died.
When Jesus therefore saw her weeping, and the Jews 33
also weeping which came with her, he groaned in the
spirit, and was troubled, and said, Where have ye laid 34
him? They say unto him, Lord, come and see. Jesus 35

36 wept.   The Jews therefore said, Behold how he loved Lk. 19. 41.
37 him ! But some of them said, Could not this man,
   which opened the eyes of him that was blind, have Jn. 9. 6.
38 caused that this man also should not die?   Jesus therefore again groaning in himself cometh to the tomb.
39 Now it was a cave, and a stone lay against it.   Jesus Mt. 27. 60.
   saith, Take ye away the stone.   Martha, the sister of him
   that was dead, saith unto him, Lord, by this time he
40 stinketh : for he hath been dead four days.   Jesus saith
   unto her, Said I not unto thee, that, if thou believedst,
41 thou shouldest see the glory of God?   So they took
   away the stone.   And Jesus lifted up his eyes, and said,
42 Father, I thank thee that thou heardest me.   And I
   knew that thou hearest me always : but because of the Jn. 12. 30.
   multitude which standeth around I said it, that they may
43 believe that thou didst send me.   And when he had thus Lk. 7. 14.
   spoken, he cried with a loud voice, Lazarus, come forth. Mt. 9. 26.
44 He that was dead came forth, bound hand and foot with **45. 57**
   grave-clothes; and his face was bound about with a napkin. Jn. 20. 7.
   Jesus saith unto them, Loose him, and let him go.
45   Many therefore of the Jews, which came to Mary and
46 beheld that which he did, believed on him.   But some
   of them went away to the Pharisees, and told them the
   things which Jesus had done.
47   The chief priests therefore and the Pharisees gathered
   a council, and said, What do we? for this man doeth
48 many signs. If we let him thus alone, all men will Acts 4. 16.
   believe on him : and the Romans will come and take
49 away both our place and our nation.   But a certain one
   of them, Caiaphas, being high priest that year, said unto Jn. 18. 14.
50 them, Ye know nothing at all, nor do ye take account
   that it is expedient for you that one man should die for
51 the people, and that the whole nation perish not.   Now
   this he said not of himself: but being high priest that
   year, he prophesied that Jesus should die for the nation;
52 and not for the nation only, but that he might also Is. 49. 6.
   gather together into one the children of God that are 1 Jn. 2. 2.
53 scattered abroad.   So from that day forth they took Ep. 2. 14..
   counsel that they might put him to death.
54   Jesus therefore walked no more openly among the
   Jews, but departed thence into the country near to the
   wilderness, into a city called Ephraim ; and there he
   tarried with the disciples.

S. Luke vii. 14, 15.

And he came nigh and touched the bier: and the bearers 14
*stood still.   And he said, Young man, I say unto thee, Arise.
And he that was dead sat up, and began to speak.   And he* 15
gave him to his mother.

S. Mark v. 40—42.

But he * * * goeth in where the child was.   And taking 40, 41
*the child by the hand, he saith unto her, Talitha cumi; which
is, being interpreted, Damsel, I say unto thee, Arise.   And* 42
*straightway the damsel rose up, and walked; for she was
twelve years old.*

1 Kings xvii. 21—23.

And he stretched himself upon the child three times, and 21
*cried unto the Lord, and said, O Lord my God, I pray thee,
let this child's soul come into him again.   And the Lord* 22
*hearkened unto the voice of Elijah; and the soul of the
child came into him again, and he revived.   And Elijah* 23
*took the child, and brought him down out of the chamber
into the house, and delivered him unto his mother: and
Elijah said, See, thy son liveth.*

2 Kings iv. 33—35.

He went in therefore, and shut the door upon them twain, 33
and prayed unto the Lord.   And he went up, and lay upon 34
*the child, and put his mouth upon his mouth, and his eyes
upon his eyes, and his hands upon his hands: and he stretched
himself upon him; and the flesh of the child waxed warm.
Then he returned, and walked in the house once to and fro;* 35
*and went up, and stretched himself upon him: and the child
sneezed seven times, and the child opened his eyes.*

2 Kings xiii. 21.

And it came to pass, as they were burying a man, that, 21
*behold, they spied a band; and they cast the man into the
sepulchre of Elisha: and as soon as the man touched the
bones of Elisha, he revived, and stood up on his feet.*

Acts ix. 40, 41.

But Peter put them all forth, and kneeled down, and 40
*prayed; and turning to the body, he said, Tabitha, arise.
And she opened her eyes; and when she saw Peter, she sat
up.   And he gave her his hand, and raised her up; and* 41
calling the saints and widows, he presented her alive.

Acts xx. 10—12.

And Paul went down, and fell on him (Eutychus), and 10
*embracing him said, Make ye no ado; for his life is in him.
* * *   And they brought the lad alive, and were not a* 12
little comforted.

113. *Of tempting others. Of forgiveness, faith, and service.*

S. Luke xvii. 1—10.

1   AND he said unto his disciples, It is impossible but   Mt. 18. 7.
that occasions of stumbling should come : but woe unto   **75**
2 him, through whom they come! It were well for him if   1 Co.11.19.
a millstone were hanged about his neck, and he were
thrown into the sea, rather than that he should cause one
3 of these little ones to stumble. Take heed to yourselves:
if thy brother sin, rebuke him ; and if he repent, forgive   Lev. 19.17.
4 him. And if he sin against thee seven times in the day,   Mt. 18. 21.
and seven times turn again to thee, saying, I repent;   **76**
thou shalt forgive him.

5   And the apostles said unto the Lord, Increase our
6 faith. And the Lord said, If ye have faith as a grain of   Mt. 17. 20.
mustard seed, ye would say unto this sycamine tree, Be   **127**
thou rooted up, and be thou planted in the sea; and it   1 Co. 13. 3.
7 would have obeyed you. But who is there of you, having
a servant plowing or keeping sheep, that will say unto
8 him, when he is come in from the field, Come straightway and sit down to meat ; and will not rather say unto
him, Make ready wherewith I may sup, and gird thyself,   Lk. 12. 37.
and serve me, till I have eaten and drunken; and after-
9 ward thou shalt eat and drink? Doth he thank the
servant because he did the things that were commanded?
10 Even so ye also, when ye shall have done all the things
that are commanded you, say, We are unprofitable   Job 22. 3;
servants; we have done that which it was our duty to do.   — 35. 7.

114. *Ten lepers cleansed. One gives thanks.*

S. Luke xvii. 11—19.

11   AND it came to pass, as they were on the way to
Jerusalem, that he was passing through the midst of
12 Samaria and Galilee. And as he entered into a certain   **36**
village, there met him ten men that were lepers, which
13 stood afar off: and they lifted up their voices, saying,   Lev.13.46.
14 Jesus, Master, have mercy on us. And when he saw
them, he said unto them, Go and shew yourselves unto   Lev. 14. 2..
the priests. And it came to pass, as they went, they
15 were cleansed. And one of them, when he saw that he

was healed, turned back, with a loud voice glorifying
God; and he fell upon his face at his feet, giving him 16
thanks: and he was a Samaritan.   And Jesus answering 17
said, Were not the ten cleansed? but where are the
nine?   Were there none found that returned to give 18
glory to God, save this stranger?   And he said unto him, 19
Lk. 8. 48. Arise, and go thy way: thy faith hath made thee whole.

115. *How the kingdom of God cometh.*

S. Luke xvii. 20—37.

AND being asked by the Pharisees, when the kingdom 20
of God cometh, he answered them and said, The kingdom of God cometh not with observation: neither shall 21
they say, Lo, here! or, There! for lo, the kingdom of
Ro. 14. 17. God is within you.

And he said unto the disciples, The days will come, 22
Mt. 9. 15. when ye shall desire to see one of the days of the Son of
man, and ye shall not see it.   And they shall say to you, 23
Mt. 24.23.. Lo, there! Lo, here! go not away, nor follow after
137   them: for as the lightning, when it lighteneth out of the 24
one part under the heaven, shineth unto the other part
under heaven; so shall the Son of man be in his day.
Lk. 9. 22. But first must he suffer many things and be rejected of 25
this generation.   And as it came to pass in the days of 26
Gen. 7.   Noah, even so shall it be also in the days of the Son of
man.   They ate, they drank, they married, they were 27
given in marriage, until the day that Noah entered into
the ark, and the flood came, and destroyed them all.
Gen. 19. Likewise even as it came to pass in the days of Lot: 28
they ate, they drank, they bought, they sold, they planted,
they builded; but in the day that Lot went out from 29
Sodom it rained fire and brimstone from heaven, and
destroyed them all: after the same manner shall it be in 30
2 The. 1. 7. the day that the Son of man is revealed.   In that day, 31
Mt. 24. 17. he which shall be on the housetop, and his goods in the
house, let him not go down to take them away: and let
him that is in the field likewise not return back.   Re- 32
Gen.19.26. member Lot's wife.   Whosoever shall seek to gain his 33
Mt. 16. 25. life shall lose it: but whosoever shall lose his life shall
71   preserve it.   I say unto you, In that night there shall be 34
two men on one bed; the one shall be taken, and the

35 other shall be left.   There shall be two women grinding Mt. 24. 40.
together; the one shall be taken, and the other shall be
37 left.   And they answering say unto him, Where, Lord?
And he said unto them, Where the body is, thither will Mt. 24. 28.
the eagles also be gathered together.   **137**

116.   *Pray without ceasing.   How to pray.*

8. Luke xviii. 1—14.

1   AND he spake a parable unto them to the end that
 2 they ought always to pray, and not to faint; saying, 1 Th. 5. 17.
There was in a city a judge, which feared not God,
 3 and regarded not man: and there was a widow in that
city; and she came oft unto him, saying, Avenge me of
 4 mine adversary.   And he would not for a while: but
afterward he said within himself, Though I fear not God,
 5 nor regard man; yet because this widow troubleth me, I Lk. 11. 8.
will avenge her, lest she wear me out by her continual 1 Cor. 9. 17.
 6 coming.   And the Lord said, Hear what the unrighteous   Gk.
 7 judge saith.   And shall not God avenge his elect, which
cry to him day and night, and he is longsuffering over Rev. 6. 9..
 8 them?   I say unto you, that he will avenge them Ecclus.
speedily.   Howbeit when the Son of man cometh, shall 35. 17...
he find faith on the earth?   2 Pe. 3. 8...
 9   And he spake also this parable unto certain which
trusted in themselves that they were righteous, and set Is. 65. 5.
10 all others at nought: Two men went up into the temple
to pray; the one a Pharisee, and the other a publican.
11 The Pharisee stood and prayed thus with himself, God,
I thank thee, that I am not as the rest of men, extor- Rev. 3. 17.
12 tioners, unjust, adulterers, or even as this publican.   I
fast twice in the week; I give tithes of all that I get.
13 But the publican, standing afar off, would not lift up so
much as his eyes unto heaven, but smote his breast, Jn. 17. 1.
14 saying, God, be merciful to me a sinner.   I say unto
you, This man went down to his house justified rather
than the other: for every one that exalteth himself shall Mt. 23. 12.
be humbled; but he that humbleth himself shall be   **135**
exalted.

117. *Of marriage, adultery, and divorce.*

S. Matthew xix. 1—12.

AND it came to pass when Jesus had finished these 1 words, he departed from Galilee, and came into the borders of Judæa beyond Jordan; and great multitudes 2 followed him; and he healed them there.

And there came unto him Pharisees, tempting him, 3 and saying, Is it lawful for a man to put away his wife for every cause? And he answered and said, Have ye 4 not read, that he which made them from the beginning

Gen. 1. 27. made them male and female, and said, For this cause 5
— 2. 24. shall a man leave his father and mother, and shall
Gr. cleave to his wife; and the twain shall become one flesh?
Mal. 2. 14.. So that they are no more twain, but one flesh. What 6
Eph. 5. 28.. therefore God hath joined together, let not man put asunder. They say unto him, Why then did Moses 7
Deu. 24. command to give a bill of divorcement, and to put her away? He saith unto them, Moses for your hardness of 8 heart suffered you to put away your wives: but from the beginning it hath not been so. And I say unto you, 9
Mt. 5. 32. Whosoever shall put away his wife, except for fornication,
43* and shall marry another, committeth adultery: and he
Lk. 16. 18. that marrieth her when she is put away committeth
110 adultery. The disciples say unto him, If the case of the 10 man is so with his wife, it is not expedient to marry.
1 Cor. 7. 1. But he said unto them, All men cannot receive this 11 saying, but they to whom it is given. For there are 12 eunuchs, which were so born from their mother's womb:
Is. 39. 7. and there are eunuchs, which were made eunuchs by
1 Cor. 7. 7. men: and there are eunuchs, which made themselves eunuchs for the kingdom of heaven's sake. He that is able to receive it, let him receive it.

S. Mark x. 1—12.

And he arose from thence, and cometh into the 1 borders of Judæa and beyond Jordan: and multitudes come together unto him again; and, as he was wont, he taught them again. And there came unto him Pharisees, 2 and asked him, Is it lawful for a man to put away his wife? tempting him. And he answered and said unto 3 them, What did Moses command you? And they said, 4 Moses suffered to write a bill of divorcement, and to put

5 her away. But Jesus said unto them, For your hardness
6 of heart he wrote you this commandment. But from
the beginning of the creation, Male and female made he
7 them. For this cause shall a man leave his father and
8 mother, and shall cleave to his wife; and the twain shall
become one flesh: so that they are no more twain, but
9 one flesh. What therefore God hath joined together,
10 let no man put asunder. And in the house the disciples 1 Cor.7.11.
11 asked him again of this matter. And he saith unto them,
Whosoever shall put away his wife, and marry another, 1 Cor.7.10,
12 committeth adultery against her: and if she herself shall — 39.
put away her husband, and marry another, she committeth adultery.

118. *Babes brought to Christ.*

S. Mark x. 13—16.

13 AND they brought unto him little children, that he
should touch them: and the disciples rebuked them.
14 But when Jesus saw it, he was moved with indignation,
and said unto them, Suffer the little children to come Mt. 18.3...
unto me, forbid them not: for of such is the kingdom **75**
15 of God. Verily I say unto you, Whosoever shall not 1Co.14.20.
receive the kingdom of God as a little child, he shall 1 Pet. 2.2.
16 in no wise enter therein. And he took them in his arms,
and blessed them, laying his hands upon them.

S. Luke xviii. 15—17.

15 And they brought unto him also their babes, that he
should touch them: but when the disciples saw it, they
16 rebuked them. But Jesus called them unto him, saying,
Suffer the little children to come unto me, and forbid
17 them not: for of such is the kingdom of God. Verily I
say unto you, Whosoever shall not receive the kingdom
of God as a little child, he shall in no wise enter therein.

S. Matthew xix. 13—15.

13 Then were there brought unto him little children,
that he should lay his hands on them, and pray: and the
14 disciples rebuked them. But Jesus said, Suffer the little
children, and forbid them not, to come unto me: for of
15 such is the kingdom of heaven. And he laid his hands
on them, and departed thence.

119.   *Counsel of perfection.   Riches a hindrance.*

S. Mark x. 17—27.

AND as he was going forth into the way, there ran 17
one to him, and kneeled to him, and asked him, Good
Master, what shall I do that I may inherit eternal life?
And Jesus said unto him, Why callest thou me good? 18
none is good save one, even God.   Thou knowest the 19
commandments, Do not kill, Do not commit adultery,
Do not steal, Do not bear false witness, Do not defraud,
Honour thy father and mother.   And he said unto him, 20
Master, all these things have I observed from my youth.
And Jesus looking upon him loved him, and said unto 21
him, One thing thou lackest: go, sell whatsoever thou
hast, and give to the poor, and thou shalt have treasure
in heaven: and come, follow me.   But his countenance 22
fell at the saying, and he went away sorrowful: for he
was one that had great possessions.

And Jesus looked round about, and saith unto his 23
disciples, How hardly shall they that have riches enter
into the kingdom of God!   And the disciples were 24
amazed at his words.   But Jesus answereth again, and
saith unto them, Children, how hard is it for them that
trust in riches to enter into the kingdom of God!   It 25
is easier for a camel to go through a needle's eye, than
for a rich man to enter into the kingdom of God.   And 26
they were astonished exceedingly, saying unto him,
Then who can be saved?   Jesus looking upon them 27
saith, With men it is impossible, but not with God: for
all things are possible with God.

Marginal references:
Ex. 20. 13..
Deu. 5. 16.
Lk. 12. 33.
98
Acts 4. 34..
Job 31. 24.
Ps. 62. 10.
1 Tim. 6. 17.
Gen. 18. 14.
Job 42. 2.
Zech. 8. 6.

S. Matthew xix. 16—26.

And behold, one came to him and said, Master, 16
what good thing shall I do, that I may have eternal life?
And he said unto him, Why askest thou me concerning 17
that which is good?   One there is who is good: but if
thou wouldest enter into life, keep the commandments.
He saith unto him, Which?   And Jesus said, Thou shalt 18
not kill, Thou shalt not commit adultery, Thou shalt not
steal, Thou shalt not bear false witness, Honour thy 19

father and thy mother : and, Thou shalt love thy neigh- Lev. 19. 18.
20 bour as thyself. The young man saith unto him, All Rom. 13. 9.
21 these things have I observed : what lack I yet ? Jesus
said unto him, If thou wouldest be perfect, go, sell that
thou hast, and give to the poor, and thou shalt have
22 treasure in heaven : and come, follow me. But when
the young man heard the saying, he went away sorrowful :
for he was one that had great possessions.
23   And Jesus said unto his disciples, Verily I say unto
you, It is hard for a rich man to enter into the kingdom
24 of heaven. And again I say unto you, It is easier for a
camel to go through a needle's eye, than for a rich man
25 to enter into the kingdom of God. And when the
disciples heard it, they were astonished exceedingly,
26 saying, Who then can be saved ? And Jesus looking
upon them said to them, With men this is impossible ;
but with God all things are possible.

S. Luke xviii. 18—27.

18   And a certain ruler asked him, saying, Good Master,
19 what shall I do to inherit eternal life ? And Jesus said
unto him, Why callest thou me good ? none is good,
20 save one, even God. Thou knowest the commandments, Do not commit adultery, Do not kill, Do not
steal, Do not bear false witness, Honour thy father and
21 mother. And he said, All these things have I observed
22 from my youth up. And when Jesus heard it, he said
unto him, One thing thou lackest yet : sell all that thou
hast, and distribute unto the poor, and thou shalt have
23 treasure in heaven : and come, follow me. But when he
heard these things, he became exceeding sorrowful ; for
24 he was very rich. And Jesus seeing him said, How
hardly shall they that have riches enter into the kingdom
25 of God ! For it is easier for a camel to enter in through
a needle's eye, than for a rich man to enter into the
26 kingdom of God. And they that heard it said, Then
27 who can be saved ? But he said, The things which are
impossible with men are possible with God.

120. *Of those who have left all.   The labourers in the vineyard.*

S. Matthew xix. 27—xx. 16.

THEN answered Peter and said unto him, Lo, we 27
have left all, and followed thee; what then shall we
have? And Jesus said unto them, Verily I say unto 28
Re. 21.1,5. you, that ye which have followed me, in the regeneration
Acts 3. 21. when the Son of man shall sit on the throne of his
1 Co. 6. 2. glory, ye also shall sit upon twelve thrones, judging the
Lk. 22. 30. twelve tribes of Israel. And every one that hath left 29
145 houses, or brethren, or sisters, or father, or mother, or
children, or lands, for my name's sake, shall receive a
hundredfold, and shall inherit eternal life. But many 30
shall be last that are first; and first that are last. For 1 20
the kingdom of heaven is like unto a man that is a
householder, which went out early in the morning to hire
labourers into his vineyard. And when he had agreed 2
Tob. 5. 14. with the labourers for a penny a day, he sent them into
Lk. 10. 35. his vineyard. And he went out about the third hour, 3
and saw others standing in the marketplace idle; and 4
to them he said, Go ye also into the vineyard, and whatsoever is right I will give you. And they went their
way. Again he went out about the sixth and the ninth 5
hour, and did likewise. And about the eleventh hour he 6
went out, and found others standing; and he saith unto
them, Why stand ye here all the day idle? They say 7
unto him, Because no man hath hired us. He saith
unto them, Go ye also into the vineyard. And when 8
Lev. 19.13. even was come, the lord of the vineyard saith unto his
Deu. 24.15 steward, Call the labourers, and pay them their hire,
Tob. 4. 14. beginning from the last unto the first. And when they 9
came that were hired about the eleventh hour, they received every man a penny. And when the first came, 10
they supposed that they would receive more; and they
likewise received every man a penny. And when they 11
received it, they murmured against the householder, say- 12
ing, These last have spent but one hour, and thou hast
made them equal unto us, which have borne the burden

13 of the day and the scorching heat. But he answered *Jas.* 1. 11.
   and said to one of them, Friend, I do thee no wrong: Gr.
14 didst not thou agree with me for a penny? Take up
   that which is thine, and go thy way; it is my will to give *Eze.* 18. 4.
15 unto this last, even as unto thee. Is it not lawful for me *Rom.* 9.20.
   to do what I will with mine own? or is thine eye evil, *Deu.* 15. 9.
16 because I am good? So the last shall be first, and the *Pro.* 28. 22.
   first last.   *Tob.* 4. 7.

8. Mark x. 28—31.

28   Peter began to say unto him, Lo, we have left all,
29 and have followed thee. Jesus said, Verily I say unto
   you, There is no man that hath left house, or brethren,
   or sisters, or mother, or father, or children, or lands, for
30 my sake, and for the gospel's sake, but he shall receive a *2 Ch.* 25.9.
   hundredfold now in this time, houses, and brethren, and *1 Tim.* 4. 8.
   sisters, and mothers, and children, and lands, with per- *2 Tim.* 3.12.
31 secutions; and in the world to come eternal life. But
   many that are first shall be last; and the last first.

8. Luke xviii. 28—30.

28   And Peter said, Lo, we have left our own, and
29 followed thee. And he said unto them, Verily I say
   unto you, There is no man that hath left house, or wife,
   or brethren, or parents, or children, for the kingdom of
30 God's sake, who shall not receive manifold more in this
   time, and in the world to come eternal life.

121. *The passion foretold. The request of James and John.*

S. Mark x. 32—45.

AND they were in the way, going up to Jerusalem; 32
and Jesus was going before them: and they were amazed;
and they that followed were afraid.   And he took again
Mt. 16. 21. the twelve, and began to tell them the things that were
71   to happen unto him, saying, Behold, we go up to 33
Jerusalem; and the Son of man shall be delivered unto
the chief priests and the scribes; and they shall condemn him to death, and shall deliver him unto the
Gentiles: and they shall mock him, and shall spit upon 34
him, and shall scourge him, and shall kill him; and
after three days he shall rise again.

Mt. 27. 56.   And there come near unto him James and John, the 35
Mk. 15. 40. sons of Zebedee, saying unto him, Master, we would
that thou shouldest do for us whatsoever we shall ask of
thee.   And he said unto them, What would ye that I 36
should do for you?   And they said unto him, Grant 37
Mt. 19. 28. unto us that we may sit, one on thy right hand, and
120   one on thy left hand, in thy glory.   But Jesus said unto 38
Mt. 26. 39. them, Ye know not what ye ask.   Are ye able to drink
Lk. 12. 50. the cup that I drink? or to be baptized with the baptism
that I am baptized with?   And they said unto him, We 39
are able.   And Jesus said unto them, The cup that I
Acts 12. 2. drink ye shall drink; and with the baptism that I am
Rev. 1. 9. baptized withal shall ye be baptized: but to sit on my 40
right hand or on my left hand is not mine to give: but
it is for them for whom it hath been prepared.   And 41
when the ten heard it, they began to be moved with
indignation concerning James and John.   And Jesus 42
called them to him, and saith unto them, Ye know that
they which are accounted to rule over the Gentiles lord
1 Pet. 5. 3. it over them; and their great ones exercise authority
Mt. 18. 1... over them.   But it is not so among you: but whosoever 43
75. 145   would become great among you, shall be your minister:
and whosoever would be first among you, shall be ser- 44
Phil. 2. 7. vant of all.   For verily the Son of man came not to be 45
ministered unto, but to minister, and to give his life a
ransom for many.

S. Matthew xx. 17—28.

17 And as Jesus was going up to Jerusalem, he took the twelve disciples apart, and in the way he said unto
18 them, Behold, we go up to Jerusalem ; and the Son of man shall be delivered unto the chief priests and scribes;
19 and they shall condemn him to death, and shall deliver him unto the Gentiles to mock, and to scourge, and to crucify : and the third day he shall be raised up.
20 Then came to him the mother of the sons of Zebedee with her sons, worshipping him, and asking a certain
21 thing of him. And he said unto her, What wouldest thou? She saith unto him, Command that these my two sons may sit, one on thy right hand, and one on thy
22 left hand, in thy kingdom. But Jesus answered and said, Ye know not what ye ask. Are ye able to drink the cup
23 that I am about to drink? They say unto him, We are able. He saith unto them, My cup indeed ye shall drink : but to sit on my right hand, and on my left hand, is not mine to give, but it is for them for whom it hath
24 been prepared of my Father. And when the ten heard it, they were moved with indignation concerning the two
25 brethren. But Jesus called them unto him, and said, Ye know that the rulers of the Gentiles lord it over them, and their great ones exercise authority over them.
26 Not so shall it be among you : but whosoever would
27 become great among you shall be your minister; and whosoever would be first among you shall be your
28 servant : even as the Son of man came not to be ministered unto, but to minister, and to give his life a ransom for many.

S. Luke xviii. 31—34.

31 And he took unto him the twelve, and said unto them, Behold, we go up to Jerusalem, and all the things that are written by the prophets shall be accomplished
32 unto the Son of man. For he shall be delivered up unto the Gentiles, and shall be mocked, and shamefully
33 entreated, and spit upon : and they shall scourge and
34 kill him : and the third day he shall rise again. And they understood none of these things ; and this saying was hid from them, and they perceived not the things that were said.

Lk. 9. 45-
73

122. *Two blind men at Jericho. Zacchæus.*

S. Luke xviii. 35—xix. 10.

AND it came to pass, as he drew nigh unto Jericho, a 35
certain blind man sat by the way side begging : and hear- 36
ing a multitude going by, he enquired what this meant.
And they told him, that Jesus of Nazareth passeth by. 37
And he cried, saying, Jesus, thou son of David, have 38
mercy on me.   And they that went before rebuked him, 39
that he should hold his peace : but he cried out the
Mt. 15. 22. more a great deal, Thou son of David, have mercy on
me.   And Jesus stood, and commanded him to be 40
brought unto him : and when he was come near, he
asked him, What wilt thou that I should do unto thee? 41
And he said, Lord, that I may receive my sight.   And 42
Mk. 5. 34. Jesus said unto him, Receive thy sight : thy faith hath
made thee whole.   And immediately he received his 43
sight, and followed him, glorifying God : and all the
people, when they saw it, gave praise unto God.

And he entered and was passing through Jericho. 1 **19**
And behold, a man called by name Zacchæus; and he 2
was a chief publican, and he was rich.   And he sought 3
to see Jesus who he was ; and could not for the crowd,
because he was little of stature.   And he ran on before, 4
and climbed up into a sycomore tree to see him : for he
was to pass that way.   And when Jesus came to the 5
place, he looked up, and said unto him, Zacchæus, make
Lk. 4. 43; haste, and come down ; for to-day I must abide at thy
— 13. 33. house.   And he made haste, and came down, and re- 6
ceived him joyfully.   And when they saw it, they all 7
Lk. 5. 30; murmured, saying, He is gone in to lodge with a man
— 15. 4. that is a sinner.   And Zacchæus stood, and said unto 8
109 the Lord, Behold, Lord, the half of my goods I give to
Lk. 3. 13. the poor ; and if I have wrongfully exacted aught of any
Ex. 22.1, 4. man, I restore fourfold.   And Jesus said unto him, To- 9
day is salvation come to this house, forasmuch as he also
Lk. 13. 16; is a son of Abraham.   For the Son of man came to seek 10
— 15. 4, 7. and to save that which was lost.

S. Mark x. 46—52.

46 And they come to Jericho: and as he went out from Jericho, with his disciples and a great multitude, the son of Timæus, Bartimæus, a blind beggar, was sitting by 47 the way side. And when he heard that it was Jesus of Nazareth, he began to cry out, and say, Jesus, thou son 48 of David, have mercy on me. And many rebuked him, that he should hold his peace: but he cried out the more a great deal, Thou son of David, have mercy on 49 me. And Jesus stood still, and said, Call ye him. And they call the blind man, saying unto him, Be of good 50 cheer: rise, he calleth thee. And he, casting away his 51 garment, sprang up, and came to Jesus. And Jesus answered him, and said, What wilt thou that I should do unto thee? And the blind man said unto him, 52 Rabboni, that I may receive my sight. And Jesus said Jn. 20. 16. unto him, Go thy way; thy faith hath made thee whole. And straightway he received his sight, and followed him in the way.

S. Matthew xx. 29—34.

29 And as they went out from Jericho, a great multitude 30 followed him. And behold, two blind men sitting by the way side, when they heard that Jesus was passing by, cried out, saying, Lord, have mercy on us, thou son of 31 David. And the multitude rebuked them, that they should hold their peace: but they cried out the more, saying, Lord, have mercy on us, thou son of David. 32 And Jesus stood still, and called them, and said, What 33 will ye that I should do unto you? They say unto him, 34 Lord, that our eyes may be opened. And Jesus, being moved with compassion, touched their eyes: and straight- Mk. 7. 33. way they received their sight, and followed him. Lk. 22. 51.

123. *The parable of the pounds.*

S. Luke xix. 11—28.

AND as they heard these things, he added and spake 11
a parable, because he was nigh to Jerusalem, and because
Acts 1. 6. they supposed that the kingdom of God was immediately to appear.   He said therefore, A certain nobleman 12
went into a far country, to receive for himself a kingdom,
Mt.25.14.. and to return.   And he called ten servants of his, and 13
139   gave them ten pounds, and said unto them, Trade ye
herewith till I come.   But his citizens hated him, and 14
Jn. 1. 11. sent an ambassage after him, saying, We will not that
this man reign over us.   And it came to pass, when he 15
was come back again, having received the kingdom, that
he commanded these servants, unto whom he had given
the money, to be called to him, that he might know what
they had gained by trading.   And the first came before 16
him, saying, Lord, thy pound hath made ten pounds
more.   And he said unto him, Well done, thou good 17
Lk.16.10.. servant: because thou wast found faithful in a very little,
have thou authority over ten cities.   And the second 18
139   came, saying, Thy pound, Lord, hath made five pounds.
And he said unto him also, Be thou also over five cities. 19
And another came, saying, Lord, behold, here is thy 20
pound, which I kept laid up in a napkin : for I feared 21
thee, because thou art an austere man : thou takest up
that thou layedst not down, and reapest that thou didst
Job 15. 6. not sow.   He saith unto him, Out of thine own mouth 22
Mt. 12. 37. will I judge thee, thou wicked servant.   Thou knewest
that I am an austere man, taking up that I laid not
down, and reaping that I did not sow ; then wherefore 23
gavest thou not my money into the bank, and I at my
coming should have required it with interest?   And he 24
said unto them that stood by, Take away from him the
pound, and give it unto him that hath the ten pounds.
And they said unto him, Lord, he hath ten pounds.   I 25, 26
Mt. 13. 12. say unto you, that unto every one that hath shall be
49   given ; but from him that hath not, even that which he
hath shall be taken away from him.   Howbeit these 27

mine enemies, which would not that I should reign over Mt. 21. 41;
them, bring hither, and slay them before me. — 22. 7.

28   And when he had thus spoken, he went on before, 129. 130
going up to Jerusalem.

---

124.   *The passover at hand.   Conspiracy of the Jews
to kill Jesus and Lazarus.*

S. John xi. 55—xii. 2, and xii. 9—11.

55   Now the passover of the Jews was at hand: and
many went up to Jerusalem out of the country before
56 the passover, to purify themselves.   They sought there- Lev. 7. 21.
fore for Jesus, and spake one with another, as they stood Jn. 18. 28.
in the temple, What think ye?   That he will not come Act. 21. 24.
57 to the feast?   Now the chief priests and the Pharisees Jn. 7. 11.
had given commandment, that, if any man knew where
he was, he should shew it, that they might take him.

12 1   Jesus therefore six days before the passover came to
Bethany, where Lazarus was, whom Jesus raised from Jn. 11. 1...
2 the dead.   So they made him a supper there: and Martha   112
served; but Lazarus was one of them that sat at meat Lk. 10. 38.
with him.   88

9   The common people therefore of the Jews learned
that he was there: and they came, not for Jesus' sake
only, but that they might see Lazarus also, whom he had
10 raised from the dead.   But the chief priests took counsel
11 that they might put Lazarus also to death; because that Lk. 16. 31.
by reason of him many of the Jews went away, and believed on Jesus.

125. *Mary anoints Jesus. Judas plans to betray Him.*

S. John xii. 3—8.

MARY therefore took a pound of ointment of spike- 3
nard, very precious, and anointed the feet of Jesus, and
wiped his feet with her hair: and the house was filled
with the odour of the ointment. But Judas Iscariot, one 4
of his disciples, which should betray him, saith, Why 5
was not this ointment sold for three hundred pence, and
given to the poor? Now this he said, not because he 6
Jn. 6. 70.   cared for the poor; but because he was a thief, and
Jn. 13. 29.   having the bag took away what was put therein. Jesus 7
therefore said, Suffer her to keep it against the day of
Deu.15.11.   my burying. For the poor ye have always with you; 8
but me ye have not always.

S. Mark xiv. 3—11.

And while he was in Bethany in the house of Simon 3
the leper, as he sat at meat, there came a woman having
Lk. 7. 37.   an alabaster cruse of ointment of spikenard very costly;
47   and she brake the cruse, and poured it over his head.
But there were some that had indignation among them- 4
selves, saying, To what purpose hath this waste of the
ointment been made? For this ointment might have 5
been sold for above three hundred pence, and given to
the poor. And they murmured against her. But Jesus 6
said, Let her alone; why trouble ye her? she hath
wrought a good work on me. For ye have the poor 7
always with you, and whensoever ye will ye can do them
good: but me ye have not always. She hath done what 8
she could: she hath anointed my body aforehand for
the burying. And verily I say unto you, Wheresoever 9
the gospel shall be preached throughout the whole
world, that also which this woman hath done shall be
spoken of for a memorial of her.

And Judas Iscariot, he that was one of the twelve, 10
went away unto the chief priests, that he might deliver
him unto them. And they, when they heard it, were 11
glad, and promised to give him money. And he sought
how he might conveniently deliver him unto them.

S. Matthew xxvi. 6—16.

6   Now when Jesus was in Bethany, in the house of
7 Simon the leper, there came unto him a woman having
an alabaster cruse of exceeding precious ointment, and
8 she poured it upon his head, as he sat at meat. But
when the disciples saw it, they had indignation, saying,
9 To what purpose is this waste? For this ointment might
10 have been sold for much, and given to the poor. But
Jesus perceiving it said unto them, Why trouble ye the
11 woman? for she hath wrought a good work upon me. For
ye have the poor always with you; but me ye have not
12 always.   For in that she poured this ointment upon my
13 body, she did it to prepare me for burial.   Verily I say
unto you, Wheresoever this gospel shall be preached in
the whole world, that also which this woman hath done
shall be spoken of for a memorial of her.
14   Then one of the twelve, who was called Judas
15 Iscariot, went unto the chief priests, and said, What are Gen.37.28.
ye willing to give me, and I will deliver him unto you?
16 And they weighed unto him thirty pieces of silver.   And Zec.11.12.
from that time he sought opportunity to deliver him unto Ex. 21. 32.
them.

S. Luke xxii. 3—6.

3   And Satan entered into Judas who was called Iscariot,
4 being of the number of the twelve.   And he went away,
and communed with the chief priests and captains, how
5 he might deliver him unto them.   And they were glad,
and covenanted to give him money.   And he consented,
6 and sought opportunity to deliver him unto them in the
absence of the multitude.

126. *Jesus entereth Jerusalem as King.*

S. Matthew xxi. 1—11

AND when they drew nigh unto Jerusalem, and came 1
Zec. 14. 4. unto Bethphage, unto the mount of Olives, then Jesus
sent two disciples, saying unto them, Go into the village 2
Mk. 14. 13. that is over against you, and straightway ye shall find
144 an ass tied, and a colt with her: loose them, and bring
them unto me. And if any one say aught unto you, ye 3
shall say, The Lord hath need of them; and straightway
he will send them. Now this is come to pass, that it 4
might be fulfilled which was spoken by the prophet,
saying,

Is. 62. 11.   Tell ye the daughter of Zion,   5
Zec. 9. 9.   Behold, thy King cometh unto thee,
             Meek, and riding upon an ass,
             And upon a colt the foal of an ass.
And the disciples went, and did even as Jesus appointed 6
them, and brought the ass, and the colt, and put on 7
them their garments; and he sat thereon.

[T. O.

S. Mark xi. 1—11.

And when they draw nigh unto Jerusalem, unto 1
Bethphage and Bethany, at the mount of Olives, he
sendeth two of his disciples, and saith unto them, Go 2
your way into the village that is over against you: and
straightway as ye enter into it, ye shall find a colt tied,
Num. 19. 2. whereon no man ever yet sat; loose him, and bring
Deu. 21. 3. him. And if any one say unto you, Why do ye this? 3
1 Sa. 6. 7. say ye, The Lord hath need of him; and straightway
he will send him back hither. And they went away, and 4
found a colt tied at the door without in the open street;
and they loose him. And certain of them that stood 5
there said unto them, What do ye, loosing the colt?
And they said unto them even as Jesus had said: and 6
they let them go. And they bring the colt unto Jesus, 7
and cast on him their garments; and he sat upon him.

[T. O.

S. Luke xix. 29—44.

29   And it came to pass, when he drew nigh unto
Bethpage and Bethany, at the mount that is called the
30 mount of Olives, he sent two of the disciples, saying, Go
your way into the village over against you ; in the which
as ye enter ye shall find a colt tied, whereon no man
31 ever yet sat : loose him, and bring him.   And if any one
ask you, Why do ye loose him? thus shall ye say, The
32 Lord hath need of him.   And they that were sent went
33 away, and found even as he had said unto them.   And
as they were loosing the colt, the owners thereof said
34 unto them, Why loose ye the colt?   And they said, The
35 Lord hath need of him.   And they brought him to
Jesus : and they threw their garments upon the colt, and
set Jesus thereon.   [T. O.

S. John xii. 12—19.

12   On the morrow a great multitude that had come to
the feast, when they heard that Jesus was coming to   1 Macc.
13 Jerusalem, took the branches of the palm trees, and   13. 51.
went forth to meet him, and cried out, Hosanna: Blessed Lev. 23. 40.
is he that cometh in the name of the Lord, even the   Rev. 7. 9.
14 King of Israel.   And Jesus, having found a young ass,
15 sat thereon; as it is written, Fear not, daughter of Zion :
behold, thy King cometh, sitting on an ass's colt.
                                                    [T. O.

S. Matthew xxi.

1 Ki. 9. 13. And the most part of the multitude spread their garments 8
in the way; and others cut branches from the trees, and
spread them in the way.   And the multitudes that went 9
Ps. 118. 25. before him, and that followed, cried, saying, Hosanna to
the son of David: Blessed is he that cometh in the
name of the Lord; Hosanna in the highest.   And when 10
he was come into Jerusalem, all the city was stirred,
saying, Who is this?   And the multitudes said, This is 11
the prophet, Jesus, from Nazareth of Galilee.

S. Mark xi.

And many spread their garments upon the way; and 8
others branches, which they had cut from the fields.
And they that went before, and they that followed, cried, 9
Hosanna; Blessed is he that cometh in the name of the 10
Lord: Blessed is the kingdom that cometh, the kingdom
of our father David: Hosanna in the highest.

Lk. 2. 59.   And he entered into Jerusalem, into the temple; and 11
when he had looked round about upon all things, it being
now eventide, he went out unto Bethany with the twelve.

S. Luke xix.

36 And as he went, they spread their garments in the way.
37 And as he was now drawing nigh, even at the descent
of the mount of Olives, the whole multitude of the
disciples began to rejoice and praise God with a loud
voice for all the mighty works which they had seen;
38 saying, Blessed is the King that cometh in the name of
the Lord : peace in heaven, and glory in the highest. Lk. 2. 14.
39 And some of the Pharisees from the multitude said unto
40 him, Master, rebuke thy disciples. And he answered and
said, I tell you that, if these shall hold their peace, the
stones will cry out. Hab. 2.11.
41   And when he drew nigh, he saw the city and wept Jn. 11. 35.
42 over it, saying, If thou hadst known in this day, even
thou, the things which belong unto peace ! but now they
43 are hid from thine eyes. For the days shall come upon
thee, when thine enemies shall cast up a bank about Is. 29. 3.
thee, and compass thee round, and keep thee in on Deu.28.52.
44 every side, and shall dash thee to the ground, and thy Ps. 137. 7..
children within thee ; and they shall not leave in thee
one stone upon another ; because thou knewest not the
time of thy visitation. Lk. 1. 68.

S. John xii.

16 These things understood not his disciples at the first : Jn. 2. 22.
but when Jesus was glorified, then remembered they that — 7. 39.
these things were written of him, and that they had done
17 these things unto him. The multitude therefore that
was with him when he called Lazarus out of the tomb, Jn. 11. 43.
18 and raised him from the dead, bare witness. For this   112
cause also the multitude went and met him, for that they.
19 heard that he had done this sign. The Pharisees therefore said among themselves, Behold how ye prevail
nothing : lo, the world is gone after him.

127. *The barren fig tree cursed. The temple cleansed.*

S. Mark xi. 12—25.

AND on the morrow, when they were come out from 12
Bethany, he hungered. And seeing a fig tree afar off 13
having leaves, he came, if haply he might find anything
Lk. 13. 7. thereon: and when he came to it, he found nothing but
100 leaves; for it was not the season of figs. And he an- 14
Lk. 3. 9. swered and said unto it, No man eat fruit from thee
henceforward for ever. And his disciples heard it.
Jn. 2. 13... And they come to Jerusalem: and he entered into 15
21 the temple, and began to cast out them that sold and
De. 14. 24.. them that bought in the temple, and overthrew the
tables of the money-changers, and the seats of them
that sold the doves; and he would not suffer that any 16
man should carry a vessel through the temple. And he 17
taught, and said unto them, Is it not written, My house
Is. 56. 7. shall be called a house of prayer for all the nations? but
Jer. 7. 11. ye have made it a den of robbers. And the chief priests 18
and the scribes heard it, and sought how they might
destroy him: for they feared him, for all the multitude
was astonished at his teaching.
And every evening he went forth out of the city. 19
And as they passed by in the morning, they saw the 20
fig tree withered away from the roots. And Peter calling 21
to remembrance saith unto him, Rabbi, behold, the fig
tree which thou cursedst is withered away. And Jesus 22
1 Co. 13. 2. answering saith unto them, Have faith in God. Verily I 23
say unto you, Whosoever shall say unto this mountain,
Be thou taken up and cast into the sea; and shall not
1 Jn. 5. 15. doubt in his heart, but shall believe that what he saith
cometh to pass; he shall have it. Therefore I say unto 24
Mt. 6. 14.. you, All things whatsoever ye pray and ask for, believe
43*. 76 that ye have received them, and ye shall have them.
Ecclus. And whensoever ye stand praying, forgive, if ye have 25
28. 2... aught against any one; that your Father also which is in
heaven may forgive you your trespasses.

S. Matthew xxi. 12—22.

12   And Jesus entered into the temple of God, and cast
out all them that sold and bought in the temple, and
overthrew the tables of the money-changers, and the
13 seats of them that sold the doves; and he saith unto
them, It is written, My house shall be called a house
14 of prayer: but ye make it a den of robbers.   And
the blind and the lame came to him in the temple: and
15 he healed them.   But when the chief priests and the
scribes saw the wonderful things that he did, and the
children that were crying in the temple and saying,
Hosanna to the son of David; they were moved with Ps. 118.26.
16 indignation, and said unto him, Hearest thou what these
are saying?   And Jesus saith unto them, Yea: did ye
never read, Out of the mouth of babes and sucklings Ps. 8. 2.
17 thou hast perfected praise?   And he left them, and went   Gr.
forth out of the city to Bethany, and lodged there.
18   Now in the morning as he returned to the city, he
19 hungered.   And seeing a fig tree by the way side, he
came to it, and found nothing thereon, but leaves only;
and he saith unto it, Let there be no fruit from thee
henceforward for ever.   And immediately the fig tree
20 withered away.   And when the disciples saw it, they
marvelled, saying, How did the fig tree immediately
21 wither away?   And Jesus answered and said unto them,
Verily I say unto you, If ye have faith, and doubt not,
ye shall not only do what is done to the fig tree, but
even if ye shall say unto this mountain, Be thou taken
22 up and cast into the sea, it shall be done.   And all
things, whatsoever ye shall ask in prayer, believing, ye
shall receive.

S. Luke xix. 45—48.

45   And he entered into the temple, and began to cast
46 out them that sold, saying unto them, It is written, And
my house shall be a house of prayer: but ye have made
it a den of robbers.
47   And he was teaching daily in the temple.   But the
chief priests and the scribes and the principal men of
48 the people sought to destroy him: and they could not
find what they might do; for the people all hung upon
him, listening.

128. *Authority questioned.   The two sons.*

S. Matthew xxi. 23—32.

AND when he was come into the temple, the chief 23
priests and the elders of the people came unto him as
Acts 4. 7. he was teaching, and said, By what authority doest thou
these things? and who gave thee this authority? And 24
Jesus answered and said unto them, I also will ask you
one question, which if ye tell me, I likewise will tell you
by what authority I do these things.   The baptism of 25
John, whence was it? from heaven or from men?   And
they reasoned with themselves, saying, If we shall say,
From heaven; he will say unto us, Why then did ye not
believe him?   But if we shall say, From men; we fear 26
Lk. 7. 29. the multitude; for all hold John as a prophet.   And 27
Mt. 14. 5. they answered Jesus, and said, We know not.   He also
said unto them, Neither tell I you by what authority I
do these things.   But what think ye?   A man had two 28
sons; and he came to the first, and said, Son, go work
to-day in the vineyard.   And he answered and said, I 29
will not: but afterward he repented himself, and went.
And he came to the second, and said likewise.   And he 30
answered and said, I go, sir: and went not.   Whether 31
of the twain did the will of his father?   They say, The
Lk. 7. 29.. first.   Jesus saith unto them, Verily I say unto you, that
46   the publicans and the harlots go into the kingdom of
God before you.   For John came unto you in the way 32
of righteousness, and ye believed him not: but the
publicans and the harlots believed him: and ye, when
ye saw it, did not even repent yourselves afterward,
that ye might believe him.

S. Mark xi. 27—33.

27 And they come again to Jerusalem : and as he was walking in the temple, there come to him the chief
28 priests, and the scribes, and the elders; and they said unto him, By what authority doest thou these things?
29 or who gave thee this authority to do these things? And Jesus said unto them, I will ask of you one question, and answer me, and I will tell you by what authority I
30 do these things. The baptism of John, was it from
31 heaven, or from men? answer me. And they reasoned with themselves saying, If we shall say, From heaven;
32 he will say, Why then did ye not believe him? But should we say, From men—they feared the people : for
33 all verily held John to be a prophet. And they answered Jesus and say, We know not. And Jesus saith unto them, Neither tell I you by what authority I do these things.

S. Luke xx. 1—8.

1 And it came to pass, on one of the days, as he was teaching the people in the temple, and preaching the gospel, there came upon him the chief priests and the
2 scribes with the elders; and they spake, saying unto him, Tell us : By what authority doest thou these things?
3 or who is he that gave thee this authority? And he answered and said unto them, I also will ask you a
4 question; and tell me : The baptism of John, was it
5 from heaven, or from men? And they reasoned with themselves, saying, If we shall say, From heaven; he
6 will say, Why did ye not believe him? But if we shall say, From men; all the people will stone us : for they
7 be persuaded that John was a prophet. And they an-
8 swered, that they knew not whence it was. And Jesus said unto them, Neither tell I you by what authority I do these things.

129.   *The wicked husbandmen.*

S. Matthew xxi. 33—46.

HEAR another parable: There was a man that was a 33
Is. 5. 1... householder, which planted a vineyard, and set a hedge
Jer. 2. 21. about it, and digged a winepress in it, and built a tower,
Ps. 80. 8... and let it out to husbandmen, and went into another
Can. 8. 11. country.   And when the season of the fruits drew near, 34
he sent his servants to the husbandmen, to receive his
Lk. 16. 5... fruits.   And the husbandmen took his servants, and beat 35
Acts 7. 52. one, and killed another, and stoned another.   Again, he 36
He. 11. 37. sent other servants more than the first: and they did
unto them in like manner.   But afterward he sent unto 37
them his son, saying, They will reverence my son.   But 38
Jn. 11. 48... the husbandmen, when they saw the son, said among
themselves, This is the heir; come, let us kill him, and
He. 13. 12. take his inheritance.   And they took him, and cast him 39
forth out of the vineyard, and killed him.   When there- 40
fore the lord of the vineyard shall come, what will he do
unto those husbandmen?   They say unto him, He will 41
miserably destroy those miserable men, and will let out
the vineyard unto other husbandmen, which shall render
him the fruits in their seasons.   Jesus saith unto them, 42
Did ye never read in the scriptures,
Ps. 118. 22.   The stone which the builders rejected,
Acts 4. 11.   The same was made the head of the corner:
This was from the Lord,
And it is marvellous in our eyes?
Therefore say I unto you, The kingdom of God shall be 43
taken away from you, and shall be given to a nation
Acts 28. 28. bringing forth the fruits thereof.   And he that falleth on 44
this stone shall be broken to pieces; but on whomsoever
it shall fall, it will scatter him as dust.   [T. O.

S. Mark xii. 1—12.

And he began to speak unto them in parables.   A 1
man planted a vineyard, and set a hedge about it, and
digged a pit for the winepress, and built a tower, and let
it out to husbandmen, and went into another country.
And at the season he sent to the husbandmen a servant, 2
that he might receive from the husbandmen of the fruits
of the vineyard.   And they took him, and beat him, and 3
sent him away empty.   And again he sent unto them 4
another servant; and him they wounded in the head,

5 and handled shamefully. And he sent another; and
him they killed: and many others; beating some, and
6 killing some. He had yet one, a beloved son: he sent
him last unto them, saying, They will reverence my son.
7 But those husbandmen said among themselves, This is
the heir; come, let us kill him, and the inheritance shall
8 be ours. And they took him, and killed him, and cast
9 him forth out of the vineyard. What therefore will the
lord of the vineyard do? he will come and destroy the
husbandmen, and will give the vineyard unto others.
10 Have ye not read even this scripture;
> The stone which the builders rejected,
> The same was made the head of the corner:
11   This was from the Lord,
> And it is marvellous in our eyes?   [T. O.

S. Luke xx. 9—19.

9   And he began to speak unto the people this parable:
A man planted a vineyard, and let it out to husbandmen,
10 and went into another country for a long time. And at
the season he sent unto the husbandmen a servant, that
they should give him of the fruit of the vineyard: but
the husbandmen beat him, and sent him away empty.
11 And he sent yet another servant: and him also they
beat, and handled him shamefully, and sent him away
12 empty. And he sent yet a third: and him also they
13 wounded, and cast him forth. And the lord of the
vineyard said, What shall I do? I will send my beloved
14 son: it may be they will reverence him. But when the
husbandmen saw him, they reasoned one with another,
saying, This is the heir: let us kill him, that the in-
15 heritance may be ours. And they cast him forth out of
the vineyard, and killed him. What therefore will the
16 lord of the vineyard do unto them? He will come and
destroy these husbandmen, and will give the vineyard
unto others. And when they heard it, they said, God
17 forbid. But he looked upon them, and said, What then
is this that is written,
> The stone which the builders rejected,
> The same was made the head of the corner?
18 Every one that falleth on that stone shall be broken to Is. 8. 14...
pieces; but on whomsoever it shall fall, it will scatter Dan. 2. 35.
him as dust.   Job 27. 21.
                                               [T. O. 1 Pet. 2. 7..

S. Matthew xxi.

And when the chief priests and the Pharisees heard 45
his parables, they perceived that he spake of them.   And 46
when they sought to lay hold on him, they feared the
multitudes, because they took him for a prophet.

S. Mark xii.

And they sought to lay hold on him; and they feared 12
the multitude; for they perceived that he spake the
parable against them: and they left him, and went
away.

S. Luke xx.

And the scribes and the chief priests sought to lay 19
hands on him in that very hour; and they feared the
people: for they perceived that he spake this parable
against them.

130.   *The King's marriage feast.*

S. Matthew xxii. 1—14.

Lk.14.15..   AND Jesus answered and spake again in parables 1
  107   unto them, saying, The kingdom of heaven is likened 2
Rev. 19. 9. unto a certain king, which made a marriage feast for his
Est. 6. 14. son, and sent forth his servants to call them that were 3
bidden to the marriage feast: and they would not come.
Again he sent forth other servants, saying, Tell them that 4
Pro. 9. 2. are bidden, Behold, I have made ready my dinner: my
oxen and my fatlings are killed, and all things are ready:
2Ch.30.10. come to the marriage feast.   But they made light of it, 5
and went their ways, one to his own farm, another to his
merchandise: and the rest laid hold on his servants, and 6
entreated them shamefully, and killed them.   But the 7
De.28.49.. king was wroth; and he sent his armies, and destroyed
Dan. 9. 26. those murderers, and burned their city.   Then saith he 8
to his servants, The wedding is ready, but they that were
Acts 13.46. bidden were not worthy.   Go ye therefore unto the 9
partings of the highways, and as many as ye shall find,
bid to the marriage feast.   And those servants went out 10
into the highways, and gathered together all as many as

they found, both bad and good: and the wedding was Mt. 13. 47.
11 filled with guests.   But when the king came in to behold
the guests, he saw there a man which had not on a wedding- Zeph. 1. 8.
12 garment: and he saith unto him, Friend, how camest Gal. 3. 27.
thou in hither not having a wedding-garment?   And he Rev. 19. 8.
13 was speechless.   Then the king said to the servants,
Bind him hand and foot, and cast him out into the
outer darkness; there shall be the weeping and gnashing
14 of teeth.   For many are called, but few chosen.

The great supper.   (**107**)

S. Luke xiv. 15—24.

15   *And when one of them that sat at meat with him
heard these things, he said unto him, Blessed is he that*
16 *shall eat bread in the kingdom of God.   But he said unto
him, A certain man made a great supper; and he bade*
17 *many: and he sent forth his servant at supper time to say
to them that were bidden, Come; for all things are now*
18 *ready.   And they all with one consent began to make
excuse.   The first said unto him, I have bought a field,
and I must needs go out and see it: I pray thee have me*
19 *excused.   And another said, I have bought five yoke of
oxen, and I go to prove them: I pray thee have me ex-*
20 *cused.   And another said, I have married a wife, and*
21 *therefore I cannot come.   And the servant came, and told
his lord these things.   Then the master of the house being
angry said to his servant, Go out quickly into the streets
and lanes of the city, and bring in hither the poor and*
22 *maimed and blind and lame.   And the servant said, Lord,
what thou didst command is done, and yet there is room.*
23 *And the lord said unto the servant, Go out into the
highways and hedges, and constrain them to come in, that*
24 *my house may be filled.   For I say unto you, that none of
those men which were bidden shall taste of my supper.*

131. *Question of the tribute to Cæsar.*

S. Matthew xxii. 15—22.

THEN went the Pharisees, and took counsel how they 15
might ensnare him in his talk.   And they send to him 16
Mk. 8. 15. their disciples, with the Herodians, saying, Master, we
know that thou art true, and teachest the way of God in
Acts 10.34. truth, and carest not for any one: for thou regardest
not the person of men.   Tell us therefore, what thinkest 17
thou?   Is it lawful to give tribute unto Cæsar, or
not?   But Jesus perceived their wickedness, and said, 18
Why tempt ye me, ye hypocrites?   Shew me the tribute 19
money.   And they brought unto him a penny.   And he 20
saith unto them, Whose is this image and superscription?
They say unto him, Cæsar's.   Then saith he unto them, 21
Rom. 13.7. Render therefore unto Cæsar the things that are Cæsar's;
1 Ch. 29.14. and unto God the things that are God's.   And when 22
they heard it, they marvelled, and left him, and went
their way.

S. Mark xii. 13—17.

And they send unto him certain of the Pharisees and 13
of the Herodians, that they might catch him in talk.
And when they were come, they say unto him, Master, 14
we know that thou art true, and carest not for any one:
for thou regardest not the person of men, but of a truth
teachest the way of God: Is it lawful to give tribute
unto Cæsar, or not?   Shall we give, or shall we not give?
But he, knowing their hypocrisy, said unto them, Why 15
tempt ye me?   bring me a penny, that I may see it.
And they brought it.   And he saith unto them, Whose 16
is this image and superscription?   And they said unto
him, Cæsar's.   And Jesus said unto them, Render unto 17
Cæsar the things that are Cæsar's, and unto God the
things that are God's.   And they marvelled greatly
at him.

S. Luke xx. 20—26.

20 And they watched him, and sent forth spies, which feigned themselves to be righteous, that they might take hold of his speech, so as to deliver him up to the rule 21 and to the authority of the governor. And they asked him, saying, Master, we know that thou sayest and teachest rightly, and acceptest not the person of any, but 22 of a truth teachest the way of God: Is it lawful for us 23 to give tribute unto Cæsar, or not? But he perceived their craftiness, and said unto them, Shew me a penny. 24 Whose image and superscription hath it? And they 25 said, Cæsar's. And he said unto them, Then render unto Cæsar the things that are Cæsar's, and unto God 26 the things that are God's. And they were not able to take hold of the saying before the people: and they marvelled at his answer, and held their peace.

132.   *Question of the resurrection.*

S. Luke xx. 27—40.

AND there came to him certain of the Sadducees, 27
Acts 23. 8. they which say that there is no resurrection; and they
asked him, saying, Master, Moses wrote unto us, that if 28
Deu. 25. 5. a man's brother die, having a wife, and he be childless,
Gen. 38. 8. his brother should take the wife, and raise up seed unto
Ruth 1. 13. his brother.   There were therefore seven brethren : and 29
— 4. 5, 10. the first took a wife, and died childless; and the second ; 30
and the third took her ; and likewise the seven also left 31
no children, and died.   Afterward the woman also died. 32
In the resurrection therefore whose wife of them shall 33
she be ? for the seven had her to wife.   And Jesus said 34
unto them, The sons of this world marry, and are given
in marriage : but they that are accounted worthy to 35
attain to that world, and the resurrection from the dead,
1 Co. 7. 29. neither marry, nor are given in marriage: for neither can 36
they die any more : for they are equal unto the angels ;
1 Jn. 3. 2. and are sons of God, being sons of the resurrection.
But that the dead are raised ; even Moses shewed, in 37
the place concerning the Bush, when he calleth the Lord
Ex. 3. 6. the God of Abraham, and the God of Isaac, and the
He. 11. 16. God of Jacob.   Now he is not the God of the dead, but 38
Ro. 14. 8.. of the living : for all live unto him.   And certain of the 39
scribes answering said, Master, thou hast well said.   For 40
they durst not any more ask him any question.

S. Mark xii. 18—27.

And there come unto him Sadducees, which say that 18
there is no resurrection ; and they asked him, saying,
Master, Moses wrote unto us, If a man's brother die, 19
and leave a wife behind him, and leave no child, that
his brother should take his wife, and raise up seed unto
his brother.   There were seven brethren : and the first 20
took a wife, and dying left no seed ; and the second 21

22 took her, and died, leaving no seed behind him; and
the third likewise : and the seven left no seed.   Last of
23 all the woman also died.   In the resurrection whose
wife shall she be of them? for the seven had her to
24 wife.   Jesus said unto them, Is it not for this cause that
ye err, that ye know not the scriptures, nor the power of
25 God? For when they shall rise from the dead, they
neither marry, nor are given in marriage; but are as
26 angels in heaven.   But as touching the dead, that they
are raised; have ye not read in the book of Moses, in
the place concerning the Bush, how God spake unto him,
saying, I am the God of Abraham, and the God of Isaac,
27 and the God of Jacob? He is not the God of the dead,
but of the living : ye do greatly err.

S. Matthew xxii. 23—33.

23   On that day there came to him Sadducees, which
say that there is no resurrection : and they asked him,
24 saying, Master, Moses said, If a man die, having no
children, his brother shall marry his wife, and raise up
25 seed unto his brother.   Now there were with us seven
brethren : and the first married and deceased, and having
26 no seed left his wife unto his brother; in like manner
27 the second also, and the third, unto the seventh.   And
28 after them all the woman died.   In the resurrection
therefore whose wife shall she be of the seven? for they
29 all had her.   But Jesus answered and said unto them,
Ye do err, not knowing the scriptures, nor the power of
30 God.   For in the resurrection they neither marry, nor
31 are given in marriage, but are as angels in heaven.   But
as touching the resurrection of the dead, have ye not
32 read that which was spoken unto you by God, saying, I
am the God of Abraham, and the God of Isaac, and the
God of Jacob? God is not the God of the dead, but of
33 the living.   And when the multitudes heard it, they were
astonished at his teaching.

133. *Question of the great commandment.*

S. Mark xii. 28—34.

AND one of the Scribes came, and heard them 28
questioning together, and knowing that he had answered
them well, asked him, What commandment is the first of
Deu.6.4... all? Jesus answered, The first is, Hear, O Israel; The 29
Mt. 4. 10. Lord our God, the Lord is one : and thou shalt love the 30
Lk.10.26.. Lord thy God with all thy heart, and with all thy soul,
87 and with all thy mind, and with all thy strength. The 31
Lev. 19.18. second is this, Thou shalt love thy neighbour as thyself.
Ro. 13. 8.. There is none other commandment greater than these.
And the scribe said unto him, Of a truth, Master, thou 32
Deu. 4. 35. hast well said that he is one; and there is none other
but he : and to love him with all the heart, and with all 33
the understanding, and with all the strength, and to love
1 Sa.15.22. his neighbour as himself, is much more than all whole
burnt offerings and sacrifices. And when Jesus saw that 34
he answered discreetly, he said unto him, Thou art not
far from the kingdom of God. And no man after that
durst ask him any question.

S. Matthew xxii. 34—40.

But the Pharisees, when they heard that he had put 34
the Sadducees to silence, gathered themselves together.
And one of them, a lawyer, asked him a question, 35
tempting him, Master, which is the great commandment 36
in the law? And he said unto him, Thou shalt love the 37
Lord thy God with all thy heart, and with all thy soul,
and with all thy mind. This is the great and first com- 38
mandment. And a second like unto it is this, Thou 39
shalt love thy neighbour as thyself. On these two com- 40
mandments hangeth the whole law, and the prophets.

134. *Christ's question of the Son of David.*

S. Matthew xxii. 41—46.

41 Now while the Pharisees were gathered together,
42 Jesus asked them a question, saying, What think ye of
the Christ? whose son is he? They say unto him, The
43 son of David. He saith unto them, How then doth Ps. 132. 11.
David in the Spirit call him Lord, saying,
44   The Lord said unto my Lord,   Ps. 110. 1.
      Sit thou on my right hand,   Acts 2. 34.
      Till I put thine enemies underneath thy feet?   Heb. 1. 3.
45 If David then calleth him Lord, how is he his son? Eph. 1. 20.
46 And no one was able to answer him a word, neither Ro. 1. 3...
durst any man from that day forth ask him any more
questions.

S. Mark xii. 35—37.

35 And Jesus answered and said, as he taught in the
temple, How say the scribes that the Christ is the son of
36 David? David himself said in the Holy Spirit,
      The Lord said unto my Lord,
      Sit thou on my right hand,
      Till I make thine enemies the footstool of thy feet.
37 David himself calleth him Lord: and whence is he his
son? And the common people heard him gladly.   Lk. 4. 22.

S. Luke xx. 41—44.

41 And he said unto them, How say they that the Christ
42 is David's son? For David himself saith in the book of
Psalms,
      The Lord said unto my Lord,
      Sit thou on my right hand,
43   Till I make thine enemies the footstool of thy feet.
44 David therefore calleth him Lord, and how is he his
son?

135. *The scribes and Pharisees condemned.*

S. Luke xx. 45—47.

AND in the hearing of all the people he said unto his 45
disciples, Beware of the scribes, which desire to walk in 46
long robes, and love salutations in the marketplaces, and
chief seats in the synagogues, and chief places at feasts;
which devour widows' houses, and for a pretence make 47
long prayers: these shall receive greater condemnation.

S. Mark xii. 38—40.

And in his teaching he said, Beware of the scribes, 38
which desire to walk in long robes, and to have salutations in the marketplaces, and chief seats in the 39
2 Ki. 4. 1. synagogues, and chief places at feasts: they which de- 40
Mt. 6. 5. vour widows' houses, and for a pretence make long
prayers; these shall receive greater condemnation.

S. Matthew xxiii. 1—39.

Then spake Jesus to the multitudes and to his 1
Mal. 2. 7.. disciples, saying, The scribes and the Pharisees sit on 2
Moses' seat: all things therefore whatsoever they bid 3
you, these do and observe: but do not ye after their
Lk. 11. 46. works; for they say, and do not. Yea, they bind heavy 4
96 burdens and grievous to be borne, and lay them on
Acts 15.10. men's shoulders; but they themselves will not move
Mt. 6. 1. them with their finger. But all their works they do for 5
Nu. 15.38.. to be seen of men: for they make broad their phylac-
Deu.22.12. teries, and enlarge the borders of their garments, and 6
Lk. 11. 43. love the chief places at feasts, and the chief seats
in the synagogues, and the salutations in the market- 7
places, and to be called of men, Rabbi. But be not ye 8

called Rabbi: for one is your teacher, and all ye are Jas. 3. 1.
9 brethren.   And call no man your father on the earth:
10 for one is your Father, which is in heaven.   Neither be Is. 63. 16.
ye called masters: for one is your master, even the
11 Christ.   But he that is greatest among you shall be your
12 servant.   And whosoever shall exalt himself shall be Lk. 14. 11.
humbled; and whosoever shall humble himself shall be   **108**
exalted.   Jas. 4. 6, 10.

13   But woe unto you, scribes and Pharisees, hypocrites!
because ye shut the kingdom of heaven against men: Lk. 11. 52.
for ye enter not in yourselves, neither suffer ye them that
are entering in to enter.

15   Woe unto you, scribes and Pharisees, hypocrites! for
ye compass sea and land to make one proselyte; and
when he is become so, ye make him twofold more a son
of hell than yourselves.

16   Woe unto you, ye blind guides, which say, Whosoever
shall swear by the temple, it is nothing; but whosoever Mt. 5. 34.
shall swear by the gold of the temple, he is a debtor.
17 Ye fools and blind: for whether is greater, the gold, or
18 the temple that hath sanctified the gold?   And, Whosoever shall swear by the altar, it is nothing; but whosoever shall swear by the gift that is upon it, he is a debtor. Mt. 5. 23.
19 Ye blind: for whether is greater, the gift, or the altar
20 that sanctifieth the gift?   He therefore that sweareth Ex. 29. 37.
by the altar, sweareth by it, and by all things thereon.
21 And he that sweareth by the temple, sweareth by it, and
22 by him that dwelleth therein.   And he that sweareth by 1 Ki. 8. 13.
the heaven, sweareth by the throne of God, and by him
that sitteth thereon.   Rev. 4. 2..

23   Woe unto you, scribes and Pharisees, hypocrites! for
ye tithe mint and anise and cummin, and have left undone Lk. 18. 12.
the weightier matters of the law, judgement, and mercy, Lk. 11. 42.
and faith: but these ye ought to have done, and not to   **96**
24 have left the other undone.   Ye blind guides, which
strain out the gnat, and swallow the camel.

25   Woe unto you, scribes and Pharisees, hypocrites! Lk. 11. 39.
for ye cleanse the outside of the cup and of the platter,
26 but within they are full from extortion and excess.   Thou
blind Pharisee, cleanse first the inside of the cup and of Is. 1. 16.
the platter, that the outside thereof may become clean Eze. 36. 25.
also.

27   Woe unto you, scribes and Pharisees, hypocrites! for

S. Matthew xxiii.

Acts 23. 3. ye are like unto whited sepulchres, which outwardly
Lk. 11. 44. appear beautiful, but inwardly are full of dead men's
bones, and of all uncleanness. Even so ye also out- 28
wardly appear righteous unto men, but inwardly ye are
full of hypocrisy and iniquity.

Woe unto you, scribes and Pharisees, hypocrites! for 29
Lk.11.47. ye build the sepulchres of the prophets, and garnish the
tombs of the righteous, and say, If we had been in the 30
days of our fathers, we should not have been partakers
with them in the blood of the prophets. Wherefore ye 31
witness to yourselves, that ye are sons of them that slew
the prophets. Fill ye up then the measure of your 32
Mt. 3. 7. fathers. Ye serpents, ye offspring of vipers, how shall 33
Gen. 3. 15. ye escape the judgement of hell? Therefore, behold, 34
Acts 7. 59; I send unto you prophets, and wise men, and scribes:
— 12. 2. some of them shall ye kill and crucify; and some of
Acts 5. 40. them shall ye scourge in your synagogues, and persecute
from city to city: that upon you may come all the 35
Rev.18.24. righteous blood shed on the earth, from the blood of
Abel the righteous unto the blood of Zachariah son of
2Ch.24.22. Barachiah, whom ye slew between the sanctuary and the
altar. Verily I say unto you, All these things shall come 36
Lk. 21. 20. upon this generation.

Lk. 13. 34. O Jerusalem, Jerusalem, which killeth the prophets, 37
104 and stoneth them that are sent unto her! how often
would I have gathered thy children together, even as a
Deu.32.11. hen gathereth her chickens under her wings, and ye
Jer. 22. 5. would not! Behold, your house is left unto you desolate. 38
— 12. 7. For I say unto you, Ye shall not see me henceforth, till 39
Ps.118.26. ye shall say, Blessed is he that cometh in the name of the
Ro. 11. 26. Lord.

136. *The widow's mite.*

S. Mark xii. 41—44.

41 AND he sat down over against the treasury, and ₂ Ki. 12. 9.
beheld how the multitude cast money into the treasury :
42 and many that were rich cast in much.   And there came Nu. 7. 2.
a poor widow, and she cast in two mites, which make a ₁ Sa. 9. 8.
43 farthing.   And he called unto him his disciples, and said
unto them, Verily I say unto you, this poor widow cast ₂ Co. 8. 12.
in more than all they which are casting into the treasury:
44 for they all did cast in of their superfluity ; but she of
her want did cast in all that she had, even all her living.

S. Luke xxi. 1—4.

1 And he looked up, and saw the rich men that were
2 casting their gifts into the treasury.   And he saw a
certain poor widow casting in thither two mites.   And
3 he said, Of a truth I say unto you, This poor widow
4 cast in more than they all : for all these did of their
superfluity cast in unto the gifts : but she of her want did
cast in all the living that she had.

S. Paul, 2 Cor. viii. 12.

*If the readiness be there, it is acceptable according as a
man hath, not according as he hath not.*

2 Cor. ix. 7.

God loveth a cheerful giver.

137. *Of Christ's second coming.*

S. Matthew xxiv. 1—51.

AND Jesus went out from the temple, and was going 1
on his way; and his disciples came to him to shew him
Jn. 2. 20. the buildings of the temple. But he answered and said 2
unto them, See ye not all these things? verily I say
Ps. 79. 1. unto you, There shall not be left here one stone upon
Dan. 8. 11. another, that shall not be thrown down.

And as he sat on the mount of Olives, the disciples 3
came unto him privately, saying, Tell us, when shall
1 Th. 5. 1.. these things be? and what shall be the sign of thy
coming, and of the end of the world? And Jesus an- 4
swered and said unto them, Take heed that no man
Acts 21. 38. lead you astray. For many shall come in my name, 5
Jn. 5. 43. saying, I am the Christ; and shall lead many astray.
And ye shall hear of wars and rumours of wars: see 6
that ye be not troubled: for these things must needs
come to pass; but the end is not yet. For nation shall 7
Is. 19. 2. rise against nation, and kingdom against kingdom: and
there shall be famines and earthquakes in divers places.
Ro. 8. 22. But all these things are the beginning of travail. [T. O. 8

S. Mark xiii. 1—37.

And as he went forth out of the temple, one of his 1
disciples saith unto him, Master, behold, what manner
of stones and what manner of buildings! And Jesus 2
said unto him, Seest thou these great buildings? there
shall not be left here one stone upon another, which
shall not be thrown down.

3   And as he sat on the mount of Olives over against the temple, Peter and James and John and Andrew
4 asked him privately, Tell us, when shall these things be? and what shall be the sign when these things are all
5 about to be accomplished? And Jesus began to say unto them, Take heed that no man lead you astray.
6 Many shall come in my name, saying, I am he; and
7 shall lead many astray. And when ye shall hear of wars and rumours of wars, be not troubled : these things must
8 needs come to pass; but the end is not yet. For nation shall rise against nation, and kingdom against kingdom : there shall be earthquakes in divers places; there shall be famines : these things are the beginning of travail.

[T. O.

8. Luke xxi. 5—36.

5   And as some spake of the temple, how it was
6 adorned with goodly stones and offerings, he said, As for these things which ye behold, the days will come, in which there shall not be left here one stone upon 1 Ki. 9. 7..
7 another, that shall not be thrown down. And they Mic. 3. 12. asked him, saying, Master, when therefore shall these things be? and what shall be the sign when these things
8 are about to come to pass? And he said, Take heed that ye be not led astray : for many shall come in my name, saying, I am he; and, The time is at hand : go
9 ye not after them. And when ye shall hear of wars and tumults, be not terrified : for these things must needs come to pass first; but the end is not immediately.
10   Then said he unto them, Nation shall rise against
11 nation, and kingdom against kingdom : and there shall be great earthquakes, and in divers places famines and pestilences; and there shall be terrors and great signs from heaven.   [T. O.

S. Matthew xxiv.

Then shall they deliver you up unto tribulation, and shall 9
Jn. 16. 2. kill you : and ye shall be hated of all the nations for my
Acts 28.22. name's sake. And then shall many stumble, and shall 10
1 Co. 4. 13. deliver up one another, and shall hate one another.
And many false prophets shall arise, and shall lead 11
2 Pet. 2. 1. many astray. And because iniquity shall be multiplied, 12
Ja. 1. 12. the love of the many shall wax cold. But he that en- 13
Rev. 2. 3. dureth to the end, the same shall be saved. And this 14
gospel of the kingdom shall be preached in the whole
Ro. 10. 18. world for a testimony unto all the nations; and then
Col. 1. 23. shall the end come.
Dan. 9. 27; When therefore ye see the abomination of desolation, 15
— 11. 31; which was spoken of by Daniel the prophet, standing in
— 12. 11. the holy place (let him that readeth understand), then 16
Heb. 11. 7. let them that are in Judæa flee unto the mountains : let 17
Lk. 17. 31. him that is on the housetop not go down to take out the
115 things that are in his house : and let him that is in the 18
field not return back to take his cloke.   [T. O.

S. Mark xiii.

Mt. 10. 17.. But take ye heed to yourselves : for they shall deliver 9
59 you up to councils; and in synagogues shall ye be
beaten; and before governors and kings shall ye stand
for my sake, for a testimony unto them. And the 10
gospel must first be preached unto all the nations. And 11
Mt. 10. 19. when they lead you to judgement, and deliver you up,
Lk. 12. 11.. be not anxious beforehand what ye shall speak : but
97 whatsoever shall be given you in that hour, that speak
1 Co. 2. 13. ye : for it is not ye that speak, but the Holy Ghost.
Mic. 7. 6. And brother shall deliver up brother to death, and the 12

father his child; and children shall rise up against
13 parents, and cause them to be put to death.   And ye
shall be hated of all men for my name's sake: but he
that endureth to the end, the same shall be saved.
14   But when ye see the abomination of desolation
standing where he ought not (let him that readeth understand), then let them that are in Judæa flee unto the
15 mountains: and let him that is on the housetop not go
down, nor enter in, to take any thing out of his house:
16 and let him that is in the field not return back to take
his cloke.   [T. O.

S. Luke xxi.

12 But before all these things, they shall lay their hands
on you, and shall persecute you, delivering you up to
the synagogues and prisons, bringing you before kings
13 and governors for my name's sake.   It shall turn unto you
14 for a testimony.   Settle it therefore in your hearts, not
15 to meditate beforehand how to answer: for I will give
you a mouth and wisdom, which all your adversaries
16 shall not be able to withstand or to gainsay.   But ye   Acts 6. 10.
shall be delivered up even by parents, and brethren, and
kinsfolk, and friends; and some of you shall they cause
17 to be put to death.   And ye shall be hated of all men
18 for my name's sake.   And not a hair of your head shall
19 perish.   In your patience ye shall win your souls.   Is. 26. 3..
20   But when ye see Jerusalem compassed with armies,
21 then know that her desolation is at hand.   Then let
them that are in Judæa flee unto the mountains; and let
them that are in the midst of her depart out; and let
22 not them that are in the country enter therein.   For
these are days of vengeance, that all things which are   Hos. 9. 7.
written may be fulfilled.   [T. O.

S. Matthew xxiv.

But woe unto them that are with child and to them 19
that give suck in those days! And pray ye that your 20
flight be not in the winter, neither on a sabbath: for 21
Dan. 12. 1. then shall be great tribulation, such as hath not been
from the beginning of the world until now, no, nor ever
shall be. And except those days had been shortened, 22
Is. 65. 8.. no flesh would have been saved: but for the elect's sake
Lk. 17.23.. those days shall be shortened. Then if any man shall 23
say unto you, Lo, here is the Christ, or, Here; believe
Deu. 13.1.. it not. For there shall arise false Christs, and false 24
2 Th. 2. 9... prophets, and shall shew great signs and wonders; so as
to lead astray, if possible, even the elect. Behold, I 25
2 Pet. 3. 17. have told you beforehand. If therefore they shall say 26
unto you, Behold, he is in the wilderness; go not forth:
Behold, he is in the inner chambers; believe it not.
Lk. 17. 24. For as the lightning cometh forth from the east, and is 27
seen even unto the west; so shall be the coming of the
Job 39. 30. Son of man. Wheresoever the carcase is, there will the 28
eagles be gathered together.
Ezek. 32. 7. But immediately, after the tribulation of those days, 29
Joel 2. 31. the sun shall be darkened, and the moon shall not give
Is. 13. 10. her light, and the stars shall fall from heaven, and the
— 34. 4. powers of the heavens shall be shaken: and then shall 30
Dan. 7. 13. appear the sign of the Son of man in heaven: and then
Zec. 12. 12. shall all the tribes of the earth mourn, and they shall
Rev. 1. 7. see the Son of man coming on the clouds of heaven
1 Co. 15.52. with power and great glory. And he shall send forth his 31
1 Th. 4. 16. angels with a great sound of a trumpet, and they shall
Deu. 30. 4. gather together his elect from the four winds, from one
end of heaven to the other. [T. O.

S. Mark xiii.

But woe unto them that are with child and . to them 17
that give suck in those days! And pray ye that it be not 18
in the winter. For those days shall be tribulation, such 19
as there hath not been the like from the beginning of
the creation which God created until now, and never
shall be. And except the Lord had shortened the days, 20

no flesh would have been saved: but for the elect's sake,
21 whom he chose, he shortened the days. And then if
any man shall say unto you, Lo, here is the Christ; or,
22 Lo, there; believe it not: for there shall arise false
Christs and false prophets, and shall shew signs and
wonders, that they may lead astray, if possible, the elect.
23 But take ye heed: behold, I have told you all things
beforehand.
24 But in those days, after that tribulation, the sun shall
25 be darkened, and the moon shall not give her light, and
the stars shall be falling from heaven, and the powers
26 that are in the heavens shall be shaken. And then
shall they see the Son of man coming in clouds with
27 great power and glory. And then shall he send forth
the angels, and shall gather together his elect from the
four winds, from the uttermost part of the earth to the
uttermost part of heaven. [T. O.

S. Luke xxi.

23 Woe unto them that are with child and to them that give
suck in those days! for there shall be great distress upon
24 the land, and wrath unto this people. And they shall fall
by the edge of the sword, and shall be led captive into
all the nations: and Jerusalem shall be trodden down   Zech. 12. 3.
of the Gentiles, until the times of the Gentiles be ful-   Gr.
25 filled. And there shall be signs in sun and moon and   Is. 63. 18.
stars; and upon the earth distress of nations, in per-   Dan. 8. 13..
26 plexity for the roaring of the sea and the billows; men
fainting for fear, and for expectation of the things which
are coming on the world: for the powers of the heavens
27 shall be shaken. And then shall they see the Son of
man coming in a cloud with power and great glory.
28 But when these things begin to come to pass, look up,
and lift up your heads; because your redemption draweth
nigh. [T. O.

S. Matthew xxiv.

Now from the fig tree learn her parable : when her 32
branch is now become tender, and putteth forth its leaves,
ye know that the summer is nigh ; even so ye also, when 33
Jas. 5. 9. ye see all these things, know ye that he is nigh, even at
Mt. 16. 28. the doors.   Verily I say unto you, This generation shall 34
not pass away, till all these things be accomplished.
Is. 51. 6. Heaven and earth shall pass away, but my words shall 35
Acts 1. 7. not pass away.   But of that day and hour knoweth no 36
one, not even the angels of heaven, neither the Son, but
2 Pet. 2. 5. the Father only.   And as were the. days of Noah, so 37
shall be the coming of the Son of man.   For as in those 38
Gen.6. 1... days which were before the flood they were eating and
drinking, marrying and giving in marriage, until the day
Gen. 7. 7; that Noah entered into the ark, and they knew not until 39
    21... the flood came, and took them all away ; so shall be the
coming of the Son of man.   Then shall two men be in 40
Lk.17.34.. the field ; one is taken, and one is left: two women shall 41
    115   be grinding at the mill ; one is taken, and one is left.
Watch therefore : for ye know not on what day your 42
Lk.12.39.. Lord cometh.   But know this, that if the master of the 43
    99   house had known in what watch the thief was coming, he
would have watched, and would not have suffered his
house to be broken through.   Therefore be ye also 44
Rev. 3. 3. ready: for in an hour that ye think not the Son of man
Lk. 12.42.. cometh.   Who then is the faithful and wise servant, 45
whom his lord hath set over his household, to give
them their food in due season ?   Blessed is that servant, 46
whom his lord when he cometh shall find so doing.
Lk. 19. 17. Verily I say unto you, that he will set him over all that 47
he hath.   But if that evil servant shall say in his heart, 48
2 Pet. 3. 4.. My lord tarrieth ; and shall begin to beat his fellow- 49
servants, and shall eat and drink with the drunken ; the 50
lord of that servant shall come in a day when he expecteth not, and in an hour when he knoweth not, and 51
shall cut him asunder, and appoint his portion with the
hypocrites : there shall be the weeping and gnashing of
teeth.

S. Mark xiv.

28 Now from the fig tree learn her parable: when her
branch is now become tender, and putteth forth its
29 leaves, ye know that the summer is nigh; even so ye
also, when ye see these things coming to pass, know ye
30 that he is nigh, even at the doors. Verily I say unto
you, This generation shall not pass away, until all these
31 things be accomplished. Heaven and earth shall pass
32 away: but my words shall not pass away. But of that
day or that hour knoweth no one, not even the angels
33 in heaven, neither the Son, but the Father. Take ye
heed, watch and pray: for ye know not when the time
34 is. It is as when a man, sojourning in another country, Mt. 25. 14.
having left his house, and given authority to his servants,   139
to each one his work, commanded also the porter to   ·
35 watch. Watch therefore: for ye know not when the   ·
Lord of the house cometh, whether at even, or at mid- Lk. 12. 38.
36 night, or at cockcrowing, or in the morning; lest coming   99
37 suddenly he find you sleeping. And what I say unto
you I say unto all, Watch.

S. Luke xxi.

29 And he spake to them a parable: Behold the fig
30 tree, and all the trees: when they now shoot forth, ye
see it and know of your own selves that the summer is
31 now nigh. Even so ye also, when ye see these things
coming to pass, know ye that the kingdom of God is
32 nigh. Verily I say unto you, This generation shall not
33 pass away, till all things be accomplished. Heaven and
earth shall pass away: but my words shall not pass
away.
34 But take heed to yourselves, lest haply your hearts
be overcharged with surfeiting, and drunkenness, and 1 Th. 5. 2..
cares of this life, and that day come on you suddenly as
35 a snare: for so shall it come upon all them that dwell Rev. 16. 15.
36 on the face of all the earth. But watch ye at every Is. 24. 17.
season, making supplication, that ye may prevail to
escape all these things that shall come to pass, and to
stand before the Son of man.   Ro. 13. 11.

J. H. G.   14

138. *The ten virgins.*

S. Matthew xxv. 1—13.

THEN shall the kingdom of heaven be likened unto 1
2Cor.11.2. ten virgins, which took their lamps, and went forth to
Eph.5.25.. meet the bridegroom. And five of them were foolish, 2
Rev. 21. 2. and five were wise. For the foolish, when they took 3
Lk. 12. 35. their lamps, took no oil with them : but the wise took 4
oil in their vessels with their lamps. Now while the 5
bridegroom tarried, they all slumbered and slept. But 6
at midnight there is a cry, Behold, the bridegroom!
Amos 4.12. Come ye forth to meet him. Then all those virgins arose, 7
and trimmed their lamps. And the foolish said unto the 8
wise, Give us of your oil; for our lamps are going out.
But the wise answered, saying, Peradventure there will 9
Ps. 49. 7. not be enough for us and you : go ye rather to them that
Is. 55. 1. sell, and buy for yourselves. And while they went away 10
Ps.45.14.. to buy, the bridegroom came ; and they that were ready
Lk. 13. 25. went in with him to the marriage feast : and the door was
103   shut. Afterward come also the other virgins, saying, 11
He. 3. 18.. Lord, Lord, open to us. But he answered and said, 12
Mt. 7. 22.. Verily I say unto you, I know you not. Watch there- 13
Jn. 10. 14. fore, for ye know not the day nor the hour.

139. *The talents.*

S. Matthew xxv. 14—30.

FOR it is as when a man, going into another country, 14
Lk.19.12.. called his own servants, and delivered unto them his
123   goods. And unto one he gave five talents, to another two, 15
Jas. 1. 17. to another one ; to each according to his several ability ;
1 Co. 12.4. and he went on his journey. Straightway he that 16
received the five talents went and traded with them, and
made other five talents. In like manner he also that 17
received the two gained other two. But he that received 18
the one went away and digged in the earth, and hid his
lord's money. Now after a long time the lord of those 19
servants cometh, and maketh a reckoning with them.
And he that received the five talents came and brought 20
other five talents, saying, Lord, thou deliveredst unto me
1 Th.2.19. five talents : lo, I have gained other five talents. His 21
lord said unto him, Well done, good and faithful servant :
Lk. 16. 10. thou hast been faithful over a few things, I will set thee
110

over many things: enter thou into the joy of thy lord. 2Tim.2.12.
22 And he also that received the two talents came and said, He. 12. 2.
Lord, thou deliveredst unto me two talents: lo, I have
23 gained other two talents. His lord said unto him, Well .
done, good and faithful servant; thou hast been faithful
over a few things, I will set thee over many things:
24 enter thou into the joy of thy lord. And he also that
had received the one talent came and said, Lord, I knew
thee that thou art a hard man, reaping where thou didst
not sow, and gathering where thou didst not scatter:
25 and I was afraid, and went away and hid thy talent in Rev. 21.8.
26 the earth: lo, thou hast thine own. But his lord answered and said unto him, Thou wicked and slothful
servant, thou knewest that I reap where I sowed not,
27 and gather where I did not scatter; thou oughtest therefore to have put my money to the bankers, and at my
coming I should have received back mine own with
28 interest. Take ye away therefore the talent from him,
29 and give it unto him that hath the ten talents. For unto
every one that hath shall be given, and he shall have Mt. 13. 12.
abundance: but from him that hath not, even that 50
30 which he hath shall be taken away. And cast ye out the
unprofitable servant into the outer darkness: there shall
be the weeping and gnashing of teeth. Mt. 8. 12.

S. Luke xix. 12—27.

12 *A certain nobleman went into a far country, to receive*
13 *for himself a kingdom, and to return. And he called ten*
servants of his, and gave them ten pounds, and said unto
14 *them, Trade ye herewith till I come. But his citizens*
hated him, and sent an ambassage after him, saying, We
15 *will not that this man reign over us. And it came to pass,*
when he was come back again, having received the kingdom,
that he commanded these servants, unto whom he had given
the money, to be called to him, that he might know what
16 *they had gained by trading. And the first came before*
him, saying, Lord, thy pound hath made ten pounds more.
17 *And he said unto him, Well done, thou good servant:* .
because thou wast found faithful in a very little, have thou
18 *authority over ten cities. And the second came, saying,*
19 *Thy pound, Lord, hath made five pounds. And he said*
20 *unto him also, Be thou also over five cities. · And another*
came, saying, Lord, behold, here is thy pound, which I kept
21 *laid up in a napkin: for I feared thee, &c.*

14—2

140. *The last judgement.*

S. Matthew xxv. 31—46.

Re. 20. 11..   BUT when the Son of man shall come in his glory, 31
Dan. 7. 9.. and all the angels with him, then shall he sit on the
2 Co. 5. 10. throne of his glory: and before him shall be gathered all 32
the nations: and he shall separate them one from
Mt. 13. 49. another, as the shepherd separateth the sheep from the
goats: and he shall set the sheep on his right hand, but 33
the goats on the left. Then shall the King say unto 34
1 Jn. 3. 1. them on his right hand, Come, ye blessed of my Father,
1 Co. 2. 9.. inherit the kingdom prepared for you from the foundation
Is. 58. 7. of the world: for I was an hungred, and ye gave me 35
Ezek. 18. 7. meat: I was thirsty, and ye gave me drink: I was a 36
Lk. 10. 37. stranger, and ye took me in; naked, and ye clothed me:
Job 31. 17, I was sick, and ye visited me: I was in prison, and ye
19, 32. came unto me. Then shall the righteous answer him, 37
saying, Lord, when saw we thee an hungred, and fed
thee? or athirst, and gave thee drink? And when saw 38
we thee a stranger, and took thee in? or naked, and
clothed thee? And when saw we thee sick, or in prison, 39
and came unto thee? And the King shall answer and 40
Heb. 2. 11. say unto them, Verily I say unto you, Inasmuch as ye
— 6. 10. did it unto one of these my brethren, even these least, ye
Pro. 19. 17. did it unto me. Then shall he say also unto them on 41
Mt. 7. 23. the left hand, Depart from me, ye cursed, into the
Jn. 5. 37. eternal fire which is prepared for the devil and his
angels: for I was an hungred, and ye gave me no meat: 42
I was thirsty, and ye gave me no drink: I was a stranger, 43
and ye took me not in; naked, and ye clothed me not;
sick, and in prison, and ye visited me not. Then shall 44
they also answer, saying, Lord, when saw we thee an
hungred, or athirst, or a stranger, or naked, or sick, or in
prison, and did not minister unto thee? Then shall he 45
Acts 9. 4. answer them, saying, Verily I say unto you, Inasmuch
as ye did it not unto one of these least, ye did it not
Dan. 12. 2. unto me. And these shall go away into eternal punish- 46
Jn. 5. 29. ment: but the righteous into eternal life.

141. *Greeks come to Christ. A voice from heaven.*

S. Luke xxi. 37, 38.

AND every day he was teaching in the temple; and 37

every night he went out, and lodged in the mount that is
38 called the mount of Olives.   And all the people came Zec. 11. 4.
early in the morning to him in the temple, to hear him.

S. John xii. 20—36.

20   Now there were certain Greeks among those that 1 Ki. 8. 41..
21 went up to worship at the feast: these therefore came to Acts 17. 4.
Philip, which was of Bethsaida of Galilee, and asked him,
22 saying, Sir, we would see Jesus.   Philip cometh and
telleth Andrew: Andrew cometh, and Philip, and they
23 tell Jesus.   And Jesus answereth them, saying, The
hour is come, that the Son of man should be glorified. Jn. 13. 31.
24 Verily, verily, I say unto you, Except a grain of wheat
fall into the earth and die, it abideth by itself alone; but 1Co.15.36..
25 if it die, it beareth much fruit.   He that loveth his life
loseth it; and he that hateth his life in this world shall Mt. 10. 39.
26 keep it unto life eternal.   If any man serve me, let him   59
follow me; and where I am, there shall also my servant 1 Th. 4. 17.
be: if any man serve me, him will the Father honour.
27 Now is my soul troubled; and what shall I say? Father, Ps. 42. 5;
save me from this hour.   But for this cause came I unto — 6. 3.
28 this hour.   Father, glorify thy name.   There came therefore a voice out of heaven, saying, I have both glorified Mt. 3. 17;
29 it, and will glorify it again.   The multitude therefore, — 17. 5.
that stood by, and heard it, said that it had thundered: 16. 72
30 others said, An angel hath spoken to him.   Jesus answered and said, This voice hath not come for my sake,
31 but for your sakes.   Now is the judgement of this world:
32 now shall the prince of this world be cast out.   And I, Jn. 16. 11.
if I be lifted up from the earth, will draw all men unto Jn. 3. 14;
33 myself.   But this he said, signifying by what manner of — 8. 28.
34 death he should die.   The multitude therefore answered 22. 79
him, We have heard out of the law that the Christ Ps. 110. 4.
abideth for ever: and how sayest thou, The Son of man
35 must be lifted up? who is this Son of man?   Jesus therefore said unto them, Yet a little while is the light among Jn. 9. 5.
you.   Walk while ye have the light, that darkness over- Jer. 13. 16.
take you not: and he that walketh in the darkness Eph. 5. 8.
36 knoweth not whither he goeth.   While ye have the 1 Jn. 2. 11.
light, believe on the light, that ye may become sons of 1 Th. 5. 5.
light.

142. *S. John on the unbelief of the Jews.   Of true faith.*

S. John xii. 36—50.

THESE things spake Jesus, and he departed and hid 36
himself from them.   But though he had done so many 37
signs before them, yet they believed not on him: that 38
the word of Isaiah the prophet might be fulfilled, which
he spake,

Is. 53. 1.   Lord, who hath believed our report?
Ro. 10. 16.   And to whom hath the arm of the Lord been re-
                   vealed?

For this cause they could not believe, for that Isaiah 39
said again,

Is. 6. 9...   He hath blinded their eyes, and he hardened their 40
                   heart;
                   Lest they should see with their eyes, and perceive
                   with their heart,
                   And should turn,
                   And I should heal them.

Is. 6. 1...   These things said Isaiah, because he saw his glory; 41
Jn. 8. 48.   and he spake of him.   Nevertheless even of the rulers 42
              many believed on him; but because of the Pharisees
Jn. 9. 22.   they did not confess it, lest they should be put out of the
   80   synagogue: for they loved the glory of men more than 43
Jn. 5. 44.   the glory of God.
   28
              And Jesus cried and said, He that believeth on me, 44
              believeth not on me, but on him that sent me.   And he 45
Jn. 14. 9.   that beholdeth me beholdeth him that sent me.   I am 46
Jn. 3. 19.   come a light into the world, that whosoever believeth on
   15   me may not abide in the darkness.   And if any man hear 47
Jn. 3. 17;   my sayings, and keep them not, I judge him not: for I
— 8. 15.   came not to judge the world, but to save the world.   He 48
              that rejecteth me, and receiveth not my sayings, hath
De. 18. 19.   one that judgeth him: the word that I spake, the same
              shall judge him in the last day.   For I spake not from 49
Jn. 5. 19.   myself; but the Father which sent me, he hath given
De. 18. 18.   me a commandment, what I should say, and what I should
              speak.   And I know that his commandment is life eternal: 50
              the things therefore which I speak, even as the Father hath
              said unto me, so I speak.

143. *Christ declares his death at hand. The conspiracy.*

S. Matthew xxvi. 1—5.

1 AND it came to pass, when Jesus had finished all
2 these words, he said unto his disciples, Ye know that
   after two days the passover cometh, and the Son of man
3 is delivered up to be crucified. Then were gathered
   together the chief priests, and the elders of the people,
   unto the court of the high priest, who was called Caiaphas; Ps. 2. 2.
4 and they took counsel together that they might take Jesus
5 by subtilty, and kill him. But they said, Not during the
   feast, lest a tumult arise among the people.

S. Mark xiv. 1, 2.

1 Now after two days was the feast of the passover
   and the unleavened bread: and the chief priests and
   the scribes sought how they might take him with subtilty,
2 and kill him: for they said, Not during the feast, lest
   haply there shall be a tumult of the people.

S. Luke xxii. 1, 2.

1 Now the feast of unleavened bread drew nigh, which
2 is called the Passover. And the chief priests and the
   scribes sought how they might put him to death; for
   they feared the people.

144. *Preparation for the passover.*

S. Mark xiv. 12—16.

Ex. 12. 6.   AND on the first day of unleavened bread, when they 12
sacrificed the passover, his disciples say unto him, Where
wilt thou that we go and make ready that thou mayest
eat the passover?   And he sendeth two of his disciples, 13
Mt. 21. 2. and saith unto them, Go into the city, and there shall
126   meet you a man bearing a pitcher of water: follow him;
and wheresoever he shall enter in, say to the goodman 14
of the house, The Master saith, Where is my guest-
chamber, where I shall eat the passover with my disciples?
Acts 1. 13. And he will himself shew you a large upper room fur- 15
nished and ready: and there make ready for us.   And 16
the disciples went forth, and came into the city, and
found as he had said unto them: and they made ready
the passover.

S. Luke xxii. 7—13.

And the day of unleavened bread came, on which 7
the passover must be sacrificed.   And he sent Peter and 8
John, saying, Go and make ready for us the passover,
that we may eat.   And they said unto him, Where wilt 9
thou that we make ready?   And he said unto them, 10
Behold, when ye are entered into the city, there shall
meet you a man bearing a pitcher of water; follow him
into the house whereinto he goeth.   And ye shall say 11
unto the goodman of the house, The Master saith unto
thee, Where is the guest-chamber, where I shall eat the
passover with my disciples?   And he will shew you a 12
large upper room furnished: there make ready.   And 13
they went, and found as he had said unto them: and
they made ready the passover.

S. Matthew xxvi. 17—19.

Now on the first day of unleavened bread the dis- 17
ciples came to Jesus, saying, Where wilt thou that we
make ready for thee to eat the passover?   And he said, 18
Go into the city to such a man, and say unto him, The
Master saith, My time is at hand; I keep the passover 19
at thy house with my disciples.   And the disciples did
as Jesus appointed them; and they made ready the
passover.

145. *Jesus' love. Precedence. The first cup.*

S. John xiii. 1.

1   Now before the feast of the passover, Jesus knowing
that his hour was come that he should depart out of this
world unto the Father, having loved his own which were Eph. 5. 2.
in the world, he loved them unto the end.

S. Mark xiv. 17.

17   And when it was evening he cometh with the twelve.

S. Matthew xxvi. 20.

20   Now when even was come, he was sitting at meat
with the twelve disciples.

S. Luke xxii. 14; 24—30; 15—18.

14   And when the hour was come, he sat down, and the
apostles with him.
＊   ＊   ＊   ＊   ＊

24   And there arose also a contention among them, which Mk. 9. 34.
25 of them is accounted to be greatest.   And he said unto   75
them, The kings of the Gentiles have lordship over them; Mt. 20. 25..
and they that have authority over them are called Bene-   121
26 factors.   But ye shall not be so : but he that is the 1 Pet. 5. 3.
greater among you, let him become as the younger;
27 and he that is chief, as he that doth serve.   For whether
is greater, he that sitteth at meat, or he that serveth? is Lk. 17. 8.
not he that sitteth at meat? but I am in the midst of you Lk. 12. 37.
28 as he that serveth.   But ye are they which have con-
29 tinued with me in my temptations; and I appoint unto Heb. 4. 15.
you a kingdom, even as my Father appointed unto me,
30 that ye may eat and drink at my table in my kingdom; Rev. 19. 9.
and ye shall sit on thrones judging the twelve tribes of Mt. 19. 28.
Israel.   120
＊   ＊   ＊   ＊   ＊

15   And he said unto them, With desire I have desired to
16 eat this passover with you before I suffer: for I say unto
you, I will not eat it, until it be fulfilled in the kingdom 1 Co. 5. 7..
17 of God.   And he received a cup, and when he had given
thanks, he said, Take this, and divide it among your-
18 selves: for I say unto you, I will not drink from henceforth of the fruit of the vine, until the kingdom of God
shall come.

146. *Jesus washes his disciples' feet.*

S. John xiii. 2—20.

Mt. 26. 14.. AND during supper, the devil having already put into 2
  125 the heart of Judas Iscariot, Simon's son, to betray him,
Heb. 2. 8. Jesus, knowing that the Father had given all things into 3
his hands, and that he came forth from God, and goeth
unto God, riseth from supper, and layeth aside his gar- 4
Lk. 12. 37. ments; and he took a towel, and girded himself.   Then 5
  99 he poureth water into the bason, and began to wash the
disciples' feet, and to wipe them with the towel wherewith he was girded. So he cometh to Simon Peter. He 6
saith unto him, Lord, dost thou wash my feet? Jesus 7
answered and said unto him, What I do thou knowest
not now; but thou shalt understand hereafter. Peter 8
saith unto him, Thou shalt never wash my feet. Jesus
Jn. 3. 5. answered him, If I wash thee not, thou hast no part with
1 Co. 6. 11. me. Simon Peter saith unto him, Lord, not my feet 9
only, but also my hands and my head. Jesus saith to 10
2 Pet. 1. 9. him, He that is bathed needeth not save to wash his feet,
Tit. 3. 5. but is clean every whit: and ye are clean, but not all.
Jn. 6. 64. For he knew him that should betray him; therefore said 11
he, Ye are not all clean.
So when he had washed their feet, and taken his 12
garments, and sat down again, he said unto them, Know
ye what I have done to you? Ye call me, Master, and, 13
Lord: and ye say well; for so I am. If I then, the 14
Gal. 6. 2. Lord and the Master, have washed your feet, ye also
1 Pet. 5. 5. ought to wash one another's feet. For I have given you 15
an example, that ye also should do as I have done to
Mt. 10. 24. you. Verily, verily, I say unto you, A servant is not 16
  59 greater than his lord; neither one that is sent greater
Jas. 1. 25. than he that sent him. If ye know these things, blessed 17
Jn. 6. 70... are ye if ye do them. I speak not of you all: I know 18
  64 whom I have chosen: but that the scripture may be ful-
Ps. 41. 9. filled, He that eateth my bread lifted up his heel against
me. From henceforth I tell you before it come to pass, 19
Jn. 14. 29. that, when it is come to pass, ye may believe that I am
  150 he. Verily, verily, I say unto you, He that receiveth 20
Mt. 10. 40. whomsoever I send receiveth me; and he that receiveth
  59 me receiveth him that sent me.

147. *The betrayal foretold. The traitor leaves.*

S. John xiii. 21—35.

21 WHEN Jesus had thus said, he was troubled in the Jn. 12. 27.
spirit, and testified, and said, Verily, verily, I say unto
22 you, that one of you shall betray me. The disciples Ps. 41. 9.
looked one on another, doubting of whom he spake.
23 There was at the table reclining in Jesus' bosom one of Jn. 20. 2;
24 his disciples, whom Jesus loved. Simon Peter therefore — 21.7,20.
beckoneth to him, and saith unto him, Tell us who it is
25 of whom he speaketh. He leaning back, as he was, on
[T. O.

S. Matthew xxvi. 21—25.

21 And as they were eating, he said, Verily I say unto
22 you, that one of you shall betray me. And they were
exceeding sorrowful, and began to say unto him every
23 one, Is it I, Lord? And he answered and said, He that
dipped his hand with me in the dish, the same shall
24 betray me. The Son of man goeth, even as it is written
of him : but woe unto that man through whom the Son Jn. 17. 12.
of man is betrayed ! good were it for that man if he had Mt. 18. 7.
25 not been born. And Judas, which betrayed him, answered and said, Is it I, Rabbi? He saith unto him,
Thou hast said.

S. Mark xiv. 18—21.

18 And as they sat and were eating, Jesus said, Verily I
say unto you, One of you shall betray me, even he that
19 eateth with me. They began to be sorrowful, and to say
20 unto him one by one, Is it I? And he said unto them,
It is one of the twelve, he that dippeth with me in the
21 dish. For the Son of man goeth, even as it is written of
him : but woe unto that man through whom the Son of
man is betrayed ! good were it for that man if he had
not been born.

S. Luke xxii. 21—23.

21 But behold, the hand of him that betrayeth me is
22 with me on the table. For the Son of man indeed
goeth, as it hath been determined : but woe unto that
23 man through whom he is betrayed ! And they began to
question among themselves, which of them it was that
should do this thing.

S. John xiii.

Jesus' breast saith unto him, Lord, who is it? Jesus 26
therefore answereth, He it is, for whom I shall dip the
sop, and give it him. So when he had dipped the sop,
Jn. 6. 71. he taketh and giveth it to Judas, the son of Simon
Lk. 22. 3. Iscariot. And after the sop, then entered Satan into 27
him. Jesus therefore saith unto him, That thou doest,
do quickly. Now no man at the table knew for what 28
Jn. 12. 6. intent he spake this unto him. For some thought, be- 29
cause Judas had the bag, that Jesus said unto him, Buy
what things we have need of for the feast; or, that he
should give something to the poor. He then having 30
1 Th. 5. 5.. received the sop went out straightway : and it was night.
Jn. 12. 23. When therefore he was gone out, Jesus saith, Now 31
1 Pet. 4. 11. is the Son of man glorified, and God is glorified in him ;
Jn. 17. 1... and God shall glorify him in himself, and straightway 32
154 shall he glorify him. Little children, yet a little while 33
Jn. 7. 34; I am with you. Ye shall seek me: and as I said unto
— 8. 21. the Jews, Whither I go, ye cannot come; so now I say
Jn. 15. 12.. unto you. A new commandment I give unto you, that 34
151 ye love one another; even as I have loved you, that ye
1 Jn. 4. 21. also love one another. By this shall all men know that 35
ye are my disciples, if ye have love one to another.

148. *Institution of the Lord's supper.*

S. Paul, 1 Cor xi. 23—25.

For I received of the Lord that which also I delivered 23
unto you, how that the Lord Jesus in the night in which
he was betrayed took bread; and when he had given 24
thanks, he brake it, and said, This is my body, which is
for you : this do in remembrance of me. In like manner 25
also the cup, after supper, saying, This cup is the new
covenant in my blood : this do, as oft as ye drink it, in
remembrance of me.

S. Mark xiv. 22—25.

22 AND as they were eating, he took bread, and when
he had blessed, he brake it, and gave to them, and
23 said, Take ye: this is my body. And he took a cup, Jn. 6. 52...
and when he had given thanks, he gave to them: and 64
24 they all drank of it. And he said unto them, This is my 1Co.10.16.
25 blood of the covenant, which is shed for many. Verily Ex. 24. 8.
I say unto you, I will no more drink of the fruit of the Zec. 9. 11.
vine, until that day when I drink it new in the kingdom Lk. 22. 18.
of God. 145
Acts 10.41.

S. Matthew xxvi. 26—29.

26 And as they were eating, Jesus took bread, and
blessed, and brake it; and he gave to the disciples, and
27 said, Take, eat; this is my body. And he took a cup,
28 and gave thanks, and gave to them, saying, Drink ye all
of it; for this is my blood of the covenant, which is
29 shed for many unto remission of sins. But I say unto
you, I will not drink henceforth of this fruit of the vine,
until that day when I drink it new with you in my
Father's kingdom.

S. Luke xxii. 19, 20.

19 And he took bread, and when he had given thanks,
he brake it, and gave to them, saying, This is my body
which is given for you: this do in remembrance of me.
20 And the cup in like manner after supper, saying, This
cup is the new covenant in my blood, even that which is
poured out for you.

149.   *Peter warned.   Danger foretold.*

S. Luke xxii. 31—38.

Job 1. 12.
— 2. 6.

SIMON, Simon, behold, Satan asked to have you, that 31
he might sift you as wheat: but I made supplication for 32
thee, that thy faith fail not: and do thou, when once
thou hast turned again, stablish thy brethren.   And he 33
said unto him, Lord, with thee I am ready to go both to
Mt. 26. 34. prison and to death.   And he said, I tell thee, Peter, the 34
155   cock shall not crow this day, until thou shalt thrice deny
that thou knowest me.

Mt. 10. 9.
59

And he said unto them, When I sent you forth with- 35
out purse, and wallet, and shoes, lacked ye any thing?
And they said, Nothing.   And he said unto them, But 36
now, he that hath a purse, let him take it, and likewise a
wallet : and he that hath none, let him sell his cloke,
and buy a sword.   For I say unto you, that this which 37
Is. 53. 12. is written must be fulfilled in me, And he was reckoned
with transgressors : for that which concerneth me hath
fulfilment.   And they said, Lord, behold, here are two 38
swords.   And he said unto them, It is enough.

S. John xiii. 36—38.

Simon Peter saith unto him, Lord, whither goest 36
thou?   Jesus answered, Whither I go, thou canst not
Jn. 21. 18. follow me now ; but thou shalt follow afterwards.   Peter 37
183   saith unto him, Lord, why cannot I follow thee even
2 Pet. 1. 14. now? I will lay down my life for thee.   Jesus answereth, 38
Wilt thou lay down thy life for me?   Verily, verily, I
say unto thee, The cock shall not crow, till thou hast
denied me thrice.

150.   *Of hope, faith, prayer.   The Comforter.*

S. John xiv. 1—31.

LET not your heart be troubled: ye believe in God, 1
believe also in me.   In my Father's house are many 2
1 Ki. 8. 13. mansions ; if it were not so, I would have told you ; for
Nu. 10. 33. I go to prepare a place for you.   And if I go and pre- 3
Heb. 6. 20. pare a place for you, I come again, and will receive you
Jn. 12. 26. unto myself ; that where I am, there ye may be also.
1 Th. 4. 17. And whither I go, ye know the way.   Thomas saith 4, 5

unto him, Lord, we know not whither thou goest; how
6 know we the way? Jesus saith unto him, I am the way, Heb. 10. 20.
and the truth, and the life: no one cometh unto the Jn. 1. 17.
7 Father, but by me. If ye had known me, ye would have — 1. 4.
known my Father also: from henceforth ye know him, — 10. 9.
Jn. 8. 19.
8 and have seen him. Philip saith unto him, Lord, shew
9 us the Father, and it sufficeth us. Jesus saith unto him,
Have I been so long time with you, and dost thou not
know me, Philip? he that hath seen me hath seen the Col. i. 15.
10 Father; how sayest thou, Shew us the Father? Believest Heb. 1. 3.
thou not that I am in the Father, and the Father in me?
the words that I say unto you I speak not from myself:
11 but the Father abiding in me doeth his works. Believe Jn. 10. 37..
me that I am in the Father, and the Father in me: or   **89**
12 else believe me for the very works' sake. Verily, verily,
I say unto you, He that believeth on me, the works that
I do shall he do also; and greater works than these Acts 2. 41..
13 shall he do; because I go unto the Father. And what- Mt. 21. 21.
soever ye shall ask in my name, that will I do, that the Mt. 7. 7.
14 Father may be glorified in the Son. If ye shall ask me Jn. 16. 23..
15 anything in my name, that will I do. If ye love me, ye   **153**
16 will keep my commandments. And I will pray the 1 Jn. 5. 3.
Father, and he shall give you another Comforter, that he
17 may be with you for ever, even the Spirit of truth: whom 1 Jn. 5. 7.
the world cannot receive; for it beholdeth him not, 1 Cor. 2. 14.
neither knoweth him: ye know him; for he abideth with
18 you, and shall be in you. I will not leave you desolate: Mt. 28. 20.
19 I come unto you. Yet a little while, and the world
beholdeth me no more; but ye behold me: because
20 I live, ye shall live also. In that day ye shall know that Rom. 5. 10.
21 I am in my Father, and ye in me, and I in you. He Gal. 2. 20.
that hath my commandments, and keepeth them, he it is
that loveth me: and he that loveth me shall be loved of 1 Jn. 2. 3..
my Father, and I will love him, and will manifest myself
22 unto him. Judas (not Iscariot) saith unto him, Lord,
what is come to pass that thou wilt manifest thyself unto
23 us, and not unto the world? Jesus answered and said Jn. 7. 4.
unto him, If a man love me, he will keep my word: and
my Father will love him, and we will come unto him, and Rev. 3. 20.
24 make our abode with him. He that loveth me not 1 Jn. 2. 24.
keepeth not my words: and the word which ye hear is
not mine, but the Father's who sent me.   Jn. 7. 16.
25   These things have I spoken unto you, while yet

S. John xiv.

abiding with you. But the Comforter, even the Holy 26
Jn. 15. 26. Spirit, whom the Father will send in my name, he shall
Jn. 16. 13.. teach you all things, and bring to your remembrance all
152　that I said unto you. Peace I leave with you ; my peace 27
Is. 26. 3. I give unto you : not as the world giveth, give I unto
Phil. 4. 7. you. Let not your heart be troubled, neither let it be
fearful. Ye heard how I said to you, I go away, and I 28
come unto you. If ye loved me, ye would have rejoiced,
Phil. 2. 6. because I go unto the Father : for the Father is greater
Jn. 13. 19. than I. And now I have told you before it come to 29
146　pass, that, when it is come to pass, ye may believe. I 30
Jn. 12. 31 will no more speak much with you, for the prince of the
141　world cometh : and he hath nothing in me ; but that the 31
world may know that I love the Father, and as the
Heb. 5. 8. Father gave me commandment, even so I do. Arise, let
us go hence.

S. Mark xiv. 26 and S. Matthew xxvi. 30.

And when they had sung a hymn, they went out
unto the mount of Olives.

151. *The vine. Christ's commandment. Comfort.*

S. John xv. 1—25.

1 Cor. 3. 9. 　I AM the true vine, and my Father is the husband- 1
Mt. 7. 21. man. Every branch in me that beareth not fruit, he 2
Mal. 3. 3. taketh it away : and every branch that beareth fruit, he
cleanseth it, that it may bear more fruit. Already ye are 3
Jn. 13. 10. clean because of the word which I have spoken unto you.
Abide in me, and I in you. As the branch cannot bear 4
fruit of itself, except it abide in the vine ; so neither can
ye, except ye abide in me. I am the vine, ye are the 5
1 Jn. 2. 6. branches : He that abideth in me, and I in him, the
Eph. 2. 12. same beareth much fruit : for apart from me ye can do
Phil. 4. 13. nothing. If a man abide not in me, he is cast forth as 6
a branch, and is withered ; and they gather them, and
Mt. 7. 19. cast them into the fire, and they are burned. If ye 7
abide in me, and my words abide in you, ask whatsoever
1 Jn. 3. 22. ye will, and it shall be done unto you. Herein is my 8
Phil. 1. 11. Father glorified, that ye bear much fruit ; and so shall ye
be my disciples. Even as the Father hath loved me, I 9
also have loved you : abide ye in my love. If ye keep 10
Jn. 14. 21. my commandments, ye shall abide in my love ; even as

I have kept my Father's commandments, and abide in
11 his love. These things have I spoken unto you, that
my joy may be in you, and that your joy may be ful- Jn. 17. 13.
12 filled. This is my commandment, that ye love one an- I Jn. I. 4.
13 other, even as I have loved you. Greater love hath no Jn. 13. 34.
man than this, that a man lay down his life for his **147**
14 friends. Ye are my friends, if ye do the things which I I Th. 4. 9.
15 command you. No longer do I call you servants; for I Jn. 3. 16.
the servant knoweth not what his lord doeth: but I have Mt. 25. 24.
called you friends; for all things that I heard from my Jas. 2. 23.
16 Father I have made known unto you. Ye did not Ge. 18. 17..
choose me, but I chose you, and appointed you, that ye 2Tim.I.11.
should go and bear fruit, and that your fruit should
abide: that whatsoever ye shall ask of the Father in my Jn. 14. 13.
17 name, he may give it you. These things I command
18 you, that ye may love one another. If the world hateth
you, ye know that it hath hated me before it hated you. Jn. 7. 7.
19 If ye were of the world, the world would love its own: I Jn. 4. 5.
but because ye are not of the world, but I chose you out Jn. 17. 14.
20 of the world, therefore the world hateth you. Remember
the word that I said unto you, A servant is not greater Jn. 13. 16.
than his lord. If they persecuted me, they will also Mt. 10. 24.
persecute you; if they kept my word, they will keep **59**
21 yours also. But all these things will they do unto you Eze. 3. 7.
for my name's sake, because they know not him that sent
22 me. If I had not come and spoken unto them, they had Jn. 9. 41.
not had sin: but now they have no excuse for their sin. Jas. 4. 17.
23, 24 He that hateth me hateth my Father also. If I had not I Jn. 2. 23.
done among them the works which none other did, they Jn. 7. 31.
had not had sin: but now have they both seen and hated
25 both me and my Father. But this cometh to pass, that
the word may be fulfilled that is written in their law, Ps. 35. 19.
They hated me without a cause. — 69. 4.

152. *Office of the Holy Ghost.*

S. John xv. 26—xvi. 15.

26 BUT when the Comforter is come, whom I will send Jn. 14. 26.
unto you from the Father, even the Spirit of truth, which **150**
proceedeth from the Father, he shall bear witness of me: Lk. 24. 49.
27 and ye also bear witness, because ye have been with me
from the beginning.
16 1 These things have I spoken unto you, that ye should
2 not be made to stumble. They shall put you out of the Jn. 9. 22.
— 12. 42.

S. John xvi.

synagogues: yea, the hour cometh, that whosoever
Acts 26.9.. killeth you shall think that he offereth service unto God.
And these things will they do, because they have not 3
1 Cor. 2. 8. known the Father, nor me. But these things have I 4
1 Tim. 1. 13. spoken unto you, that when their hour is come, ye may
Jn. 14. 29. remember them, how that I told you. And these things
I said not unto you from the beginning, because I was
Jn. 7. 33. with you. But now I go unto him that sent me; and 5
none of you asketh me, Whither goest thou? But 6
Jn. 14. 1. because I have spoken these things unto you, sorrow
hath filled your heart. Nevertheless I tell you the truth; 7
Jn. 7. 39. It is expedient for you that I go away: for if I go not
away, the Comforter will not come unto you; but if I
Acts 2. 33. go, I will send him unto you. And he, when he is come, 8
will convict the world in respect of sin, and of righteous-
Acts 2. 37.. ness, and of judgement: of sin, because they believe not 9
Acts 2. 32. on me; of righteousness, because I go to the Father, and 10
Jn. 12. 31. ye behold me no more; of judgement, because the prince 11
Lk. 10. 18. of this world hath been judged. I have yet many things 12
1 Cor. 3. 2. to say unto you, but ye cannot bear them now. How- 13
Jn. 14. 26. beit when he, the Spirit of truth, is come, he shall guide
150 you into all the truth: for he shall not speak from him-
1 Jn. 2. 27. self; but what things soever he shall hear, these shall he
speak: and he shall declare unto you the things that are
to come. He shall glorify me: for he shall take of 14
Mt. 11. 27. mine, and shall declare it unto you. All things whatso- 15
Jn. 13. 3. ever the Father hath are mine: therefore said I, that he
taketh of mine, and shall declare it unto you.

153. *Of Christ's resurrection. Of prayer in his name.*
The disciples declare their belief, and are warned.

S. John xvi. 16—33.

Jn. 7. 33. A LITTLE while, and ye behold me no more; and 16
— 13. 33. again a little while, and ye shall see me. Some of his 17
disciples therefore said one to another, What is this that
he saith unto us, A little while, and ye behold me not;
and again a little while, and ye shall see me: and,
Because I go to the Father? They said therefore, What 18
is this that he saith, A little while? We know not what
he saith. Jesus perceiveth that they were desirous to 19
ask him, and he said unto them, Do ye inquire among

yourselves concerning this, that I said, A little while,
and ye behold me not, and again a little while, and ye
20 shall see me? Verily, verily, I say unto you, that ye
shall weep and lament, but the world shall rejoice: ye   Mt. 9. 15.
shall be sorrowful, but your sorrow shall be turned into Jn. 20. 20.
21 joy. A woman when she is in travail hath sorrow,   Gen. 3. 16.
because her hour is come: but when she is delivered Is. 26. 17.
of the child, she remembereth no more the anguish, for
22 the joy that a man is born into the world. And ye Gen. 4. 1.
therefore now have sorrow: but I will see you again, and
your heart shall rejoice, and your joy no one taketh Is. 66. 14.
23 away from you. And in that day ye shall ask me 1 Pet. 1.8.
nothing. Verily, verily, I say unto you, If ye shall ask Mt. 7. 7.
anything of the Father, he will give it you in my name. Jn. 14. 13.
24 Hitherto have ye asked nothing in my name: ask, and   **150**
ye shall receive, that your joy may be fulfilled.   Mt. 21. 22.
25   These things have I spoken unto you in proverbs:
the hour cometh, when I shall no more speak unto you
26 in proverbs, but shall tell you plainly of the Father. In
that day ye shall ask in my name: and I say not unto
27 you, that I will pray the Father for you; for the Father
himself loveth you, because ye have loved me, and have Jn. 14. 21.
28 believed that I came forth from the Father. I came out Jn. 8. 42.
from the Father, and am come into the world: again, I
29 leave the world, and go unto the Father. His disciples Jn. 13. 3.
say, Lo, now speakest thou plainly, and speakest no
30 proverb. Now know we that thou knowest all things, Jn. 21. 17.
and needest not that any man should ask thee: by this
31 we believe that thou camest forth from God. Jesus Jn. 17. 8.
32 answered them, Do ye now believe? Behold, the hour
cometh, yea, is come, that ye shall be scattered, every Mt. 26. 56.
man to his own, and shall leave me alone: and yet I am
33 not alone, because the Father is with me. These things Jn. 8. 29.
have I spoken unto you, that in me ye may have peace. Is. 26. 3.
In the world ye have tribulation: but be of good cheer;
I have overcome the world.   1 Jn. 5. 4..

154. *Christ's prayer for them and for his church.*

S. John xvii. 1—26.

1   THESE things spake Jesus; and lifting up his eyes to Lk. 18. 13.
heaven, he said, Father, the hour is come; glorify thy
2 Son, that the Son may glorify thee: even as thou gavest Phil. 2. 9..
him authority over all flesh, that whatsoever thou hast Mt. 28. 18.

S. John xvii.

Jn. 6. 37.	given him, to them he should give eternal life. And this 3
1 Jn. 5. 12.	is life eternal, that they should know thee the only true
Jn. 6. 40.	God, and him whom thou didst send, even Jesus Christ.
	I glorified thee on the earth, having accomplished the 4
Jn. 5. 36.	work which thou hast given me to do. And now, O 5
	Father, glorify thou me with thine own self with the
Jn. 1. 1..	glory which I had with thee before the world was. I 6
Jn. 1. 18.	manifested thy name unto the men whom thou gavest me
Jn. 10. 29.	out of the world: thine they were, and thou gavest them
	to me; and they have kept thy word. Now they know 7
	that all things whatsoever thou hast given me are from
Jn. 7. 16.	thee: for the words which thou gavest me I have given 8
	unto them; and they received them, and knew of a truth
Jn. 16. 27.	that I came forth from thee, and they believed that thou
	didst send me. I pray for them: I pray not for the world, 9
Jn. 10. 29.	but for those whom thou hast given me; for they are thine:
— 16. 15.	and all things that are mine are thine, and thine are mine: 10
Jn. 16. 28.	and I am glorified in them. And I am no more in the 11
	world, and these are in the world, and I come to thee.
Ps. 121. 5.	Holy Father, keep them in thy name which thou hast
Jude 1.	given me, that they may be one, even as we are. While 12
	I was with them, I kept them in thy name which thou
Jude 24.	hast given me: and I guarded them, and not one of
2 Th. 2. 3.	them perished, but the son of perdition; that the
Ps. 109. 8.	scripture might be fulfilled. But now I come to thee; 13
— 41. 9.	and these things I speak in the world, that they may
	have my joy fulfilled in themselves. I have given them 14
Jn. 15. 18.	thy word; and the world hated them, because they are
1 Jn. 3. 13.	not of the world, even as I am not of the world. I pray 15
	not that thou shouldest take them from the world, but
1 Jn. 5. 18..	that thou shouldest keep them from the evil one. They 16
	are not of the world, even as I am not of the world.
Eph. 5. 26.	Sanctify them in the truth: thy word is truth. As thou 17, 18
Jn. 20. 21.	didst send me into the world, even so sent I them into
1 Cor. 1. 30.	the world. And for their sakes I sanctify myself, that 19
Heb. 10. 10.	they themselves also may be sanctified in truth. Neither 20
	for these only do I pray, but for them also that believe
Rom. 12. 5.	on me through their word; that they may all be one; 21
Eph. 4. 4.	even as thou, Father, art in me, and I in thee, that they
	also may be in us: that the world may believe that thou
	didst send me. And the glory which thou hast given me 22
	I have given unto them; that they may be one, even as

23 we are one; I in them, and thou in me, that they may
be perfected into one; that the world may know that Col. 3. 14.
thou didst send me, and lovedst them, even as thou
24 lovedst me. Father, that which thou hast given me, I
will that, where I am, they also may be with me; that Jn. 12. 26.
they may behold my glory, which thou hast given me: 1 Th. 4. 17.
for thou lovedst me before the foundation of the world.
25 O righteous Father, the world knew thee not, but I knew Jn. 16. 3.
26 thee; and these knew that thou didst send me; and I Jn. 16.27.
made known unto them thy name, and will make it
known; that the love wherewith thou lovedst me may be
in them, and I in them. Jn. 15. 9.

155. *The disciples and Peter again warned.*

S. John xviii. 1.

WHEN Jesus had spoken these words, he went forth
with his disciples over the brook Kidron. 2 Sa. 15.23.

S. Luke xxii. 39.

And he came out, and went, as his custom was, unto
the mount of Olives; and the disciples also followed him. Zech. 14.4.

S. Mark xiv. 27—31.

27 And Jesus saith unto them, All ye shall be offended: Mt. 11. 6.
for it is written, I will smite the shepherd, and the sheep Zech. 13. 7.
28 shall be scattered abroad. Howbeit, after I am raised up,
29 I will go before you into Galilee. But Peter said unto Mt. 28. 10.
30 him, Although all shall be offended, yet will not I. And Prov.16.18.
Jesus saith unto him, Verily I say unto thee, that thou Jn.13.36...
to-day, even this night, before the cock crow twice, shalt
31 deny me thrice. But he spake exceeding vehemently, If **149**
I must die with thee, I will not deny thee. And in like
manner also said they all.

S. Matthew xxvi. 31—35.

31 Then saith Jesus unto them, All ye shall be offended
in me this night: for it is written, I will smite the
shepherd, and the sheep of the flock shall be scattered
32 abroad. But after I am raised up, I will go before you
33 into Galilee. But Peter answered and said unto him, If
all shall be offended in thee, I will never be offended.
34 Jesus said unto him, Verily I say unto thee, that this
night, before the cock crow, thou shalt deny me thrice.
35 Peter saith unto him, Even if I must die with thee, yet
will I not deny thee. Likewise also said all the disciples.

156. *Gethsemane.*

S. Mark xiv. 32—42.

Gen. 2. 8.   AND they come unto a place which was named Geth- 32
              semane: and he saith unto his disciples, Sit ye here,
Mk. 5. 37. while I pray.   And he taketh with him Peter and James 33
Mt. 17. 1. and John, and began to be greatly amazed, and sore
Ph. 2. 26. troubled.   And he saith unto them, My soul is exceeding 34
  Gr.   sorrowful even unto death: abide ye here, and watch.
            And he went forward a little, and fell on the ground, 35
            and prayed that, if it were possible, the hour might pass
Mk. 10. 27. away from him.   And he said, Abba, Father, all things 36
Mt. 20. 22. are possible unto thee; remove this cup from me: how-
            beit not what I will, but what thou wilt.   And he cometh, 37
            and findeth them sleeping, and saith unto Peter, Simon,
            sleepest thou?   couldest thou not watch one hour?
Rom. 7. 18. Watch and pray, that ye enter not into temptation: the 38
Gal. 5. 17. spirit indeed is willing, but the flesh is weak.   And 39
            again he went away, and prayed, saying the same words.
Mk. 9. 6.   And again he came, and found them sleeping, for their 40
            eyes were very heavy; and they wist not what to answer
            him.   And he cometh the third time, and saith unto 41
            them, Sleep on now, and take your rest: it is enough;
Jn. 13. 1. the hour is come; behold, the Son of man is betrayed
            into the hands of sinners.   Arise, let us be going: 42
            behold, he that betrayeth me is at hand.

S. John xviii. 1.

            When Jesus had spoken these words, he went forth
2 Sa. 15. 23. with his disciples over the brook Kidron, where was a
Gen. 2. 8. garden, into the which he entered, himself and his
            disciples.

S. Matthew xxvi. 36—46.

36 Then cometh Jesus with them unto a place called Gethsemane, and saith unto his disciples, Sit ye here, 37 while I go yonder and pray. And he took with him Peter and the two sons of Zebedee, and began to be 38 sorrowful and sore troubled. Then saith he unto them, My soul is exceeding sorrowful, even unto death : abide 39 ye here, and watch with me. And he went forward a little, and fell on his face, and prayed, saying, O my Father, if it be possible, let this cup pass away from me : 40 nevertheless, not as I will, but as thou wilt. And he cometh unto the disciples, and findeth them sleeping, and saith unto Peter, What, could ye not watch with me 41 one hour? Watch and pray, that ye enter not into temptation : the spirit indeed is willing, but the flesh is 42 weak. Again a second time he went away, and prayed, saying, O my Father, if this cannot pass away, except I 43 drink it, thy will be done. And he came again and 44 found them sleeping, for their eyes were heavy. And he left them again, and went away, and prayed a third time, 45 saying again the same words. Then cometh he to the disciples, and saith unto them, Sleep on now, and take your rest : behold, the hour is at hand, and the Son of 46 man is betrayed unto the hands of sinners. Arise, let us be going : behold he is at hand that betrayeth me.

S. Luke xxii. 40—46.

40 And when he was at the place, he said unto them, 41 Pray that ye enter not into temptation. And he was parted from them about a stone's cast ; and he kneeled Dan. 6. 10. 42 down and prayed, saying, Father, if thou be willing, Acts20.36. remove this cup from me : nevertheless not my will, but — 21. 5. 43 thine, be done. And there appeared unto him an angel Mt. 4. 11. 44 from heaven, strengthening him. And being in an agony he prayed more earnestly : and his sweat became Heb. 5. 7. as it were great drops of blood falling down upon the 45 ground. And when he rose up from his prayer, he came unto the disciples, and found them sleeping for 46 sorrow, and said unto them, Why sleep ye? rise and pray, that ye enter not into temptation.

157. *The betrayal and arrest.*

S. John xviii. 2—11.

Now Judas also, which betrayed him, knew the place: 2
for Jesus oft-times resorted thither with his disciples.
Judas then, having received the band of soldiers, and 3
officers from the chief priests and the Pharisees, cometh
Acts 1. 16. thither with lanterns and torches and weapons. Jesus 4
therefore, knowing all the things that were coming upon
him, went forth, and saith unto them, Whom seek ye?
They answered him, Jesus of Nazareth. Jesus saith 5
unto them, I am he. And Judas also, which betrayed
him, was standing with them. When therefore he said 6
Jn. 7. 45... unto them, I am he, they went backward, and fell to
the ground. Again therefore he asked them, Whom seek 7
ye? And they said, Jesus of Nazareth. Jesus answered, 8
I told you that I am he: if therefore ye seek me, let
these go their way: that the word might be fulfilled 9
Jn. 17. 12. which he spake, Of those whom thou hast given me I
lost not one. Simon Peter therefore having a sword 10
drew it, and struck the high priest's servant, and cut off
his right ear. Now the servant's name was Malchus.
Jesus therefore said unto Peter, Put up the sword into 11
Mt. 20. 22. the sheath: the cup which the Father hath given me,
156   shall I not drink it?

S. Mark xiv. 43—52.

And straightway, while he yet spake, cometh Judas, 43
one of the twelve, and with him a multitude with swords
and staves, from the chief priests and the scribes and
the elders. Now he that betrayed him had given them a 44
token, saying, Whomsoever I shall kiss, that is he; take
him, and lead him away safely. And when he was come, 45
straightway he came to him, and saith, Rabbi; and
2 Sa. 20. 9. kissed him. And they laid hands on him, and took 46
him. But a certain one of them that stood by drew his 47
sword, and smote the servant of the high priest, and
struck off his ear. And Jesus answered and said unto 48
them, Are ye come out, as against a robber, with swords
and staves to seize me? I was daily with you in the 49
temple teaching, and ye took me not: but this is done
that the scriptures might be fulfilled. And they all left 50
him, and fled.

And a certain young man followed with him, having 51

a linen cloth cast about him, over his naked body: and
52 they lay hold on him; but he left the linen cloth, and
fled naked.

S. Matthew xxvi. 47—56.

47   And while he yet spake, lo, Judas, one of the
twelve, came, and with him a great multitude with swords
and staves, from the chief priests and elders of the
48 people. Now he that betrayed him gave them a sign,
saying, Whomsoever I shall kiss, that is he: take him.
49 And straightway he came to Jesus, and said, Hail,
50 Rabbi; and kissed him. And Jesus said unto him,
Friend, do that for which thou art come. Then they Mt. 22. 12.
51 came and laid hands on Jesus, and took him. And
behold, one of them that were with Jesus stretched out
his hand, and drew his sword, and smote the servant of
52 the high priest, and struck off his ear. Then saith
Jesus unto him, Put up again thy sword into its place:
for all they that take the sword shall perish with the Rev. 13. 10.
53 sword. Or thinkest thou that I cannot beseech my
Father, and he shall even now send me more than twelve 2 Ki. 6. 17.
54 legions of angels? How then should the scriptures be
55 fulfilled, that thus it must be? In that hour said Jesus
to the multitudes, Are ye come out as against a robber
with swords and staves to seize me? I sat daily in Jn. 7. 44...
56 the temple teaching, and ye took me not. But all this   77
is come to pass, that the scriptures of the prophets might
be fulfilled. Then all the disciples left him, and fled.   Jn. 16. 32.

S. Luke xxii. 47—53.

47   While he yet spake, behold, a multitude, and he that
was called Judas, one of the twelve, went before them;
48 and he drew near unto Jesus to kiss him. But Jesus
said unto him, Judas, betrayest thou the Son of man
49 with a kiss? And when they that were about him saw
what would follow, they said, Lord, shall we smite with Lk. 22. 35.
50 the sword? And a certain one of them smote the
servant of the high priest, and struck off his right ear.
51 But Jesus answered and said, Suffer ye thus far. And
52 he touched his ear and healed him. And Jesus said
unto the chief priests, and captains of the temple, and Acts 5. 24.
elders, which were come against him, Are ye come out,
53 as against a robber, with swords and staves? When I
was daily with you in the temple, ye stretched not forth
your hands against me: but this is your hour, and the
power of darkness.

158. *Jesus before Annas.*

S. John xviii. 12—14 ; 19—24.

So the band and the chief captain, and the officers of 12
the Jews, seized Jesus and bound him, and led him to
Lk. 3. 2. Annas first ; for he was father in law to Caiaphas, which 13
Acts 4. 6. was high priest that year.   Now Caiaphas was he which 14
Jn.11.49... gave counsel to the Jews, that it was expedient that one
112 man should die for the people.

*   *   *   *   *

The high priest therefore asked Jesus of his disciples, 19
and of his teaching.   Jesus answered him, I have spoken 20
Lk. 4. 15. openly to the world; I ever taught in synagogues, and
Jn. 7. 28. in the temple, where all the Jews come together ; and in
Jn. 8. 26. secret spake I nothing.   Why askest thou me? ask them 21
that have heard me, what I spake unto them : behold,
these know the things which I said.   And when he had 22
Acts 23. 2. said this, one of the officers standing by struck Jesus
with his hand, saying, Answerest thou the high priest so ? 23
Jesus answered him, If I have spoken evil, bear witness
of the evil : but if well, why smitest thou me?   Annas 24
therefore sent him bound unto Caiaphas the high priest.

S. Luke xxii. 54; 63—65.

54   And they seized him, and led him away, and brought him into the high priest's house.

           *   *   *   *   *

63   And the men that held Jesus mocked him, and beat
64 him. And they blindfolded him, and asked him, saying,
65 Prophesy: who is he that struck thee? And many other Is. 53. 7.
things spake they against him, reviling him.   1 Pet.2.23.

S. Matthew xxvi. 57.

57   And they that had taken Jesus led him away to the house of Caiaphas the high priest, where the scribes and the elders were gathered together.

S. Mark xiv. 53.

53   And they led Jesus away to the high priest: and there come together with him all the chief priests and the elders and the scribes.

159. *Peter thrice denies him.*

S. John xviii. 15—18; 25—27.

AND Simon Peter followed Jesus, and so did another 15

Mk. 1. 20. disciple. Now that disciple was known unto the high
priest, and entered in with Jesus into the court of the
high priest; but Peter was standing at the door without. 16
So the other disciple, which was known unto the high

Acts 12.13. priest, went out and spake unto her that kept the door,
and brought in Peter. The maid therefore that kept the 17
door saith unto Peter, Art thou also one of this man's
disciples? He saith, I am not. Now the servants and 18
the officers were standing there, having made a fire of
coals; for it was cold; and they were warming themselves: and Peter also was with them, standing and
warming himself.

*   *   *   *   *

Now Simon Peter was standing and warming him- 25
self. They said therefore unto him, Art thou also one

Mt.10. 32.. of his disciples? He denied, and said, I am not. One 26
of the servants of the high priest, being a kinsman of
him whose ear Peter cut off, saith, Did not I see thee in
the garden with him? Peter therefore denied again: and 27
straightway the cock crew.

S. Mark xiv. 54; 66—72.

And Peter had followed him afar off, even within, 54
into the court of the high priest; and he was sitting
with the officers, and warming himself in the light of
the fire.

*   *   *   *   *

And as Peter was beneath in the court, there cometh 66
one of the maids of the high priest; and seeing Peter 67
warming himself, she looked upon him, and saith, Thou
also wast with the Nazarene, even Jesus. But he denied, 68
saying, I neither know, nor understand what thou sayest:
and he went out into the porch; and the cock crew.
And the maid saw him, and began again to say to them 69
that stood by, This is one of them. But he again denied 70
it. And after a little while again they they that stood
by said to Peter, Of a truth thou art one of them; for
thou art a Galilæan. But he began to curse, and to 71
swear, I know not this man of whom ye speak. And 72
straightway the second time the cock crew. And Peter

called to mind the word, how that Jesus said unto him,
Before the cock crow twice, thou shalt deny me thrice.
And when he thought thereon, he wept.

S. Matthew xxvi. 58; 69—75.

58   But Peter followed him afar off, unto the court of the
high priest, and entered in, and sat with the officers, to
see the end.

     *   *   *   *   *

69   Now Peter was sitting without in the court: and a
maid came unto him, saying, Thou also wast with Jesus
70 the Galilæan. But he denied before them all, saying, I   Jn. 13. 38.
71 know not what thou sayest. And when he was gone out   **149**
into the porch, another maid saw him, and saith unto   Mt. 26. 34.
them that were there, This man also was with Jesus the   **155**
72 Nazarene. And again he denied with an oath, I know
73 not the man. And after a little while they that stood by
came and said to Peter, Of a truth thou also art one of
74 them; for thy speech bewrayeth thee. Then began he   Jud. 12. 6.
to curse and to swear, I know not the man. And
75 straightway the cock crew. And Peter remembered the
word which Jesus had said, Before the cock crow, thou
shalt deny me thrice. And he went out, and wept
bitterly.

S. Luke xxii. 54—62.

54, 55   But Peter followed afar off. And when they had
kindled a fire in the midst of the court, and had sat
56 down together, Peter sat in the midst of them. And a
certain maid seeing him as he sat in the light of the fire,
and looking stedfastly upon him, said, This man also
57 was with him. But he denied, saying, Woman, I know
58 him not. And after a little while another saw him, and
said, Thou also art one of them. But Peter said, Man,
59 I am not. And after the space of about one hour
another confidently affirmed, saying, Of a truth this man
60 also was with him: for he is a Galilæan. But Peter
said, Man, I know not what thou sayest. And im-
61 mediately, while he yet spake, the cock crew. And the
Lord turned, and looked upon Peter. And Peter remembered the word of the Lord, how that he said unto
him, Before the cock crow this day, thou shalt deny   Jn. 21. 17.
62 me thrice. And he went out, and wept bitterly.

160. *Jesus before the Sanhedrin.*

S. Mark xiv. 55—65.

1 Ki. 21. 10.   Now the chief priests and the whole council sought 55
witness against Jesus to put him to death; and found it
Ps. 35. 11. not. For many bare false witness against him, and their 56
witness agreed not together. And there stood up certain, 57
and bare false witness against him, saying, We heard 58
Jn. 2. 19. him say, I will destroy this temple that is made with
21   hands, and in three days I will build another made
without hands. And not even so did their witness agree 59
together. And the high priest stood up in the midst, 60
and asked Jesus, saying, Answerest thou nothing? what
Ps. 39. 9. is it which these witness against thee? But he held his 61
Is. 53. 7. peace, and answered nothing. Again the high priest
asked him, and saith unto him, Art thou the Christ, the
Dan. 7. 13. Son of the Blessed? And Jesus said, I am : and ye shall 62
Ps. 110. 1. see the Son of man sitting at the right hand of power, and
1 Th. 4. 16. coming with the clouds of heaven. And the high priest 63
2 Ki. 19. 1. rent his clothes, and saith, what further need have we
Acts 14. 14. of witnesses? Ye have heard the blasphemy : what think 64
ye? And they all condemned him to be worthy of
Is. 50. 6. death. And some began to spit on him, and to cover 65
his face, and to buffet him, and to say unto him, Prophesy: and the officers received him with blows of
their hands.

S. Matthew xxvi. 59—68.

Now the chief priests and the whole council sought 59
false witness against Jesus, that they might put him to
death ; and they found it not, though many false wit- 60
nesses came. But afterward came two, and said, This 61
man said, I am able to destroy the temple of God, and

62 to build it in three days. And the high priest stood up,
and said unto him, Answerest thou nothing? what is it
63 which these witness against thee? But Jesus held his
peace. And the high priest said unto him, I adjure thee
by the living God, that thou tell us whether thou be the Lev. 5. 1.
64 Christ, the Son of God. Jesus saith unto him, Thou Heb. 7. 16.
hast said: nevertheless I say unto you, Henceforth ye
shall see the Son of man sitting at the right hand of
65 power, and coming on the clouds of heaven. Then the
high priest rent his garments, saying, He hath spoken
blasphemy: what further need have we of witnesses?
66 behold, now ye have heard the blasphemy: what think
ye? They answered and said, He is worthy of death.
67 Then did they spit in his face and buffet him: and some
68 smote him with the palms of their hands, saying, Prophesy unto us, thou Christ: who is he that struck thee?

S. Luke xxii. 66—71.

66   And as soon as it was day, the assembly of the elders
of the people was gathered together, both chief priests
and scribes; and they led him away into their council,
67 saying, If thou art the Christ, tell us. But he said unto
68 them, If I tell you, ye will not believe: and if I ask you,
69 ye will not answer. But from henceforth shall the Son
of man be seated at the right hand of the power of God.
70 And they all said, Art thou then the Son of God? And
71 he said unto them, Ye say that I am. And they said,
What further need have we of witness? for we ourselves
have heard from his own mouth.

161. *The suicide of Judas.*

S. Matthew xxvii. 3—10.

THEN Judas, which betrayed him, when he saw that 3
he was condemned, repented himself, and brought back
the thirty pieces of silver to the chief priests and elders,
saying, I have sinned in that I betrayed innocent blood. 4
2 Ki. 10. 9. But they said, What is that to us? see thou to it.   And 5
he cast down the pieces of silver into the sanctuary, and
2Sa.17.23. departed; and he went away and hanged himself.   And 6
1 Sa. 31. 4. the chief priests took the pieces of silver, and said, It
is not lawful to put them into the treasury, since it is
Deu.23.18. the price of blood.   And they took counsel, and bought 7
with them the potter's field, to bury strangers in.   Where- 8
fore that field was called, The field of blood, unto this
day.   Then was fulfilled that which was spoken by 9
Zec. 11.12. Jeremiah the prophet, saying, And they took the thirty
pieces of silver, the price of him that was priced, whom
certain of the children of Israel did price; and they gave 10
them for the potter's field, as the Lord appointed me.

S. Luke or S. Peter, Acts i. 18, 19.

Now this man obtained a field with the reward of his 18
iniquity; and falling headlong, he burst asunder in the
midst, and all his bowels gushed out.   And it became 19
known to all the dwellers in Jerusalem, insomuch that
in their language that field was called Akeldama, that is,
The field of blood.

Suicide of Saul.

1 Sam. xxxi. 1—6.

1   Now the Philistines fought against Israel: and the men of Israel fled from before the Philistines, and fell 2 down slain in mount Gilboa.   And the Philistines followed hard upon Saul and upon his sons; and the Philistines slew Jonathan, and Abinadab, and Malchi-shua, the sons 3 of Saul.   And the battle went sore against Saul, and the archers overtook him; and he was greatly distressed by 4 reason of the archers.   Then said Saul to his armourbearer, Draw thy sword, and thrust me through therewith; lest these uncircumcised come and thrust me through, and abuse me.   But his armourbearer would not; for he was sore afraid.   Therefore Saul took his sword, and fell upon 5 it.   And when his armourbearer saw that Saul was dead, 6 he likewise fell upon his sword, and died with him.   So Saul died, and his three sons, and his armourbearer, and all his men, that same day together.

Suicide of Ahithophel.

2 Sam. xvii. 14; 23.

14   And Absalom and all the men of Israel said, The counsel of Hushai the Archite is better than the counsel of Ahithophel.   For the LORD had ordained to defeat the good counsel of Ahithophel, to the intent that the LORD might bring evil upon Absalom.

*   *   *   *   *

23   And when Ahithophel saw that his counsel was not followed, he saddled his ass, and arose, and gat him home, unto his city, and set his house in order, and hanged himself; and he died, and was buried in the sepulchre of his father.

J. H. G.   16

162. *Jesus before Pilate.*

S. John xviii. 28—38.

THEY lead Jesus therefore from Caiaphas into the 28
Acts 10.28. palace: and it was early; and they themselves entered
— 12. 4. not into the palace, that they might not be defiled, but
might eat the passover. Pilate therefore went out unto 29
Acts 25.16. them, and saith, What accusation bring ye against this
man? They answered and said unto him, If this man 30
were not an evil-doer, we should not have delivered him
up unto thee. Pilate therefore said unto them, Take 31
Acts 24. 6. him yourselves, and judge him according to your law.
The Jews said unto him, It is not lawful for us to put
Mt. 20. 19. any man to death: that the word of Jesus might be 32
121 fulfilled, which he spake, signifying by what manner of
death he should die.
Pilate therefore entered again into the palace, and 33
called Jesus, and said unto him, Art thou the King of the
Jews? Jesus answered, Sayest thou this of thyself, or did 34
others tell it thee concerning me? Pilate answered, 35
Am I a Jew? Thine own nation and the chief priests
delivered thee unto me: what hast thou done? Jesus 36
Col. 1. 13.. answered, My kingdom is not of this world: if my
Rev.11.15. kingdom were of this world, then would my servants
fight, that I should not be delivered to the Jews: but
now is my kingdom not from hence. Pilate therefore 37
said unto him, Art thou a king then? Jesus answered,
Thou sayest that I am a king. To this end have I been
1 Ti. 6. 13. born, and to this end am I come into the world, that I
1 Jn. 4. 6. should bear witness unto the truth. Every one that is
of the truth heareth my voice. Pilate saith unto him, 38
What is truth?

S. Matthew xxvii. 1, 2; 11—14.

1 Now when morning was come, all the chief priests
and the elders of the people took counsel against
2 Jesus to put him to death: and they bound him, and
led him away, and delivered him up to Pilate the
governor.

＊   ＊   ＊   ＊   ＊

11 Now Jesus stood before the governor: and the
governor asked him, saying, Art thou the King of the
12 Jews? And Jesus said unto him, Thou sayest. And
when he was accused by the chief priests and elders, he
13 answered nothing.   Then saith Pilate unto him, Hearest Is. 53. 7.
thou not how many things they witness against thee?
14 And he gave him no answer, not even to one word:
insomuch that the governor marvelled greatly.

S. Mark xv. 1—5.

1 And straightway in the morning the chief priests
with the elders and scribes, and the whole council, held
a consultation, and bound Jesus, and carried him away,
2 and delivered him up to Pilate.   And Pilate asked him,
Art thou the King of the Jews?   And he answering
3 saith unto him, Thou sayest.   And the chief priests
4 accused him of many things.   And Pilate again asked
him, saying, Answerest thou nothing? behold how many
5 things they accuse thee of.   But Jesus no more answered
anything; insomuch that Pilate marvelled.

S. Luke xxiii. 1—4.

1 And the whole company of them rose up, and brought
2 him before Pilate.   And they began to accuse him, saying,
We found this man perverting our nation, and forbidding Mt. 22. 21.
to give tribute to Cæsar, and saying that he himself is   **131**
3 Christ a king.   And Pilate asked him, saying, Art thou
the King of the Jews?   And he answered him and said,
4 Thou sayest.   And Pilate said unto the chief priests and
the multitudes, I find no fault in this man.

163. *Jesus before Herod.*

S. Luke xxiii. 5—12.

BUT they were the more urgent, saying, He stirreth 5
up the people, teaching throughout all Judæa, and beginning from Galilee even unto this place. But when 6
Pilate heard it, he asked whether the man were a Gali-
Lk. 3. 1. læan. And when he knew that he was of Herod's 7
jurisdiction, he sent him unto Herod, who himself also
was at Jerusalem in these days.

Now when Herod saw Jesus, he was exceeding glad: 8
Lk. 9. 9. for he was of a long time desirous to see him, because
Mk. 6. 20. he had heard concerning him; and he hoped to see
Jn. 4. 48. some miracle done by him. And he questioned him in 9
many words; but he answered him nothing. And the 10
chief priests and the scribes stood, vehemently accusing
Acts 4. 27. him. And Herod with his soldiers set him at nought, 11
and mocked him, and arraying him in gorgeous apparel
sent him back to Pilate. And Herod and Pilate became 12
friends with each other that very day: for before they
were at enmity between themselves.

164. *Barabbas preferred. Jesus condemned.*

S. Matthew xxvii. 15—26.

Now at the feast the governor was wont to release 15
unto the multitude one prisoner, whom they would. And 16
they had then a notable prisoner, called Barabbas.
When therefore they were gathered together, Pilate said 17
Jos. 24. 15. unto them, Whom will ye that I release unto you?
Barabbas, or Jesus which is called Christ? For he knew 18
that for envy they had delivered him up. And while he 19
was sitting on the judgement-seat, his wife sent unto
him, saying, Have thou nothing to do with that righteous
man: for I have suffered many things this day in a
dream because of him. Now the chief priests and the 20
elders persuaded the multitudes that they should ask for
Barabbas, and destroy Jesus. But the governor answered 21
and said unto them, Whether of the twain will ye that I
release unto you? And they said, Barabbas.   [T. O.

S. Luke xxiii. 13—25.

13 And Pilate called together the chief priests and the
14 rulers and the people, and said unto them, Ye brought
  unto me this man, as one that perverteth the people:
  and behold, I, having examined him before you, found
  no fault in this man touching those things whereof ye
15 accuse him: no, nor yet Herod: for he sent him back
  unto us; and behold, nothing worthy of death hath
16 been done by him.   I will therefore chastise him, and
18 release him.   But they cried out altogether, saying,
19 Away with this man, and release unto us Barabbas: one
  who for a certain insurrection made in the city, and for
  murder, was cast into prison.   [T. O.

S. Mark xv. 6—15.

6 Now at the feast he used to release unto them one
7 prisoner, whom they asked of him.   And there was one
  called Barabbas, lying bound with them that had made
  insurrection, men who in the insurrection had committed
8 murder.   And the multitude went up and began to ask
9 him to do as he was wont to do unto them.   And Pilate
  answered them, saying, Will ye that I release unto you
10 the King of the Jews?   For he perceived that for envy
11 the chief priests had delivered him up.   But the chief
  priests stirred up the multitude, that he should rather
  release Barabbas unto them.   [T. O.

S. John xviii. 38—40.

38 And when he had said this, he went out again unto
  the Jews, and saith unto them, I find no crime in him.
39 But ye have a custom, that I should release unto you one
  at the passover: will ye therefore that I release unto you
  the King of the Jews? They cried out therefore again,
40 saying, Not this man, but Barabbas.   Now Barabbas was
  a robber.

S. Matthew xxvii.

Pilate saith unto them, What then shall I do unto 22 Jesus which is called Christ? They all say, Let him be crucified. And he said, Why, what evil hath he done? 23
Is. 5. 7.   But they cried out exceedingly, saying, Let him be cruci-fied. So when Pilate saw that he prevailed nothing, but 24 rather that a tumult was arising, he took water, and
Deu. 21.6.. washed his hands before the multitude, saying, I am in-nocent of the blood of this righteous man: see ye to it. 25
Deu. 19.10. And all the people answered and said, His blood be
Acts 5. 28. on us, and on our children. Then released he unto 26 them Barabbas: but Jesus he scourged and delivered to be crucified.

S. Luke xxiii.

Acts 3. 13.   And Pilate spake unto them again, desiring to release 20 Jesus; but they shouted, saying, Crucify, crucify him. 21 And he said unto them the third time, Why, what evil 22 hath this man done? I have found no cause of death in him: I will therefore chastise him and release him. But they were instant with loud voices, asking that he 23 might be crucified. And their voices prevailed. And 24 Pilate gave sentence that what they asked for should be done. And he released him that for insurrection and 25
Acts 3. 14. murder had been cast into prison, whom they asked for; but Jesus he delivered up to their will.

S. Mark xv.

And Pilate again answered and said unto them, 12 What then shall I do unto him whom ye call the King of the Jews? And they cried out again, Crucify him. 13 And Pilate said unto them, Why, what evil hath he 14 done? But they cried out exceedingly, Crucify him. And Pilate, wishing to content the multitude, released 15 unto them Barabbas, and delivered Jesus, when he had scourged him, to be crucified.

S. Peter, Acts ii. 22, 23.

22 *Ye men of Israel, hear these words : Jesus of Nazareth,*
a man approved of God unto you by mighty works and
wonders and signs, which God did by him in the midst of
23 *you, even as ye yourselves know ; him, being delivered up*
by the determinate counsel and foreknowledge of God, ye by
the hand of lawless men did crucify and slay.

Acts iii. 13—15.

13 *The God of Abraham, and of Isaac, and of Jacob, the*
God of our fathers, hath glorified his Servant Jesus ; whom
ye delivered up, and denied before the face of Pilate, when
14 *he had determined to release him. But ye denied the Holy*
and Righteous One, and asked for a murderer to be granted
15 *unto you, and killed the Prince of life.*

Acts v. 27, 28.

27, 28 *And the high priest asked them, saying, We straitly*
charged you not to teach in this name : and behold, ye have
filled Jerusalem with your teaching, and intend to bring
this man's blood upon us.

165. *Jesus is scourged, mocked, sentenced.*

S. John xix. 1—16.

THEN Pilate therefore took Jesus, and scourged him. 1
And the soldiers plaited a crown of thorns, and put it 2
on his head, and arrayed him in a purple garment;
and they came unto him, and said, Hail, King of the 3
Jews! And they struck him with their hands. And 4
Pilate went out again, and saith unto them, Behold, I
bring him out to you, that ye may know that I find no
crime in him. Jesus therefore came out, wearing the 5
crown of thorns and the purple garment. And Pilate
saith unto them, Behold, the man! When therefore the 6
chief priests and the officers saw him, they cried out,
saying, Crucify him, crucify him. Pilate saith unto
them, Take him yourselves, and crucify him : for I find
no crime in him. The Jews answered him, We have a 7
law, and by that law he ought to die, because he made
himself the Son of God. When Pilate therefore heard 8
this saying, he was the more afraid ; and he entered into 9
the palace again, and saith unto Jesus, Whence art thou?
But Jesus gave him no answer. Pilate therefore saith 10
unto him, Speakest thou not unto me? knowest thou
not that I have power to release thee, and have power to
crucify thee? Jesus answered him, Thou wouldest have 11
no power against me, except it were given thee from
above : therefore he that delivered me unto thee hath
greater sin. Upon this Pilate sought to release him : 12
but the Jews cried out, saying, If thou release this man,
thou art not Cæsar's friend : every one that maketh himself a king speaketh against Cæsar. When Pilate there- 13
fore heard these words, he brought Jesus out, and sat
down on the judgement-seat at a place called The Pave-
ment, but in Hebrew, Gabbatha. Now it was the 14
Preparation of the passover : it was about the sixth hour.
And he saith unto the Jews, Behold, your King! They 15
therefore cried out, Away with him, away with him,
crucify him. Pilate saith unto them, Shall I crucify your
King? The chief priests answered, We have no king
but Cæsar. Then therefore he delivered him unto them 16
to be crucified.

163

Jn. 18. 31.

Lev. 24. 16.

Jn. 7. 30.

Acts 3. 13.

S. Matthew xxvii. 27—81.

27   Then the soldiers of the governor took Jesus into the palace, and gathered unto him the whole band.
28 And they stripped him, and put on him a scarlet robe.
29 And they plaited a crown of thorns and put it upon his head, and a reed in his right hand; and they kneeled down before him, and mocked him, saying, Hail, King
30 of the Jews! And they spat upon him, and took the Is. 50. 6.
31 reed and smote him on the head. And when they had mocked him, they took off from him the robe, and put on him his garments, and led him away to crucify him.

S. Mark xv. 16—20.

16   And the soldiers led him away within the court, which is the Prætorium; and they call together the whole band.
17 And they clothe him with purple, and plaiting a crown
18 of thorns, they put it on him; and they began to salute
19 him, Hail, King of the Jews! And they smote his head with a reed, and did spit upon him, and bowing their
20 knees worshipped him. And when they had mocked him, they took off from him the purple, and put on him his garments. And they led him out to crucify him.

166. *Jesus is led to Calvary.*

S. Luke xxiii. 26—32.

AND when they led him away, they laid hold upon 26 one Simon of Cyrene, coming from the country, and laid on him the cross, to bear it after Jesus.

And there followed him a great multitude of the 27 people, and of women who bewailed and lamented him. But Jesus turning unto them said, Daughters of Jerusalem, 28 weep not for me, but weep for yourselves, and for your children. For behold, the days are coming, in which 29 they shall say, Blessed are the barren, and the wombs that never bare, and the breasts that never gave suck.

Hos. 10. 8. Then shall they begin to say to the mountains, Fall on 30
Rev. 6. 16. us; and to the hills, Cover us. For if they do these 31
Eze. 20. 47. things in the green tree, what shall be done in the dry?
1 Pet. 4. 18.   And there were also two others, malefactors, led with 32 him to be put to death.

S. Mark xv. 21—23.

Mt. 5. 41.   And they compel one passing by, Simon of Cyrene, 21
Gr.   coming from the country, the father of Alexander and Rufus, to go with them, that he might bear his cross.
Nu. 15. 36. And they bring him unto the place Golgotha, which is, 22
He. 13. 12. being interpreted, The place of a skull. And they 23 offered him wine mingled with myrrh: but he received it not.

S. Matthew xxvii. 32—34.

And as they came out, they found a man of Cyrene, 32 Simon by name: him they compelled to go with them, that he might bear his cross. And when they were come 33 unto a place called Golgotha, that is to say, The place of a skull, they gave him wine to drink mingled with gall: 34 and when he had tasted it, he would not drink.

S. John xix. 17.

They took Jesus therefore: and he went out, bearing 17
Mt. 16. 24. the cross for himself, unto the place called The place of a skull, which is called in Hebrew Golgotha:

167. *He is crucified.*

S. John xix. 18—25.

18 WHERE they crucified him, and with him two others, Gal. 3. 13.
19 on either side one, and Jesus in the midst. And Pilate Ps. 22. 16.
wrote a title also, and put it on the cross. And there
was written, JESUS OF NAZARETH, THE KING OF THE
20 JEWS. This title therefore read many of the Jews:
for the place where Jesus was crucified was nigh to the
city: and it was written in Hebrew, and in Latin, and
21 in Greek. The chief priests of the Jews therefore said
to Pilate, Write not, The King of the Jews; but, that he
22 said, I am King of the Jews. Pilate answered, What I
have written I have written.

23   The soldiers therefore, when they had crucified Jesus,
took his garments, and made four parts, to every soldier
a part; and also the coat: now the coat was without
24 seam, woven from the top throughout. They said therefore one to another, Let us not rend it, but cast lots for
it, whose it shall be: that the scripture might be fulfilled,
which saith,

They parted my garments among them, Ps. 22. 18.
And upon my vesture did they cast lots.
25 These things therefore the soldiers did.

S. Mark xv. 24—27.

24   And they crucify him, and part his garments among
them, casting lots upon them, what each should take.
25, 26 And it was the third hour, and they crucified him. And
the superscription of his accusation was written over,
27 THE KING OF THE JEWS. And with him they crucify two Is. 53. 9.
robbers; one on his right hand, and one on his left.

S. Matthew xxvii. 35—38.

35   And when they had crucified him, they parted his
36 garments among them, casting lots: and they sat and
37 watched him there. And they set up over his head his
accusation written, THIS IS JESUS THE KING OF THE JEWS.
38 Then are there crucified with him two robbers, one on
the right hand, and one on the left.

S. Luke xxiii. 33—34, 38.

33   And when they came unto the place which is called
The skull, there they crucified him, and the malefactors,

[T. O.

one on the right hand and the other on the left.　And 34
Acts 7. 60. Jesus said, Father, forgive them ; for they know not what
Acts 3. 17. they do.　And parting his garments among them, they
cast lots.　　　*　　　*　　　*　　　*
And there was also a superscription over him, THIS IS 38
THE KING OF THE JEWS.

168.　*Conduct of priests, people, soldiers, robbers.*

S. Matthew xxvii. 39—44.

Ps. 22. 7.　　AND they that passed by railed on him, wagging their 39
Ps. 109.25. heads, and saying, Thou that destroyest the temple, and 40
160　　buildest it in three days, save thyself: if thou art the
Son of God, come down from the cross.　In like manner 41
also the chief priests mocking him, with the scribes and
elders, said, He saved others ; himself he cannot save. 42
He is the King of Israel ; let him now come down from
the cross, and we will believe on him.　He trusteth on 43
Ps. 22. 8.　God ; let him deliver him now, if he desireth him : for
he said, I am the Son of God.　And the robbers also 44
that were crucified with him cast upon him the same
reproach.

S. Mark xv. 29—32.

And they that passed by railed on him, wagging their 29
heads, and saying, Ha ! thou that destroyest the temple,
and buildest it in three days, save thyself, and come 30
down from the cross.　In like manner also the chief 31
priests mocking him among themselves with the scribes
said, He saved others ; himself he cannot save.　Let the 32
Christ, the King of Israel, now come down from the
cross, that we may see and believe.　And they that were
crucified with him reproached him.

S. Luke xxiii. 35—37.

And the people stood beholding.　And the rulers 35
also scoffed at him, saying, He saved others ; let him
save himself, if this is the Christ of God, his chosen.
And the soldiers also mocked him, coming to him, 36
offering him vinegar, and saying, If thou art the King 37
of the Jews, save thyself.

169. *Of Jesus himself.*

S. Luke xxiii. 39—43.

39 AND one of the malefactors which were hanged
railed on him, saying, Art not thou the Christ? save thy-
40 self and us. But the other answered, and rebuking him said,
Dost thou not even fear God, seeing thou art in the same
41 condemnation?   And we indeed justly; for we receive
the due reward of our deeds: but this man hath done
42 nothing amiss.   And he said, Jesus, remember me when
43 thou comest in thy kingdom.   And he said unto him,
Verily I say unto thee, To-day shalt thou be with me in 2 Co. 12. 4.
Paradise.   Lk. 16. 22.

S. John xix. 25—27.

25 But there were standing by the cross of Jesus his
mother, and his mother's sister, Mary the wife of Clopas,
26 and Mary Magdalene.   When Jesus therefore saw his
mother, and the disciple standing by, whom he loved, he Jn. 21. 20.
27 saith unto his mother, Woman, behold, thy son!   Then
saith he to the disciple, Behold, thy mother!   And from
that hour the disciple took her unto his own home.

170. *His death.*

S. Matthew xxvii. 45—56.

Amos 8. 9.   Now from the sixth hour there was darkness over all 45
the land until the ninth hour. And about the ninth 46
hour Jesus cried with a loud voice, saying, Eli, Eli,
Ps. 22. 1.   lama sabachthani? that is, My God, my God, why hast
thou forsaken me? And some of them that stood there, 47
when they heard it, said, This man calleth Elijah.
And straightway one of them ran, and took a sponge, 48
Ps. 69. 21. and filled it with vinegar, and put it on a reed, and gave
him to drink. And the rest said, Let be; let us see 49
whether Elijah cometh to save him. And Jesus cried 50
again with a loud voice, and yielded up his spirit. And 51
Lev. 16. 2. behold, the veil of the temple was rent in twain from the
Heb.9.8... top to the bottom; and the earth did quake; and the
rocks were rent; and the tombs were opened; and many 52
bodies of the saints that had fallen asleep were raised;
1 Co.15.20. and coming forth out of the tombs after his resurrection 53
they entered into the holy city and appeared unto many.
Now the centurion, and they that were with him watching 54
Jesus, when they saw the earthquake, and the things that
were done, feared exceedingly, saying, Truly this was the
Ps. 88. 8; Son of God. And many women were there beholding 55
— 38. 11. from afar, which had followed Jesus from Galilee, mini-
Lk. 8. 3.   stering unto him: among whom was Mary Magdalene, 56
and Mary the mother of James and Joses, and the
mother of the sons of Zebedee.

S. Mark xv. 33—41.

And when the sixth hour was come, there was dark- 33
ness over the whole land until the ninth hour. And at 34
the ninth hour Jesus cried with a loud voice, Eloi, Eloi,
lama sabachthani? which is, being interpreted, My God,
my God, why hast thou forsaken me? And some of 35
them that stood by, when they heard it, said, Behold, he
calleth Elijah. And one ran, and filling a sponge full of 36

vinegar, put it on a reed, and gave him to drink, saying,
Let be; let us see whether Elijah cometh to take him
37 down.   And Jesus uttered a loud voice, and gave up the
38 ghost.   And the veil of the temple was rent in twain
39 from the top to the bottom.   And when the centurion,
which stood by over against him, saw that he so gave up
the ghost, he said, Truly this man was the Son of God.
40 And there were also women beholding from afar: among
whom were both Mary Magdalene, and Mary the mother
of James the less and of Joses, and Salome ; who, when
41 he was in Galilee, followed him, and ministered unto
him ; and many other women which came up with him
unto Jerusalem.

S. Luke xxiii. 44—49.

44   And it was now about the sixth hour, and a darkness
came over the whole land until the ninth hour, the sun's
45 light failing : and the veil of the temple was rent in the
46 midst.   And when Jesus had cried with a loud voice, he
said, Father, into thy hands I commend my spirit : and Ps. 31. 5.
47 having said this, he gave up the ghost.   And when the
centurion saw what was done, he glorified God, saying,
48 Certainly this was a righteous man.   And all the multitudes that came together to this sight, when they
beheld the things that were done, returned smiting their
49 breasts.   And all his acquaintance, and the women that Lk. 8. 3.
followed with him from Galilee, stood afar off, seeing
these things.

S. John xix. 28—30.

28   After this Jesus, knowing that all things are now
finished, that the scripture might be accomplished, saith,
29 I thirst.   There was set there a vessel full of vinegar : so
they put a sponge full of the vinegar upon hyssop, and
30 brought it to his mouth.   When Jesus therefore had
received the vinegar, he said, It is finished : and he Jn. 17. 4.
bowed his head, and gave up his spirit.

171.   *His death made certain.*

S. John xix. 31—37.

THE Jews therefore, because it was the Preparation, 31
Deu.21.23. that the bodies should not remain on the cross upon the
sabbath (for the day of that sabbath was a high day),
asked of Pilate that their legs might be broken, and that
they might be taken away. The soldiers therefore came, 32
and brake the legs of the first, and of the other which
was crucified with him : but when they came to Jesus, 33
and saw that he was dead already, they brake not his
legs : howbeit one of the soldiers with a spear pierced 34
1 Jn.5.6... his side, and straightway there came out blood and
water.   And he that hath seen hath borne witness, and 35
his witness is true : and he knoweth that he saith true,
Ex. 12.46. that ye also may believe. For these things came to 36
Num.9.12. pass, that the scripture might be fulfilled, A bone of him
Ps. 34. 20. shall not be broken. And again another scripture saith, 37
Zec. 12.10. They shall look on him whom they pierced.

172.   *His burial.*

S. John xix. 38—42.

AND after these things Joseph of Arimathæa, being a 38
Jn. 12. 42. disciple of Jesus, but secretly for fear of the Jews, asked
of Pilate that he might take away the body of Jesus :
and Pilate gave him leave. He came therefore, and
Jn. 3. 1; took away his body. And there came also Nicodemus, 39
— 7. 50. he who at the first came to him by night, bringing a
Mt. 2. 11. mixture of myrrh and aloes, about a hundred pound
weight.   So they took the body of Jesus, and bound it 40
Gen.50.2.. in linen cloths with the spices, as the custom of the Jews
Jn. 11. 44. is to bury. Now in the place where he was crucified 41
there was a garden ; and in the garden a new tomb
2 Ki.13.21. wherein was never man yet laid. There then because of 42
the Jews' Preparation (for the tomb was nigh at hand)
they laid Jesus.

S. Mark xv. 42—47.

And when even was now come, because it was the 42
Preparation, that is, the day before the sabbath, there 43

came Joseph of Arimathæa, a councillor of honourable
estate, who also himself was looking for the kingdom of
God; and he boldly went in unto Pilate, and asked for
44 the body of Jesus.   And Pilate marvelled if he were
already dead: and calling unto him the centurion, he
45 asked him whether he had been any while dead.   And
when he learned it of the centurion, he granted the
46 corpse to Joseph.   And he bought a linen cloth, and
taking him down, wound him in the linen cloth, and laid
him in a tomb which had been hewn out of a rock; and
47 he rolled a stone against the door of the tomb.   And
Mary Magdalene and Mary the mother of Joses beheld
where he was laid.

S. Luke xxiii. 50—56.

50   And behold, a man named Joseph, who was a coun-
51 cillor, a good man and a righteous (he had not consented
to their counsel and deed), a man of Arimathæa, a city
of the Jews, who was looking for the kingdom of God:
52 this man went to Pilate, and asked for the body of Jesus.
53 And he took it down, and wrapped it in a linen cloth,
and laid him in a tomb that was hewn in stone, where
54 never man had yet lain.   And it was the day of the
55 Preparation, and the sabbath drew on.   And the women, Lk. 8. 2.
·   which had come with him out of Galilee, followed after,
56 and beheld the tomb, and how his body was laid.   And
they returned, and prepared spices and ointments.
    And on the sabbath they rested according to the
commandment.

S. Matthew xxvii. 57—61.

57   And when even was come, there came a rich man
from Arimathæa, named Joseph, who also himself was I Sam. 1. 1.
58 Jesus' disciple: this man went to Pilate, and asked for
the body of Jesus.   Then Pilate commanded it to be
59 given up.   And Joseph took the body, and wrapped it
60 in a clean linen cloth, and laid it in his own new tomb, Is. 22. 16.
which he had hewn out in the rock: and he rolled a
great stone to the door of the tomb, and departed. Jn. 11. 38.
61 And Mary Magdalene was there, and the other Mary,
sitting over against the sepulchre.

J. H. G.   17

173. *Precautions against the removal of His body.*

S. Matthew xxvii. 62—66.

Now on the morrow, which is the day after the 62
Preparation, the chief priests and the Pharisees were
gathered together unto Pilate, saying, Sir, we remember 63
Jn. 2. 19... that that deceiver said, while he was yet alive, After three
days I rise again. Command therefore that the sepulchre 64
be made sure until the third day, lest haply his disciples
come and steal him away, and say unto the people, He
is risen from the dead: and the last error will be worse
than the first. Pilate said unto them, Ye have a guard:
go your way, make it as sure as ye can. So they went, 65
Dan. 6. 17. and made the sepulchre sure, sealing the stone, the 66
guard being with them.

174. *An angel rolls away the stone.*

S. Matthew xxviii. 2—4.

2   AND behold, there was a great earthquake; for an
angel of the Lord descended from heaven, and came
3 and rolled away the stone, and sat upon it. His appearance was as lightning, and his raiment white as snow: Dan. 10. 6.
4 and for fear of him the watchers did quake, and became
as dead men.

175. *The tomb empty. Angels declare that He is risen.*

S. John xx. 1—10.

Now on the first day of the week cometh Mary 1
Magdalene early, while it was yet dark, unto the tomb,
and seeth the stone taken away from the tomb. She 2
runneth therefore, and cometh to Simon Peter, and to
Jn. 21. 20. the other disciple, whom Jesus loved, and saith unto
them, They have taken away the Lord out of the tomb,
and we know not where they have laid him. Peter 3
therefore went forth, and the other disciple, and they
went toward the tomb. And they ran both together : 4
and the other disciple outran Peter, and came first to
the tomb ; and stooping and looking in, he seeth the 5
Jn. 19. 40. linen cloths lying ; yet entered he not in. Simon Peter 6
therefore also cometh, following him, and entered into
the tomb ; and he beholdeth the linen cloths lying, and 7
Jn. 11. 44. the napkin, that was upon his head, not lying with the
linen cloths, but rolled up in a place by itself. Then 8
entered in therefore the other disciple also, which came
first to the tomb, and he saw, and believed. For as yet 9
Ps. 16. 10. they knew not the scripture, that he must rise again from
Acts 2. 31. the dead. So the disciples went away again unto their 10
own home.

S. Mark xvi. 1—8.

Lk. 8. 2.   And when the sabbath was past, Mary Magdalene, 1
and Mary the mother of James, and Salome, bought
Lk. 23. 55. spices, that they might come and anoint him. And very 2
Gen. 50. 2. early on the first day of the week, they come to the
tomb when the sun was risen. And they were saying 3
among themselves, Who shall roll us away the stone
from the door of the tomb ? and looking up, they see 4
that the stone is rolled back : for it was exceeding great.
And entering into the tomb, they saw a young man 5
sitting on the right side, arrayed in a white robe ; and
they were amazed. And he saith unto them, Be not 6
amazed : ye seek Jesus, the Nazarene, which hath been
crucified : he is risen ; he is not here : behold, the place
where they laid him ! But go, tell his disciples and 7
Peter, He goeth before you into Galilee : there shall ye
see him, as he said unto you. And they went out, and 8

fled from the tomb; for trembling and astonishment had come upon them: and they said nothing to any one; for they were afraid.

S. Luke xxiv. 1—12.

1 But on the first day of the week, at early dawn, they came unto the tomb, bringing the spices which they had 2 prepared. And they found the stone rolled away from 3 the tomb. And they entered in, and found not the 4 body of the Lord Jesus. And it came to pass, while they were perplexed thereabout, behold, two men stood 5 by them in dazzling apparel: and as they were affrighted, and bowed down their faces to the earth, they said unto them, Why seek ye the living among the dead? Is. 8. 19. 6 He is not here, but is risen: remember how he spake 7 unto you when he was yet in Galilee, saying that the Mk. 9. 31. Son of man must be deilvered up into the hands of **73** sinful men, and be crucified, and the third day rise 8, 9 again. And they remembered his words, and returned from the tomb, and told all these things to the eleven, 10 and to all the rest. Now they were Mary Magdalene, and Joanna, and Mary the mother of James: and the other women with them told these things unto the 11 apostles. And these words appeared in their sight as 12 idle talk; and they disbelieved them. But Peter arose, and ran unto the tomb; and stooping and looking in, he seeth the linen cloths by themselves; and he departed to his home, wondering at that which was come to pass.

S. Matthew xxviii. 1; 5—8.

1 Now late on the sabbath day, as it began to dawn toward the first day of the week, came Mary Magdalene and the other Mary to see the sepulchre.

     *   *   *   *   *

5 And the angel answered and said unto the women, Fear not ye: for I know that ye seek Jesus, which hath been 6 crucified. He is not here; for he is risen, even as he 7 said. Come, see the place where the Lord lay. And go quickly, and tell his disciples, He is risen from the Mt. 26. 32. dead; and lo, he goeth before you into Galilee; there Mt. 28. 16. 8 shall ye see him: lo, I have told you. And they de- **184** parted quickly from the tomb with fear and great joy, and ran to bring his disciples word.

176. *Jesus appears to Mary Magdalene.*

S. John xx. 11—18.

BUT Mary was standing without at the tomb weeping: 11
so, as she wept, she stooped and looked into the tomb;
and she beholdeth two angels in white sitting, one at the 12
head, and one at the feet, where the body of Jesus had
lain.   And they say unto her, Woman, why weepest thou? 13
She saith unto them, Because they have taken away my
Lord, and I know not where they have laid him.   When 14
she had thus said, she turned herself back, and beholdeth
Lk. 24. 16. Jesus standing, and knew not that it was Jesus.   Jesus 15
Jn. 21. 4. saith unto her, Woman, why weepest thou? whom seekest
thou?   She, supposing him to be the gardener, saith unto
him, Sir, if thou hast borne him hence, tell me where
thou hast laid him, and I will take him away.   Jesus 16
saith unto her, Mary.   She turneth herself, and saith
Mk. 10. 51. unto him in Hebrew, Rabboni; which is to say, Master.
Jesus saith to her, Touch me not; for I am not yet 17
Rom. 8. 29. ascended unto the Father: but go unto my brethren,
Heb. 2. 11. and say to them, I ascend unto my Father and your
Eph. 1. 17. Father, and my God and your God.   Mary Magdalene 18
1 Pet. 1. 3. cometh and telleth the disciples, I have seen the Lord;
and how that he had said these things unto her.

S. Mark xvi. 9—11.

Now when he was risen early on the first day of the 9
week, he appeared first to Mary Magdalene, from whom
he had cast out seven devils.   She went and told them 10
that had been with him, as they mourned and wept.
And they, when they heard that he was alive, and had 11
been seen of her, disbelieved.

177. *Jesus appears to the other women.*

S. Matthew xxviii. 8—10.

8 AND they departed quickly from the tomb with fear
9 and great joy, and ran to bring his disciples word. And
behold, Jesus met them, saying, All hail. And they came
10 and took hold of his feet, and worshipped him. Then
saith Jesus unto them, Fear not: go tell my brethren Mt. 26. 32.
that they depart into Galilee, and there shall they see me. Mt. 28. 16.

184

S. Luke xxiv. 8, 9, 11.

8, 9 And they remembered his words, and returned from
the tomb, and told all these things unto the eleven, and
to all the rest.

* * * * *

11 And these words appeared in their sight as idle talk ;
they disbelieved them.

178. *Report and bribery of the guards.*

S. Matthew xxviii. 11—15.

11 · Now while they were going, behold, some of the Mt. 27. 65.
guard came into the city, and told unto the chief priests **173**
12 all the things that were come to pass. And when they
were assembled with the elders, and had taken counsel,
13 they gave large money unto the soldiers, saying, Say ye,
His disciples came by night, and stole him away while
14 we slept. And if this come to the governor's ears, we Acts 12.19.
15 will persuade him, and rid you of care. So they took 1 Sam. 8. 3.
the money, and did as they were taught : and this saying
was spread abroad among the Jews, and continueth until
this day.

179. *Jesus appears to Cleopas and another;*
also to Peter.

S. Luke xxiv. 13—35.

AND behold, two of them were going that very 13
day to a village named Emmaus, which was three-
score furlongs from Jerusalem. And they communed 14
with each other of all these things which had happened.
And it came to pass, while they communed and ques- 15
tioned together, that Jesus himself drew near, and went
Jn. 20. 14. with them. But their eyes were holden that they should 16
— 21. 4. not know him. And he said unto them, What communi- 17
cations are these that ye have one with another, as ye
walk? And they stood still, looking sad. And one of 18
Jn. 19. 25. them, named Cleopas, answering said unto him, Dost
thou alone sojourn in Jerusalem and not know the things
which are come to pass there in these days? And he 19
said unto them, What things? And they said unto him,
The things concerning Jesus of Nazareth, which was a
prophet mighty in deed and word before God and all
the people: and how the chief priests and our rulers 20
delivered him up to be condemned to death, and cruci-
Lk. 1. 68. fied him. But we hoped that it was he which should 21
Acts 1. 6. redeem Israel. Yea and beside all this, it is now the
third day since these things came to pass. Moreover 22
certain women of our company amazed us, having been
early at the tomb; and when they found not his body, 23
they came, saying, that they had also seen a vision of
angels, which said that he was alive. And certain of 24
them that were with us went to the tomb, and found it
even so as the women had said: but him they saw not.
And he said unto them, O foolish men, and slow of heart 25
to believe in all that the prophets have spoken! Be- 26
Acts 17. 3. hoved it not the Christ to suffer these things, and to
enter into his glory? And beginning from Moses and 27

from all the prophets, he interpreted to them in all the Acts 3. 22..
28 scriptures the things concerning himself. And they drew
nigh unto the village, whither they were going: and he
29 made as though he would go further. And they con- Gen. 32. 26.
strained him, saying, Abide with us: for it is toward Jn. 1. 39.
30 evening, and the day is now far spent. And he went
in to abide with them. And it came to pass, when he
had sat down with them to meat, he took the bread, and Lk. 9. 16.
31 blessed it, and brake, and gave to them. And their Lk. 22. 19.
eyes were opened, and they knew him ; and he vanished Lk. 4. 30.
32 out of their sight. And they said one to another, Was Jn. 8. 59.
not our heart burning within us, while he spake to us in
33 the way, while he opened to us the scriptures? And
they rose up that very hour, and returned to Jerusalem,
and found the eleven gathered together, and them that
34 were with them, saying, The Lord is risen indeed, and
35 hath appeared to Simon. And they rehearsed the things 1 Cor. 15. 5.
that happened in the way, and how he was known of them
in the breaking of the bread.

S. Mark xvi. 12, 13.

12 And after these things he was manifested in another
form unto two of them, as they walked, on their way
13 into the country. And they went away and told it unto
the rest : neither believed they them.

S. Paul, 1 Cor. xv. 5.

And that he appeared to Cephas.

180. *Jesus appears to His disciples the same evening.*

S. Luke xxiv. 36—49.

AND as they spake these things, he himself stood in 36
Jn. 14. 27. the midst of them, and saith unto them, Peace be unto
Mt. 14. 26. you. But they were terrified and affrighted, and sup- 37
63 posed that they beheld a spirit. And he said unto them, 38
Why are ye troubled? and wherefore do reasonings arise
in your heart? See my hands and my feet, that it is I 39
Jn. 20. 27. myself: handle me, and see; for a spirit hath not flesh
181 and bones, as ye behold me having. And when he had 40
1 Jn. 1. 1. said this, he shewed them his hands and his feet. And 41
while they still disbelieved for joy, and wondered, he
Gen.45.26. said unto them, Have ye here anything to eat? And 42
Jn. 21. 5. they gave him a piece of a broiled fish. And he took 43
Acts 10.41. it, and did eat before them.

And he said unto them, These are my words which 44
I spake unto you, while I was yet with you, how that all
things must needs be fulfilled, which are written in the
law of Moses, and the prophets, and the psalms, concern-
Acts 16.14. ing me. Then opened he their mind, that they might 45
understand the scriptures; and he said unto them, Thus 46
Acts 26.23. it is written, that the Christ should suffer, and rise again
from the dead the third day; and that repentance and 47
remission of sins should be preached in his name unto
Acts 1. 8. all the nations, beginning from Jerusalem. Ye are wit- 48
Acts 3. 15. nesses of these things. And behold, I send forth the 49
Jn. 14. 16. promise of my Father upon you: but tarry ye in the
— 15. 26. city, until ye be clothed with power from on high.

S. John xx. 19—23.

When therefore it was evening, on that day, the first 19
Jn. 20. 26. day of the week, and when the doors were shut where
the disciples were, for fear of the Jews, Jesus came and
stood in the midst, and saith unto them, Peace be unto
you. And when he had said this, he shewed unto them 20
his hands and his side. The disciples therefore were
glad, when they saw the Lord. Jesus therefore said to 21
Jn. 17. 18. them again, Peace be unto you: as the Father hath sent
2 Tim. 2. 2. me, even so send I you. And when he had said this, he 22
breathed on them, and saith unto them, Receive ye the
Mt. 16. 19. Holy Ghost: whose soever sins ye forgive, they are 23
Mt. 18. 18. forgiven unto them; whose soever sins ye retain, they are
71. 76 retained.

S. Mark xvi. 14—18.

14 And afterward he was manifested unto the eleven themselves as they sat at meat; and he upbraided them with their unbelief and hardness of heart, because they believed not them which had seen him after he was 15 risen. And he said unto them, Go ye into all the world, Mt. 28. 19. 16 and preach the gospel to the whole creation. He that **184** believeth and is baptized shall be saved; but he that 17 disbelieveth shall be condemned. And these signs shall follow them that believe: in my name shall they cast out Acts 16. 18. 18 devils; they shall speak with new tongues; they shall Acts 2. 4. take up serpents, and if they drink any deadly thing, it Acts 28. 5. shall in no wise hurt them; they shall lay hands on the Acts 28. 8. sick, and they shall recover.

S. Paul, 1 Cor. xv. 5.

Then *he appeared* to the twelve.

181. *Again, a week later. Thomas.*

S. John xx. 24—31.

24 BUT Thomas, one of the twelve, called Didymus, was Jn. 11. 16. 25 not with them when Jesus came. The other disciples therefore said unto him, We have seen the Lord. But he said unto them, Except I shall see in his hands the print of the nails, and put my finger into the print of the nails, and put my hand into his side, I will not believe. 26 And after eight days again his disciples were within, and Thomas with them. Jesus cometh, the doors being Jn. 20. 19. shut, and stood in the midst, and said, Peace be unto Jn. 14. 27. 27 you. Then saith he to Thomas, Reach hither thy finger, and see my hands; and reach hither thy hand, and put Lk. 24. 39. it into my side: and be not faithless, but believing. **180** 28 Thomas answered and said unto him, My Lord and my 29 God. Jesus saith unto him, Because thou hast seen me, thou hast believed: blessed are they that have not seen, 1 Pet. 1. 8. and yet have believed. 30 Many other signs therefore did Jesus in the presence Jn. 21. 25 of the disciples, which are not written in this book: but **183** 31 these are written, that ye may believe that Jesus is the Christ, the Son of God; and that believing ye may have 1 Jn. 5. 13. life in his name.

182. *Again at the sea of Tiberias. The draught of fishes.*

S. John xxi. 1—14.

AFTER these things Jesus manifested himself again to 1
the disciples at the sea of Tiberias; and he manifested
himself on this wise.   There were together Simon Peter, 2
Jn. 1. 45... and Thomas called Didymus, and Nathanael of Cana in
Mt. 4. 21. Galilee, and the sons of Zebedee, and two other of his
disciples.   Simon Peter saith unto them, I go a fishing. 3
They say unto him, We also come with thee.   They
went forth, and entered into the boat; and that night
Lk. 9. 5. they took nothing.   But when day was now breaking, 4
35   Jesus stood on the beach: howbeit the disciples knew
not that it was Jesus.   Jesus therefore saith unto them, 5
Lk. 24. 41. Children, have ye aught to eat?   They answered him,
No.   And he said unto them, Cast the net on the right 6
side of the boat, and ye shall find.   They cast therefore,
and now they were not able to draw it for the multitude
Jn. 13. 28. of fishes.   That disciple therefore whom Jesus loved 7
saith unto Peter, It is the Lord.   So when Simon Peter
heard that it was the Lord, he girt his coat about him
(for he was naked), and cast himself into the sea.   But 8
the other disciples came in the little boat (for they were
not far from the land, but about two hundred cubits off),
dragging the net full of fishes.   So when they got out 9
upon the land, they see a fire of coals there, and fish laid
thereon, and bread.   Jesus saith unto them, Bring of the 10
fish which ye have now taken.   Simon Peter therefore 11
went up, and drew the net to land, full of great fishes, a
hundred and fifty and three: and for all there were so
many, the net was not rent.   Jesus saith unto them, 12
Acts 10.41. Come and break your fast.   And none of the disciples
durst inquire of him, Who art thou? knowing that it was
Lk. 24. 30. the Lord.   Jesus cometh, and taketh the bread, and 13
179   giveth them, and the fish likewise.   This is now the 14
third time that Jesus was manifested to the disciples,
after that he was risen from the dead.

183. *Special charge to Peter and John.*

S. John xxi. 15—25.

15 So when they had broken their fast, Jesus saith to
Simon Peter, Simon, son of John, lovest thou me more Mt. 26. 33.
than these? He saith unto him, Yea, Lord; thou **155**
knowest that I love thee. He saith unto him, Feed
16 my lambs. He saith to him again a second time, Simon, Eze.34.2...
son of John, lovest thou me? He saith unto him, Yea,
Lord; thou knowest that I love thee. He saith unto
17 him, Tend my sheep. He saith unto him the third time, 1 Pet. 5. 2.
Simon, son of John, lovest thou me? Peter was grieved
because he said unto him the third time, Lovest thou Mt. 26. 75.
me? And he said, unto him, Lord, thou knowest all **159**
things; thou knowest that I love thee. Jesus saith unto
18 him, Feed my sheep. Verily, verily, I say unto thee, Acts 20.28.
When thou wast young, thou girdedst thyself, and
walkedst whither thou wouldest: but when thou shalt
be old, thou shalt stretch forth thy hands, and another Jn. 13. 36.
shall gird thee, and carry thee whither thou wouldest
19 not. Now this he spake, signifying by what manner of 2 Pet. 1.14.
death he should glorify God. And when he had spoken
20 this, he saith unto him, Follow me. Peter, turning
about, seeth the disciple whom Jesus loved following;
which also leaned back on his breast at the supper, and Jn.13.23...
21 said, Lord, who is he that betrayeth thee? Peter there- **147**
fore seeing him saith to Jesus, Lord, and what shall this
22 man do? Jesus saith unto him, If I will that he tarry
23 till I come, what is that to thee? follow thou me. This Mt. 16. 28.
saying therefore went forth among the brethren, that that ⌐ 24. 30.
disciple should not die: yet Jesus said not unto him,
that he should not die; but, If I will that he tarry till I
come, what is that to thee?
24 This is the disciple which beareth witness of these
things, and wrote these things: and we know that his 3 Jn. 12.
witness is true.
25 And there are also many other things which Jesus Jn. 20. 30.
did, the which if they should be written every one, I **181**
suppose that even the world itself would not contain the
books that should be written.

184. *Again in Galilee.*

S. Matthew xxviii. 16—20.

Mt. 26. 32.
— 28. 7.
175

BUT the eleven disciples went into Galilee, unto the 16
mountain where Jesus had appointed them. And when 17
they saw him, they worshipped him : but some doubted.
And Jesus came to them and spake unto them, saying, 18

Heb. 2. 8.
Mk. 16. 15.
180

All authority hath been given unto me in heaven and on
earth. Go ye therefore, and make disciples of all the 19
nations, baptizing them into the name of the Father and
of the Son and of the Holy Ghost : teaching them to 20
observe all things whatsoever I commanded you : and

Ro. 8. 35...

lo, I am with you alway, even unto the end of the world.

S. Paul, 1 Cor. xv. 6, 7.

Then he appeared to above five hundred brethren at 6
once, of whom the greater part remain until now, but
some are fallen asleep ; then he appeared to James ; 7
then to all the apostles.

185. *And in Jerusalem, during forty days.*

S. Luke, Acts 1. 3—8.

Acts 10.41.
Lk. 24. 39.

HE shewed himself alive to his apostles after his pas- 3
sion by many proofs, appearing unto them by the space
of forty days, and speaking the things concerning the
kingdom of God : and, being assembled together with 4
them, he charged them not to depart from Jerusalem,

Lk. 24. 49.
180.

but to wait for the promise of the Father, which, said he,
ye heard from me : for John indeed baptized with water ;

Mt. 3. 11.
15

but ye shall be baptized with the Holy Ghost not many 5
days hence.
They therefore, when they were come together, asked 6

Dan. 7. 27.
Mt. 24. 36.
137

him, saying, Lord, dost thou at this time restore the
kingdom to Israel? And he said unto them, It is not 7
for you to know times or seasons, which the Father hath

Acts 2. 2.

set within his own authority. But ye shall receive power, 8
when the Holy Ghost is come upon you : and ye shall

Acts 2. 14,
— 8. 1,
— 8. 4,
— 13. 4.

be my witnesses both in Jerusalem, and in all Judæa and
Samaria, and unto the uttermost part of the earth.

186. *His Ascension.*

S. Luke xxiv. 50—53.

50   AND he led them out until they were over against
Bethany : and he lifted up his hands, and blessed them.
51 And it came to pass, while he blessed them, he parted   2 Ki. 2. 11.
52 from them, and was carried up into heaven.   And they
worshipped him, and returned to Jerusalem with great
53 joy : and were continually in the temple, blessing God.   Acts 2. 46.

Acts 1. 9—12.

9   And when he had said these things, as they were
looking, he was taken up ; and a cloud received him out
10 of their sight.   And while they were looking stedfastly   Mt. 28. 3.
into heaven as he went, behold, two men stood by them   Acts 13.31.
11 in white apparel; which also said, Ye men of Galilee, why
stand ye looking into heaven ? this Jesus, which was
received up from you into heaven, shall so come in like   Mt. 25. 31.
manner as ye beheld him going into heaven.
12   Then returned they unto Jerusalem from the mount
called Olivet, which is nigh unto Jerusalem, a sabbath
day's journey off.

S. Mark xvi. 19, 20.

19   So then the Lord Jesus, after he had spoken unto
them, was received up into heaven, and sat down at the   Eph. 1. 20.
20 right hand of God.   And they went forth, and preached   Ps. 110. 1.
everywhere, the Lord working with them, and confirming   Acts 5. 12.
the word by the signs that followed.   Amen.

187. *Of giving and receiving.*

S. Paul, Acts xx. 35.

REMEMBER the words of the Lord Jesus, how he
himself said, It is more blessed to give than to receive.

AND EVERY CREATED THING WHICH IS IN THE
HEAVEN, AND ON THE EARTH, AND UNDER THE EARTH,
AND ON THE SEA, AND ALL THINGS THAT ARE IN THEM,
HEARD I SAYING, UNTO HIM THAT SITTETH ON THE
THRONE, AND UNTO THE LAMB, BE THE BLESSING, AND
THE HONOUR, AND THE GLORY, AND THE DOMINION, FOR
EVER AND EVER.   AND THE FOUR LIVING CREATURES
SAID, AMEN.   AND THE ELDERS FELL DOWN AND WOR-
SHIPPED.   REV. V. 13, 14.

INDEX OF PROPER NAMES.

N.B. The names occurring only in the two Genealogies (2 and 3) are not given. The numbers refer to the sections.

A. Authorised Version. R. Revised Version. V. Table of Variations.

CAMBRIDGE: PRINTED BY C. J. CLAY, M.A., AND SONS, AT THE UNIVERSITY PRESS.

BY THE SAME EDITOR.

UNIFORM WITH THIS VOLUME.

———

THE GOSPEL HISTORY

OF OUR LORD AND SAVIOUR

JESUS CHRIST

IN A CONNECTED NARRATIVE

IN THE WORDS OF THE REVISED VERSION.

———

London: C. J. CLAY AND SONS,
CAMBRIDGE UNIVERSITY PRESS WAREHOUSE,
AVE MARIA LANE.

1892

CPSIA information can be obtained
at www.ICGtesting.com
Printed in the USA
LVHW08*1026210818
587625LV00007B/43/P

9 781340 561895